THE
JEWISH
HOLIDAY
TABLE

THE
JEWISH
HOLIDAY
TABLE

A World of Recipes, Traditions & Stories to Celebrate All Year Long

Naama Shefi
and the Jewish Food Society
with Devra Ferst

ARTISAN | NEW YORK

Library of Congress Cataloging-in-Publication Data is on file.

ISBN 978-1-64829-097-8

Design by Toni Tajima
Cover design by Talmor & Talmor & Talmor
Original floral designs (cover and pages 4–5, 16–17, 128–129, 200–201,
304–305) by Emily Parkinson
Food styling by Judy Haubert
Additional food styling by Mariana Velásquez (pages 106–116, 168–175,
310–328, 352–362, 388, 398–399), Nurit Kariv (pages 154–155 and
384), and Chaya Rappoport (pages 84–85 and 248)
Prop styling by Vanessa Vazquez
Additional prop styling by Mariana Velásquez (pages 2–3 and 22–37)
Tableware pages 84–85 courtesy of Porta NYC

Artisan books may be purchased in bulk for business, educational,
or promotional use. For information, please contact your local
bookseller or the Hachette Book Group Special Markets Department
at special.markets@hbgusa.com.

The publisher is not responsible for websites (or their content) that are
not owned by the publisher.

The Hachette Speakers Bureau provides a wide range of authors for
speaking events. To find out more, go to hachettespeakersbureau.com
or email HachetteSpeakers@hbgusa.com.

Published by Artisan,
an imprint of Workman Publishing,
a division of Hachette Book Group, Inc.
1290 Avenue of the Americas
New York, NY 10104
artisanbooks.com

The Artisan name and logo are registered trademarks of
Hachette Book Group, Inc.

Printed in China on responsibly sourced paper

10 9 8 7 6 5 4 3 2

To the cooks of our tradition—
most often women—who have
built the Jewish kitchen and
tended to its flame, making sure
its light never goes out

Contents

PREFACE:
The Grandmother Who Started It All

THE FIRST TIME I met my husband's family was at his grandmother Ketty's snug four-hundred-square-foot apartment outside Tel Aviv. Ilan and I arrived early on a Friday afternoon to find Nonna, as the family called her in Ladino, in her kitchen. She was tending to simmering pots on every burner—with a tray of just-baked savory pastries called borekitas ready for us to snack on.

Another twenty guests were coming in a couple of hours for Shabbat dinner, and I couldn't fathom how everyone would fit. But Ilan told me, "Wait, you'll see, it's like magic." As aunts, uncles, and cousins arrived, each of them found a seat at the table, which Ketty covered with what seemed like an endless array of dishes: an eggplant salad with just the right amount of garlic, a tangle of green zucchini ribbons dressed with paprika and lemon, tomatoes and onion sleeves stuffed with beef and rice, a chard-and-potato pie, and many more.

I was spellbound by Ketty, by her spirit, hospitality, and cooking. The menu was a map of her life: She was born in Izmir on Turkey's coast in 1927, but her family moved across the water to the Greek island of Rhodes when she

was two years old, and later to Rhodesia (present-day Zimbabwe), to escape the Nazis. Finally, in 1976, she settled in Israel. Each dish told a part of her story: the albondigas (meatballs) in tomato sauce nodded to her community's roots in Spain generations ago, while the eggplant salad came from the time when her family lived in the Ottoman Empire, and a salad of Swiss chard stems echoed Israel's era of austerity.

Dinners like this one are a hallmark of many Jewish homes, but that's not how I grew up. I ate all of my meals in the communal dining hall on Kibbutz Givat HaShlosha, where my parents still live. The community part was lovely, the repetitive menu less so. During the week, there were calves' liver, sad stuffed peppers, and spaghetti that had sat in sauce for far too long. On Shabbat, things were a bit better, with freshly fried schnitzel and roast chicken. There was also a perfect cholent with kishke for Saturday lunch that a woman named Batsheva made. And the most exciting thing in the dining hall: a herring cart overseen by a sweet old man named Schnitzer, whom I always jokingly called "Schnitzel." But most of our meals on the

Meeting Nonna for the first time, Givatayim, 2006

kibbutz were divorced from the cooks, their stories, and their traditions.

At Ketty's table, those connections were inescapable. Her life and spirit were wrapped up in every dish she served. She was in her eighties when I met her, and I knew then that I wanted to do everything I could to help protect her legacy.

That evening planted a seed.

———————

GROWING UP IN ISRAEL, I never had to think about what it means to be Jewish—it was baked into the cake. But when I moved to New York City in 2005, I realized I needed to seek out ways to connect to my Jewish identity. I started curating events like a conference about gefilte fish, an Israeli-Moroccan Seder, and the Kubbeh Project, a monthlong pop-up starring an Iraqi Jewish comfort food in the East Village. I found that through them, I could realize my Jewish identity and help others feel connected to our community, instilling a sense of pride and joy.

I started to imagine a home for Jewish food and thought back to that meal I had experienced years before at Ketty's apartment. There are countless cooks like her whose recipes tell the stories not only of their lives and those who came before them, but also of their communities and the Jewish experience. I knew that if those recipes and stories disappeared, so too would a crucial and irreplaceable part of our history and culture.

In 2016, I was fortunate to meet philanthropist Terry Kassel, who believed in that vision, and she generously and passionately supported the creation of a new home for Jewish food. A year later, I launched the Jewish Food Society, a nonprofit organization dedicated to preserving and celebrating Jewish culinary heritage from around the world. At the heart of our work is a digital archive with family recipes and stories. We bring them to life through events like pop-up dinners, cooking classes, and our podcast, *Schmaltzy*.

Since I created JFS, I've seen how food can enable those who identify as Jewish to feel proud of their roots and find a place for themselves within the community. And for those who are not Jewish, it can make them feel welcome at our table.

INTRODUCTION:
A Year of Celebrations

THERE'S TIME and space for so many celebrations in the Jewish calendar: The year starts in the fall with a trio of holidays—Rosh Hashanah, Yom Kippur, and Sukkot—and a season for forgiveness and setting intentions. In the winter, Hanukkah brings light into the darkness and Purim gives us a chance to party. And when spring and Passover finally arrive, we rejoice in freedom at Seder and relish the season at Shavuot. Throughout the year, Jewish life is marked by Shabbat, a weekly chance to slow down and connect with one another. Each holiday offers us an opportunity to find personal meaning in an ancient tradition that's always evolving. And at their core is time to spend around a table with the people we love most.

My friend and cookbook author Mitchell Davis once told me that for him, the meal *is* the holiday. Rosh Hashanah starts in his kitchen before the guests arrive, as he makes his mother's matzah balls and gefilte fish (see page 38).

What we cook for these meals reveals much about the Jewish people and our journey. Some dishes, for example, reflect ancient commandments and customs that are still observed throughout the Jewish world: During the Passover Seder, we eat bitter herbs and charoset, a sweet paste made from fruits and nuts, to help recall the story of the Exodus of the Jews from slavery in ancient Egypt. On Rosh Hashanah, the Jewish New Year, we dot our tables with fruits like apples, dates, and pomegranates in the hope of ensuring a sweet and plentiful year ahead.

How we interpret these customs often reflects where our family's community settled in the Diaspora centuries ago. On Hanukkah, it's traditional to fry foods in oil to recall the miracle of light in the Temple in ancient Jerusalem. But which types of foods are fried depends on our background. In chef Nir Mesika's family (see page 148), his Moroccan grandmother made ring-shaped doughnuts called sfenj for the holiday, and his Egyptian grandmother fried gumball-sized zalabia, a type of doughnut she'd learned to make from a Muslim neighbor who prepared them during Ramadan. By interpreting holiday traditions with local ingredients and culinary customs, Jewish cooks imbued many of the foods they encountered in the Diaspora with new meaning.

Passed down from generation to generation, the dishes we serve help tell stories of love and celebrations past, of wars and loss, of moves to faraway places, of survival, and of so much more.

Cooks are often the keepers of these stories and our traditions. They are the ones who make sure that a relative lost in the Holocaust is remembered with her Hungarian desserts on Purim (see page 178); that even when a family had to hide their Jewish identity in Milan, doughnuts and apple fritters were still made around Hanukkah time (see page 132); and that dishes from a family who moved from Iraq to India in the nineteenth century were taught to the next generation (see page 58).

This book is a celebration of these cooks, their traditions and lives, and the holidays where they left indelible marks on the table.

What Is Jewish Food?

In New York City, if you ask someone on the street that question, you're likely to get responses like deli, bagels, gefilte fish, or matzah ball soup. In Israel, you might be told it's the Shabbat stew cholent, challah, or chopped liver. In a Sephardi community, the answer could be pastelicos, leek fritters, or mina, the Passover pie. No matter where you ask this question, though, the answer will almost always include holiday classics, which are the backbone of Jewish cooking.

There are countless definitions and visions of Jewish food—it's not a static thing; it's always evolving. At its core, it lives at the intersection of Jewish rituals and holidays, kosher laws, and the food traditions and ingredients that cooks have encountered in a Diaspora that started more than two thousand years ago, even before the destruction of the Second Temple in Jerusalem.

In the centuries that followed, Jewish families emigrated to flee persecution and seek out opportunities, establishing communities in many corners of the world. You can read about those journeys in the pages of this book and see how the places where families settled shaped and seasoned their cooking.

While this migration continues today, Jewish families often identify with one of two main groups—Ashkenazi and Sephardi—that evolved in the Diaspora, each with their own culinary traditions. Ashkenazi Jews, like my coauthor Devra Ferst's family (see page 96), settled in Germany and France, where their culture first developed in the Middle Ages and later spread eastward through Europe. In the face of harsh winters when little could grow, preserved foods like pickles became a hallmark of their cuisine, as did hearty root vegetables and fruit like apples. Sephardi Jews, like Alexandra Zohn's ancestors (see page 264), were exiled from the Iberian Peninsula during the Spanish Expulsion in 1492. As they settled in parts of the Mediterranean and the Ottoman Empire—bringing savory pies and sweets like marzipan with them—many of these immigrants encountered Jewish communities that had lived in North Africa and the Middle East for centuries. And when their descendants arrived in Israel generations later, they were labeled Mizrahim, or Eastern Jews—no matter their actual roots.

Jewish communities like those of Persia (and later, Iran), Central Asia, Ethiopia, Rome, and the Bene Israel of

India have their own histories, cuisines, and holiday dishes. And with migrations like those of Iraqi Jews to India, Moroccan Jews to Brazil, and Eastern European Jews to Mexico, new ones emerged. Today the greatest diversity of Jewish food can be found in Israel, where cooks from the far corners of the world not only set their own tables at home but also bring their culinary traditions to the communal table.

Across the Diaspora, cooks adopted and adapted dishes and culinary techniques from non-Jewish neighbors and those they had commercial ties to, making them kosher. Rather than pork, Jews cooked beef. Rather than fry or bake with lard, they used oil, butter, or goose fat, taking care not to mix milk and meat. They also developed unique dishes made with local ingredients, such as Ashkenazi cholent, Sephardi adafina, and other dishes that are cooked or kept warm overnight so that families can enjoy hot meals on Shabbat, when work, including cooking, is forbidden.

Holiday cooking is at the heart of the Jewish kitchen. These holidays have developed over thousands of years, taking on more and more layers of meaning and symbolism with age. Many have agricultural roots, but some commemorate key moments in Jewish history as well—like the springtime harvest festival Shavuot, which also marks receiving the Torah from God. As the holidays evolved, so did the foods made for these celebrations.

Hardship has shaped the Jewish kitchen, too, and made its cooks resourceful. Elizaveta Vigonskaia remembers her mother frying potatoes in fish oil to keep the family alive during a famine in Ukraine (see page 158). And my husband's grandmother Ketty made a wonderful salad from chard stems for Shabbat so that nothing would go to waste. Jewish cooks have always found creative ways to turn whatever is available into a meal worthy of a celebration.

Cooking the dishes our ancestors made connects us not only to them, but also to our larger community's richly layered past and traditions that evolve with every generation.

The Jewish Food Society

Since launching the nonprofit Jewish Food Society in 2017, my team and I have dedicated ourselves to preserving and celebrating Jewish culinary heritage from around the world. We've gathered more than a thousand family recipes and the stories behind them for our digital archive and brought them to life through events and our podcast, *Schmaltzy*. We believe they carry the marrow of who we are as Jewish individuals and families. And when we look at them as a whole, they help tell a vital part of the story of the Jewish people.

Many of the best family recipes call for a pinch of this and a teacup of that—and some are never even written down. At JFS, we collaborate closely with cooks to translate their family treasures into working professional recipes, testing and retesting them, sometimes adjusting them ever so slightly to reflect how we eat today, while maintaining their integrity and honoring the spirit of the

original dish. Asking families to share their personal traditions is intimate work that's often best done while a cook is making plov (page 126) or frying fish for escabeche (page 376). When we can, we spend time in the kitchen with them—and when we can't, we chat on the phone, over WhatsApp, or by any means possible to get to the core of a family's most cherished recipes and stories.

So many of the best Jewish family recipes are rooted in holiday traditions and stories. They offer a tangible link to places and people that sometimes exist only in our memories, passed down l'dor v'dor, Hebrew for "from generation to generation."

About This Book

This book invites you to the holiday tables of thirty wonderful cooks and exceptional hosts. They share menus for a Persian Rosh Hashanah feast (page 20) and a Moroccan-Brazilian Shabbat lunch (page 372), dessert recipes from medieval Spain (page 166), and a gefilte fish recipe that weathered the Soviet Union (page 208). They share family stories of playing cards and snacking on Purim in Baghdad (see page 190), traveling from Yemen to Israel by camel (see page 88), and fleeing a village in Ethiopia in the middle of the night (see page 342). You will find their recipes and hear their stories in their own words—written with some help from the Jewish Food Society team.

Some of these cooks are professionals in the food world, while others work in fields like tech, publishing, and design, but they all have a passion for storytelling through food. Each table's menu reflects one family's traditions, which may be shared across a Jewish community or be unique to that family. Often, these menus are a blend of dishes that are uniquely Jewish and ones a family or community adopted and sometimes adapted from non-Jewish neighbors they lived among in the Diaspora for centuries. Just as the recipes are often an amalgam of the family's journey, so are their names. You may see dishes your family knows by one name called another by the family who contributed them.

There is no one right way to celebrate the Jewish holidays—or to cook from this book. You can invite friends and family over for a Passover Seder or a springtime dinner and make every dish from baker Rinat Tzadok's Israeli-Moroccan-Yemenite menu (page 246) or celebrate Sukkot in the fall with a Bukharian spread from Dr. Svetlana Davydov (page 120). You can also mix and match recipes for different holiday meals, dinner parties, or weekend brunches. Or add dishes like Hila Alpert's cheese-filled calsones (page 293) or Anna Polonsky's herb salad (page 354) to a menu of your own.

I am deeply grateful to all of the cooks and families who so generously shared their stories and recipes. I invite you to get to know them and to try their dishes. I also hope this collection inspires you to welcome new flavors and traditions to your own table and to expand your ideas of what Jewish holiday cooking, and Jewish food, can be.

A Note on Kashrut and Pantry

Kosher laws have shaped Jewish recipes for centuries, with customs and levels of observance varying by community and household. Traditionally, pork, shellfish, and the mixing of meat and dairy ingredients are forbidden. In keeping with tradition, nearly all of the individual recipes in this book are kosher and all can easily be made kosher with adaptations we offer in the recipes. (For more information on Passover and kashrut, see page 202).

To honor both Jewish traditions and family customs, the menus in this book are presented as the families prepare them, and in the few cases where a dairy recipe appears in a meat menu, we have provided nondairy substitutions; use whichever you prefer.

SHOP SEASONALLY: Great meals are made from ingredients that are in season, so try shopping at your local farmers' market and make the recipes when their star ingredients are at their best.

SALT: These recipes were tested with Diamond Crystal kosher salt. If you are using another brand, such as Morton's, use half the amount specified in the recipe and add more to taste if necessary. This is particularly important if you are cooking with kosher meat, since it is already salted.

DAIRY: When a recipe calls for a dairy ingredient or vegan alternative, make sure to use one that is full-fat.

VEGAN DAIRY: If you are looking for a pareve or vegan alternative to butter or other dairy ingredients, we recommend Earth Balance products.

EGGS: The eggs in these recipes are always large.

ALLIUMS: Onions and garlic are always peeled unless otherwise noted.

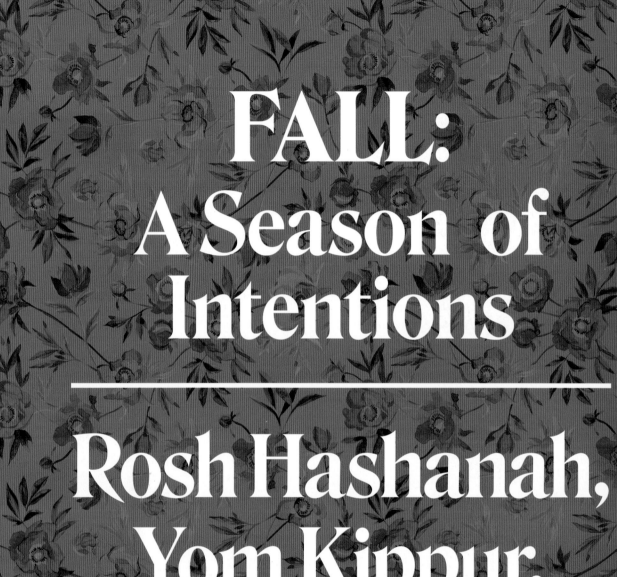

FALL:
A Season of Intentions

Rosh Hashanah, Yom Kippur, and Sukkot

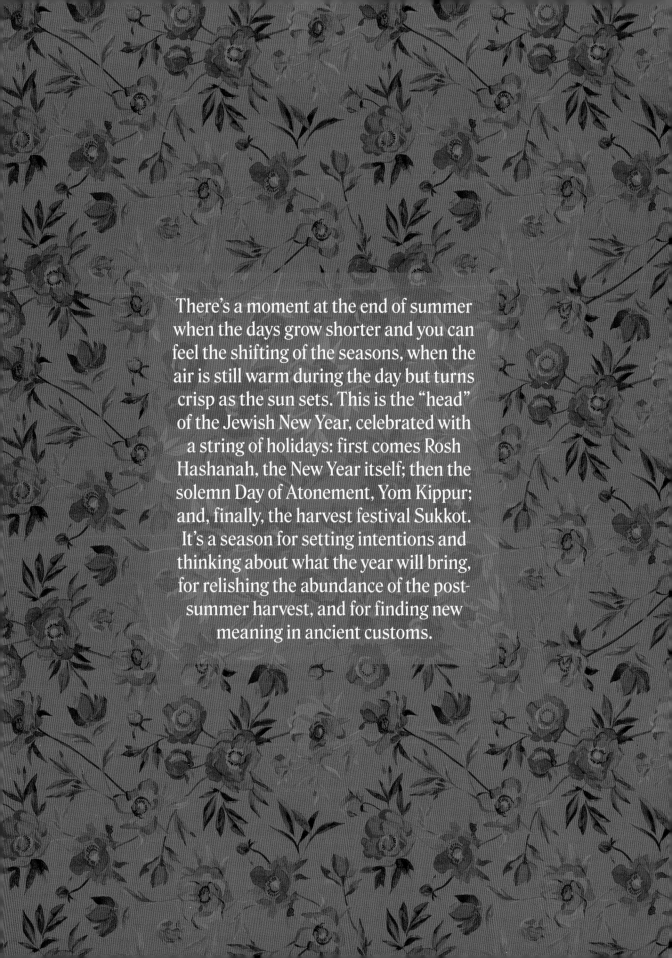

There's a moment at the end of summer when the days grow shorter and you can feel the shifting of the seasons, when the air is still warm during the day but turns crisp as the sun sets. This is the "head" of the Jewish New Year, celebrated with a string of holidays: first comes Rosh Hashanah, the New Year itself; then the solemn Day of Atonement, Yom Kippur; and, finally, the harvest festival Sukkot. It's a season for setting intentions and thinking about what the year will bring, for relishing the abundance of the post-summer harvest, and for finding new meaning in ancient customs.

Rosh Hashanah

MY FATHER AND I always ate poached fish heads in our kibbutz dining hall on the Jewish New Year, Rosh Hashanah, so we would be the heads and not the tails in the year to come. In many homes, apples are dipped in honey, originally an Ashkenazi tradition that represents sweetness, and shiny round loaves of challah are laid out to reflect the cycle of the year. No matter where you celebrate the holiday, the tables will always be full of symbolic foods eaten as good omens, meant to capture wishes for a sweet and abundant year free of obstacles. Some Rosh Hashanah foods and customs are shared across several Jewish communities, while others are unique to a place or even a family.

Before the official meal begins, it's customary in some families—most often those with Sephardi, Middle Eastern, or North African heritage—to celebrate with a series of blessings, sometimes called a Rosh Hashanah Seder, where foods like dates and pomegranates are blessed with wishes for the year ahead. Some of these foods and their connections to the New Year are based on Hebrew and Aramaic puns that, unfortunately, do not translate into English, but they are a meaningful part of the holiday's tradition. At Jessica Solnicki's Seder, olives are served for prosperity and fried spinach is meant to symbolically rid one's life of enemies. In her family the spinach is also part of the main meal, cooked in a dish called pkaila (page 76). It stands in for beet greens, which in Hebrew are called selek, which sounds like the Hebrew word for "getting rid of," and receives a blessing that asks that our enemies will leave us.

For many cooks, though, the symbolism of the food looks backward instead of forward. Recipes are made year after year as a way to keep alive the memory of loved ones who made them for the holiday before we did. For Rottem Lieberson, her Persian grandmother's legacy lives on in her lamb stewed with quinces and the refreshing apple drink called faloodeh sib (page 37). Mitchell Davis, who grew up in an Ashkenazi home in Toronto, carries the torch of his mother's cooking forward on the holiday with her recipes for chopped liver and kasha varnishkes (pages 44 and 52).

For this holiday, I love to borrow recipes from families I've met through the Jewish Food Society. I think about the families and how so much of our culture is shared, even if we are from communities that once lived very far apart. For centuries, Jews have folded their hopes for the coming year into their Rosh Hashanah dishes. As I cook, I ponder my own, setting my course.

My Persian Grandmother and Her Secret Recipes

SHARED BY

Rottem Lieberson

My grandmother Hanom's life was full of tragedy and children. She was married in Tehran when she was barely out of childhood herself and gave birth to ten children of her own. When my grandfather died, she was left without any money, but she still managed to bring the family to Israel. The transition wasn't easy. She spoke little Hebrew and deeply missed Tehran and her eldest son, who stayed back. In the years that followed, she lost him and another son.

From the time I was little, I could see how tough life had made my grandmother and how tightly she clung to her eight remaining children. She kept everyone together around her table. She would call daily to share the menu she was preparing, and aunts, uncles, and cousins would stop by for their favorite dishes, sometimes with bunches of fresh herbs in tow to fuel her cooking. Any sign of emotion from her was expressed through these meals.

I spent nearly every afternoon after school in her home, watching her in the kitchen as she added turmeric, saffron, and herbs to the large pots on her stove, skillfully making the sour and fragrant dishes of Iran.

FAMILY JOURNEY

Tehran, Iran → *Sha'ar Haliyah, Israel* → *Jerusalem* → *Tel Aviv*

Rottem and her husband, Ofer, on their wedding day, with
Rottem's grandmother Hanom Karmanian, in Tel Aviv, 1990

Guests would ask, "Hanom, what did you put in this?" She would reply,
"Nothing. Just a little bit of salt."

When it comes to Persian recipes, all the best cooks lie to guard their
secrets.

From one year to the next, her holiday menus remained exactly the
same. For Rosh Hashanah, she would cook for as many as a hundred
people, always using the most expensive ingredients as a wish for a
prosperous year ahead. My thirty or so cousins and I would have pillow
fights in her bedroom while the adults lingered over khoresh e beh, a
stew with meat and quinces; rice with tart barberries; a cold apple drink
called faloodeh sib; and more.

It was in this repetition of dishes and traditions that my grandmother
built her legacy. This was her power—her power to keep our family
together, to ensure she would not be forgotten. Today it's in my body, in
my blood. I feel it whenever I cook these dishes.

ROTTEM LIEBERSON is an acclaimed cookbook author in Israel whose work
is inspired by her Persian heritage and her grandmother Hanom's legacy.

Challah with Caramelized Quince
24

Olive Salad with Pomegranate
25

Cucumber, Mint, and Sumac Salad
26

Red Cabbage, Date, and Beet Salad
27

Fried Eggplant with Mint Dressing
28

Ash e Anar
Pomegranate Soup with Meatballs
30

Khoresh e Beh
Lamb Stew with Quince and Dried Apricot
32

Rice with Potato Tahdig
33

Tut
Marzipan
36

Faloodeh Sib
Chilled Apple Drink with Rosewater
37

—*Serve with*—

apples and honey, fresh fruit

Challah with Caramelized Quince

Rosh Hashanah challahs are most often swirled round loaves like the one Mitchell Davis bakes (page 42), but Rottem likes this festive braided loaf for the holiday, weaving in sweet caramelized quinces that have simmered for a couple of hours in a spiced syrup. It's best to begin this recipe a day in advance so the starter can rest for at least 8 hours or as long as overnight, which adds greater depth of flavor to the dough. You can also prepare the quinces up to 2 days ahead of time and store them, covered, at room temperature. *(Pictured on page 23)*

MAKES 2 loaves

FOR THE STARTER

1½ cups (195 g) all-purpose flour

¼ teaspoon active dry yeast

1 cup (240 ml) room-temperature water

FOR THE DOUGH

5½ cups (715 g) plus 1 tablespoon all-purpose flour

2 tablespoons active dry yeast

2 large eggs

5 tablespoons (60 g) sugar

¼ cup (60 ml) extra-virgin olive oil, plus more for greasing the bowl and work surface

1 to 1¼ cups (240 to 300 ml) water

1 tablespoon kosher salt

FOR THE CARAMELIZED QUINCES

2 quinces, peeled, cored, and cut into 12 wedges each

¾ cup (150 g) sugar

4 cardamom pods

1 cinnamon stick

FOR THE EGG WASH AND FINISHING

1 large egg, beaten with ½ teaspoon water

1 cup (140 g) sesame seeds

MAKE THE STARTER: Put the flour, yeast, and water in a medium bowl and stir to blend. Cover with plastic wrap and set aside at room temperature for at least 8 hours and up to overnight.

MAKE THE DOUGH: Put the flour and yeast in the bowl of a stand mixer fitted with the dough hook. Mix on low speed for a few seconds, until blended. Stop the mixer, add the starter, eggs, sugar, and olive oil, and mix on low for 3 minutes. Gradually add 1 cup (240 ml) water and mix for 3 more minutes, until a dough begins to form. If the dough feels dry, add up to ¼ cup (60 ml) more water.

Add the salt and mix on medium speed until the dough is smooth and no longer sticks to the bowl, another 8 minutes or so. Place a towel over the bowl and let the dough proof for 30 minutes.

Remove the towel and knead the dough on medium speed for 3 minutes.

Grease a large bowl with 1 to 2 teaspoons olive oil. Transfer the dough to the greased bowl and roll the dough in the bowl to coat it with oil. Cover the bowl with the towel and let the dough proof until doubled in size, 1 to 2 hours.

MEANWHILE, MAKE THE CARAMELIZED QUINCES: Put the quinces in a heavy-bottomed saucepan and add the sugar, cardamom, and cinnamon. Cook over medium heat, stirring occasionally, until all the sugar has dissolved and the quinces have started to release liquid, about 10 minutes.

Reduce the heat to low and gently simmer, stirring occasionally, until the quinces are tender and caramelized and the liquid has reduced to a thick, bright red sauce, about 1½ hours. Remove from the heat and set aside to cool.

SHAPE THE CHALLAHS: Lightly grease a clean work surface with olive oil. Turn out the proofed dough onto the surface and use a pastry scraper or large knife to divide it into 6 equal pieces. Roll each piece into a ball on the work surface. Cover the balls with a towel and let rest for 15 minutes.

Flatten each ball into an oval about 6 by 11 inches (15 by 28 cm) and then, starting from a long side, roll into a log about 20 inches (50 cm) long. Cover with a towel and let rest for 10 minutes.

Line two baking sheets with parchment paper. Make two 3-stranded challah braids: Arrange 3 logs side by side in front of you on the work surface, running vertically. Pinch together the ends farthest from you to connect the 3 logs. Gently pull the left log over the center log. Then pull the right log over the center log (which used to be the left log). Continue braiding the logs in this manner, and then pinch the near ends of the logs together and tuck both ends of the braid under to form a tidy loaf. Repeat with the second loaf.

Transfer the challahs to the baking sheets. Tightly tuck 12 pieces of the caramelized quince along the seams of each challah. Cover the loaves with towels and let rest until doubled in size, 30 to 35 minutes.

Preheat the oven to 400°F (205°C).

Brush the proofed challahs with the egg wash and sprinkle the sesame seeds on top. Bake until the challahs are golden brown and feel light and sound hollow when tapped on the bottom, 20 to 30 minutes. Remove from the oven and transfer to a wire rack to cool.

Serve warm or at room temperature.

Olive Salad with Pomegranate

Pomegranate adds a fruity note to these marinated olives. Pomegranate concentrate is thinner and less sweet than pomegranate syrup or molasses; the concentrate is worth seeking out. Look for one without added sugar. If you can't find the concentrate, you can replace it with one-third as much good-quality pomegranate molasses. *(Pictured on page 22)*

MAKES 6 to 8 servings

2 cups (300 g) pitted green olives

2 garlic cloves, finely chopped

1 cup (150 g) pomegranate seeds

⅓ cup (80 ml) pomegranate concentrate

⅓ cup (10 g) plus 1 tablespoon roughly chopped fresh mint

⅓ cup (80 ml) extra-virgin olive oil

1 teaspoon kosher salt

¼ teaspoon freshly ground black pepper

2 tablespoons chopped toasted walnuts

Put the olives, garlic, and pomegranate seeds in a bowl and mix well.

In another bowl, whisk the pomegranate concentrate, ⅓ cup (10 g) of the mint, and the olive oil until combined. Pour the dressing over the olive mixture and stir until evenly coated. Add the salt and pepper and mix again.

Put the salad in an airtight container and refrigerate until ready to serve, letting the salad rest for at least 1 hour so the flavors blend.

To serve, transfer the salad to a serving bowl and sprinkle with the walnuts and the remaining 1 tablespoon mint.

Cucumber, Mint, and Sumac Salad

"When someone comes over, the first thing you do is give them a cucumber. This is the tradition," Rottem says. The host should peel the cucumber with a knife and serve it with a pinch of salt, she explains. "This means she respects you and you respect her back."

Instead of peeling the cucumbers here, Rottem cuts them into spears and tosses them with a tangy lemon-sumac dressing for a salad that's a refreshing counterpoint to the richer dishes on her table. If you can't find Persian cucumbers, English ones will do, but they are more than twice as long, so be sure to adjust the recipe accordingly. No matter the variety you use, dress the salad just before serving so the cucumbers stay crunchy.

MAKES 6 to 8 servings

12 Persian cucumbers (about 2¼ pounds/1 kg), quartered lengthwise

1½ tablespoons ground sumac

¼ cup (60 ml) extra-virgin olive oil

¼ cup (60 ml) fresh lemon juice, or more to taste

1 teaspoon kosher salt

¼ cup (8 g) lightly packed fresh mint leaves for garnish

Flaky salt for garnish (optional)

Put the cucumbers, 1 tablespoon of the sumac, the olive oil, lemon juice, and kosher salt in a large bowl. Gently mix to coat evenly (your hands are the best tool for this). Taste and adjust the seasoning with more lemon and salt if needed.

Transfer the salad to a serving bowl, sprinkle the remaining 1½ teaspoons sumac on top, and garnish with the mint and a sprinkling of flaky salt, if using. Serve immediately.

Red Cabbage, Date, and Beet Salad

This sweet-tart slaw-like salad is best when the cabbage is sliced whisper-thin so everything comes together well. Use a mandoline slicer if you have one, and if not, make sure your chef's knife is sharp! *(Pictured on pages 22–23)*

MAKES 6 to 8 servings

1½ pounds (675 g) beets, trimmed and scrubbed

½ small red cabbage (about 13 ounces/365 g), cored and very thinly sliced crosswise, ideally on a mandoline (about 4½ cups/285 g lightly packed)

5 dates, pitted and chopped into small bits

2 jalapeños, cored, seeded, and finely chopped

½ cup (15 g) finely chopped fresh cilantro

½ cup (15 g) thinly sliced scallion greens

3 tablespoons fresh lemon juice, or more to taste

¼ cup (60 ml) extra-virgin olive oil, or more to taste

1 teaspoon kosher salt

Preheat the oven to 375°F (190°C). Line a baking sheet with parchment paper.

Put the beets on the baking sheet, cover the sheet tightly with foil, and bake until the beets are fork-tender, 40 minutes to 1 hour and 15 minutes, depending on the size of your beets. Remove from the oven and cool the beets until they can be easily handled.

Peel the beets with your fingers or a paring knife. Cut the beets into julienne: First cut each beet into slices ⅛ inch (3 mm) thick, then stack a few slices at a time and cut into strips ⅛ inch (3 mm) wide.

In a large bowl, combine the beets, cabbage, dates, jalapeños, cilantro, scallion greens, lemon juice, olive oil, and salt and mix well. Taste and adjust the seasoning if needed, adding more lemon, olive oil, and salt to make the salad nicely zingy. Serve immediately.

Fried Eggplant with Mint Dressing

Take your time when you fry the eggplant to make sure each slice is nicely browned on the outside and fully cooked and creamy on the inside. Eggplant loves to drink up oil, so be sure to use plenty and to keep the temperature steady.

MAKES 6 to 8 servings

1½ pounds (675 g) eggplant, sliced into ¼-inch (6 mm) rounds

1 tablespoon kosher salt

Vegetable or grapeseed oil for shallow-frying

FOR THE DRESSING

2 tablespoons pomegranate concentrate (see headnote on page 25)

⅓ cup (80 ml) extra-virgin olive oil, plus more if needed

1 cup (30 g) finely chopped fresh mint

1 teaspoon kosher salt

¼ teaspoon freshly ground black pepper

1 tablespoon pomegranate seeds for garnish

Sprinkle the eggplant slices on both sides with the salt and spread them in a single layer on a wire rack set over a baking sheet. Set aside for 20 minutes.

Pat the eggplant slices dry with paper towels, wiping off excess salt. Line a large plate or tray with paper towels.

Heat about ¼ cup (60 ml) vegetable oil in a large skillet over medium-high heat. Once the oil is hot, add as many eggplant rounds as will fit easily in one layer and fry, turning once, until golden brown, 3 to 5 minutes on each side. Transfer the fried eggplant to the paper towel–lined plate. Continue frying the remaining eggplant rounds in batches, adding more oil to the pan as needed and letting the new oil get hot before adding more eggplant.

MAKE THE DRESSING: In a small bowl, whisk the pomegranate concentrate, olive oil, mint, salt, and pepper together until well combined. Taste and adjust the seasoning with more salt and pepper if needed.

Arrange the fried eggplant in a few layers on a serving plate. Spoon the dressing over the eggplant and sprinkle the pomegranate seeds on top. Serve warm or at room temperature.

Ash e Anar
Pomegranate Soup with Meatballs

Generous amounts of fresh herbs and scallions lighten up this hearty soup with a tangy undercurrent of pomegranate—a classic Persian flavor combination. The meatballs can be made ahead of time and kept in the refrigerator for a day or in the freezer for up to a month.

MAKES 8 servings

FOR THE SOUP

3 tablespoons extra-virgin olive oil

3 cups (450 g) finely chopped yellow onions

8 garlic cloves, thinly sliced

½ cup (100 g) basmati rice, rinsed and drained

½ cup (90 g) yellow lentils

½ teaspoon ground turmeric

2 tablespoons kosher salt

¼ teaspoon freshly ground black pepper

3 quarts (3 L) water

1 cup (30 g) finely chopped fresh cilantro

1 cup (30 g) finely chopped fresh flat-leaf parsley

1 cup (30 g) finely chopped fresh mint, plus more for garnish

2 to 3 bunches scallions (about 20), white and light green parts, finely chopped

1 cup (240 ml) pomegranate concentrate (see headnote on page 25)

¼ to ½ cup (50 to 100 g) sugar (optional)

Pomegranate seeds for garnish

FOR THE MEATBALLS

1½ pounds (625 g) ground beef

¾ cup (115 g) finely chopped yellow onion

1 garlic clove, finely minced or crushed

1 cup (30 g) finely chopped fresh cilantro

1 teaspoon kosher salt

1 teaspoon freshly ground black pepper

MAKE THE SOUP: Heat the olive oil in a large pot over medium heat. Add the onions and cook, stirring occasionally, until soft and golden, 15 to 20 minutes.

MEANWHILE, MAKE THE MEATBALLS: Put the beef, onion, garlic, cilantro, salt, and pepper in a large bowl. Mix well (your hands are the best tool for this) until combined. Scoop up a heaping teaspoon of the mixture and roll it between your palms into a ball the size of a cherry tomato, then transfer it to a baking sheet or tray. Continue shaping the remaining meatball mixture, then set the meatballs aside.

When the onions are ready, add the garlic and cook until golden, 3 to 5 minutes. Add the rice, lentils, turmeric, salt, and pepper and stir to mix well. Stir in the water, increase the heat to high, and bring to a boil. Add the meatballs, cover the pot, adjust the heat to a simmer, and cook for 30 minutes, stirring occasionally.

Uncover the pot and stir in the cilantro, parsley, mint, and scallions. Increase the heat to high to bring the mixture back to a boil, then cover the pot again, reduce the heat to a simmer, and cook the soup for another 30 minutes, stirring occasionally.

Stir in the pomegranate concentrate and cook, covered, for another 10 minutes.

Taste the soup and adjust the seasoning with more salt and pepper if needed; add sugar to taste if the soup seems too tart.

Ladle the soup into individual bowls, garnish with pomegranate seeds, and serve hot.

Khoresh e Beh

Lamb Stew with Quince and Dried Apricot

In Persian cooking, fruits aren't reserved exclusively for dessert, Rottem explains. They can also be added to khoresh, or stews, like this beautifully spiced one where fresh and dried fruits are as prominent as the meat. If you've never cooked with quinces, this recipe and Rottem's challah (page 24) are good introductions. Quinces are astringent and unyielding when raw, but once simmered for a while, as they are here, they turn tender and a stunning deep pink color. If you can't find quinces, apples are a fine substitute.

Serve the stew with Rottem's Rice with Potato Tahdig (opposite) for a holiday meal or with plain white rice on a busier evening. *(Pictured on page 35)*

MAKES 6 to 8 servings

5 quinces or red apples, peeled, cored, and cut into eighths

2 tablespoons fresh lemon or lime juice

5 tablespoons (75 ml) extra-virgin olive oil

2 pounds (900 g) boneless lamb shoulder or neck, cut into 1½-inch (3.75 cm) cubes

1 large yellow onion, finely chopped

3 garlic cloves, thinly sliced

1 large tomato, cored and finely chopped

1 teaspoon ground turmeric

½ teaspoon dried rose petals

½ teaspoon ground cardamom

1½ teaspoons kosher salt

¼ teaspoon freshly ground black pepper

4 cups (1 L) water

1 teaspoon ground cinnamon

⅛ teaspoon ground nutmeg

⅛ teaspoon ground cloves

2 tablespoons all-purpose flour

10 dried apricots

2 tablespoons sugar

Put the quinces and lemon juice in a bowl and toss to coat the quinces with the juice. Set aside.

In a Dutch oven or other wide heavy-bottomed pot, heat 2 tablespoons of the olive oil over medium heat. Add the lamb and sauté until nicely browned on all sides, about 10 minutes total. Add the onion and sauté until golden, 6 to 8 minutes. Add the garlic, tomato, turmeric, rose petals, cardamom, salt, and pepper and mix well.

Add the water, increase the heat to high, and bring the mixture to a boil. Cover the pot with a lid, adjust the heat to low, and simmer the stew for 1 hour.

Meanwhile, in a large skillet, warm the remaining 3 tablespoons olive oil over medium heat. Pat the quince pieces dry with paper towels. Once the oil is hot, add the quinces, cinnamon, nutmeg, and cloves and scoot the quinces around in the pan to mix the spices. Sear the quinces all over until golden brown, 10 to 12 minutes. Add the flour and mix well to coat the quince pieces; remove from the heat.

Add the quinces, dried apricots, and sugar to the pot with the lamb and stir to combine. Continue cooking, covered, until the lamb and quinces are very tender, another 20 to 35 minutes.

Taste and adjust the seasoning with more salt and pepper if needed. Serve hot.

Rice with Potato Tahdig

No Persian meal is complete without rice and its tahdig, the crunchy crust from the bottom of the pot. In this rendition from Rottem's grandmother Hanom, the rice is made with a layer of potato slices on the bottom and topped with tart barberries. Mastering tahdig takes practice and confidence. To give yourself the best shot at a crust that releases easily from the pan, use a nonstick skillet. A deep 9-inch (22.5 cm) one with a lid that's slightly domed will work best for this quantity of rice. When it comes to the sauce, if you can't find barberries, don't worry; it will be excellent even without them. *(Pictured on pages 34–35)*

MAKES 6 to 8 servings

FOR THE SAUCE

¾ cup (50 g) dried barberries

Small pinch of saffron threads (about 7)

¼ cup (60 ml) boiling water

1 tablespoon vegetable oil

1 tablespoon sugar

¼ teaspoon kosher salt

FOR THE RICE

2¼ cups (450 g) basmati rice

Kosher salt

6 tablespoons (90 ml) vegetable oil

½ teaspoon ground turmeric

1 large russet potato, peeled and cut into ¼-inch (6 mm) rounds

MAKE THE SAUCE: Put the barberries, saffron, and boiling water in a small pot and set aside for 1 hour, stirring the mixture every 5 minutes or so to allow the barberries to soak up the saffron flavor.

Add the oil, sugar, and salt to the pot, set over low heat, and cook, stirring occasionally, until the sugar has dissolved and the sauce is bright orange in color, about 10 minutes. Remove from the heat and set aside.

MAKE THE RICE: Put the rice in a large bowl and cover it completely with room-temperature water. Soak for 30 minutes, then drain and rinse. Cover again with water, soak for 10 minutes, and drain; repeat this process at 10-minute intervals until the water runs clear.

Fill a large pot about three-quarters full with water and add 1 heaping tablespoon salt. Place the pot over high heat and bring the water to a boil. Add the rice and cook, uncovered, for 7 minutes. Drain and rinse the rice and set aside in a bowl.

Add the oil and turmeric to a deep 9-inch (22.5 cm) nonstick skillet with a lid, swirling to mix them together. Arrange the potato slices in an even layer to cover the bottom of the skillet completely (you may not need all the potato slices); season lightly with salt. Very gently pile the partly cooked rice onto the potatoes; do not stir the rice or pack it into the skillet. Using the handle of a wooden spoon, poke four holes, evenly spaced, into the rice, reaching all the way down to the potato layer.

Place a kitchen towel over the skillet, cover with the lid, and tie the corners of the towel together on top of the lid to keep them away from the burner. Place the skillet over medium-high heat

and cook for about 15 minutes. Reduce the heat to low and cook for an additional 25 minutes.

Remove the skillet from the heat and remove the lid and towel. To turn out the tahdig, place a large flat platter on top of the skillet and, using a thick, dry kitchen towel or pot holders to protect your hands, hold the skillet with one hand and the plate with the other and swiftly invert them, slipping the tahdig onto the plate. Carefully remove the skillet; if any potato slices are stuck to the bottom, just peel them off and reposition them with the other slices.

Pour the barberry and saffron sauce over the tahdig and rice and serve immediately.

Tut
Marzipan

The word *tut*, which means "white mulberry" in Persian, also refers to marzipan that's flavored with rosewater and formed into the shape of the berry. Rottem's grandmother Hanom shaped hers like strawberries and served them with sweets from Iran, fruit, and nuts. You can make the paste up to a week in advance, but be sure to wrap it tightly, as it dries out easily. For the best texture, form the sweets the day you plan to serve them.

MAKES about 30 pieces

1 cup (130 g) blanched almonds

1 cup (100 g) confectioners' sugar

1 tablespoon rosewater

½ cup (100 g) granulated sugar

15 roasted unsalted pistachios, split lengthwise in half

Put the almonds and confectioners' sugar in a food processor and process until a sandy mixture forms, about 2 minutes. With the processor running, add the rosewater and process until a soft, smooth dough forms, another 5 minutes or so. Transfer to a bowl.

Put the granulated sugar on a plate; set aside.

Scoop up about 1 rounded teaspoon of the marzipan and shape into a ball. Shape the ball into a rounded triangle to resemble a strawberry, using your index finger and thumb to create dimples in the sides and top of it. Put on a plate and repeat with the remaining marzipan.

Roll each piece of marzipan in the sugar to coat all sides. Poke a pistachio half into the top of each piece of marzipan, as if it were the leaf on a fresh strawberry. Transfer the marzipan to a pretty dish and serve.

Faloodeh Sib
Chilled Apple Drink with Rosewater

Faloodeh refers to an iconic cold Persian dessert made with rice noodles. In faloodeh sib, the noodles are replaced with apples for a sweet that's served at the Yom Kippur breakfast in some Persian Jewish homes. Rottem's grandmother also made it for Rosh Hashanah, when apples are traditionally eaten. "It was always in her fridge and you just took a sip whenever you wanted—it's refreshing, it's amazing!" Rottem says.

Grated apples will oxidize and brown slightly, which is just fine, but if you want to keep their flesh white, add a big squeeze of lemon juice to them as you grate them. For added festivity, spike the pitcher of faloodeh sib with ½ to 1 cup (120 to 240 ml) vodka.

MAKES 6 to 8 servings

7 red apples, unpeeled, cored and grated

1 teaspoon rosewater

2 tablespoons sugar (optional)

Cold water

1 cup (200 g) ice cubes

1 lemon, thinly sliced

Put the apples in a large glass pitcher (at least 2 quarts/2 L) and add the rosewater, sugar (if using), and enough cold water to cover the apples by an inch (2.5 cm) or so. Stir well and put the pitcher in the refrigerator for at least 2 hours and up to 4 hours.

Just before serving, add the ice and lemon slices to the pitcher. Serve in pretty glasses or small punch cups, with spoons for eating the apples.

Whether in Toronto or New York, the Meal Is the Holiday

SHARED BY

Mitchell Davis

On the days before holidays, the powerful smell of gefilte fish being made from scratch used to waft down the hallways of our apartment building in north Toronto when I was growing up. This was the 1970s, and we called our neighborhood the Jewish ghetto. There was the kosher-style butcher shop where I worked in high school, and bakeries selling challah. Orthodox, Reform, and Conservative synagogues all were within walking distance, and my junior high, despite being a public school, was virtually closed for the High Holidays.

I felt incredibly Jewish, but not in any religious way. For my family, holiday meals were our religion. They were how we were Jewish, the ritual that made us feel different from people outside the neighborhood. Everyone was welcome at my mom's table. I'm one of four siblings, and someone's roommate from college, someone's partner, and someone else's friend were always at the meal. No matter the holiday, the menu was the same—at Passover, we just substituted matzah for challah.

It looked something like this: chopped liver made in a wooden bowl, featherweight matzah balls in chicken soup (even though my mom actually preferred "sinkers"), kasha varnishkes loaded with butter,

---

FAMILY JOURNEY

London → New Jersey → Toronto → New York City

The Davis family in the kitchen of the James Beard Foundation in New York City, 1996. From left to right: brother Sheldon, niece Helen, Mitchell, mom Sondra, and sister Carrie (not present: sister Leslie).

tzimmes—and, because God forbid someone might ever starve, there were always two proteins—roast chicken and brisket.

I started helping my mom, Sondra, in the kitchen when I was very young, listening to her advice to, for example, salt a chicken "like you're salting the road" and noticing that she had a special touch—perhaps inherited from her grandmother Eva. I fell in love with the kitchen and sometimes would pretend I was sick so I could stay home from school and watch cooking shows. As my mom's health declined and her eyesight faded, she relied on me and my sister Carrie in the kitchen. Even as a teen, I did a lot of my mother's cooking, especially for the holidays.

When I started writing a Jewish cookbook in my early thirties, I asked my mother to come visit and cook with me in my New York apartment. This was how I learned that despite her always saying she used the matzah ball recipe from the back of the Streit's box, she clearly had her own ideas about measurements. Luckily, I learned them then and there—she passed away before the book came out.

Over the years, her holiday menu became our menu. I've added a few items to the table, but her dishes have remained—they need to be there. Without them, there would be no holiday.

MITCHELL DAVIS is a food innovator, writer, thought leader, and author of *The Mensch Chef: Or Why Delicious Jewish Food Isn't an Oxymoron*. He serves as a senior strategist to the Jewish Food Society's partner organization Asif: Culinary Institute of Israel.

Round Challah with Honey and Raisins

On Rosh Hashanah, it's customary to bake round loaves of challah. As with many symbolic foods in Jewish tradition, there are several theories behind this custom: Some sources say the shape represents the circular, continuous nature of the year or the cycle of life. Others argue that the round loaf represents the shape of a crown for God to wear as the King of the New Year. Raisins or other dried fruits are often worked into the dough as a symbol of a sweet year to come.

Mitchell's challah can be kneaded by hand or made in a stand mixer. No matter which method you use, be sure to start this recipe early in the day to allow for a few rises.

MAKES 1 large loaf

1 cup (240 ml) lukewarm water (around 120°F/49°C, or warm to the touch)

¼ cup (85 g) mild honey, such as acacia or wildflower, or ¼ cup (50 g) sugar

1 packet (2¼ teaspoons/7 g) active dry yeast

2 large eggs

¼ cup (60 ml) plus 1 tablespoon peanut or Crisco oil (100% soybean oil) or 4 tablespoons (60 g) unsalted butter, melted and cooled

4½ cups (585 g) unbleached all-purpose flour

1 tablespoon kosher salt

½ cup (70 g) golden raisins

1 large egg beaten with 1 teaspoon water for egg wash

TO PREPARE THE DOUGH BY HAND: In a large bowl, combine the water, honey, and yeast and stir to dissolve the yeast.

Add the eggs and the ¼ cup (60 ml) oil to the water-yeast mixture and, using a sturdy wire whisk, whisk until frothy and well blended. Add 2 cups (260 g) flour and the salt and continue whisking until a smooth batter forms. Switch to a sturdy wooden spoon and stir in 2¼ cups (290 g) more flour so you have a stiff, shaggy dough.

Dust the work surface with some of the remaining ¼ cup (30 g) flour and turn the dough out onto it. Using a dough scraper and your hands, knead the dough, folding it in half on top of itself and then pushing it down on the counter away from you to re-form a sort of blob, until it is smooth and soft, no longer sticky, and elastic enough to hold its shape, 5 to 10 minutes, depending on how vigorously you are kneading. If the dough is too sticky to handle, add some of the remaining flour in small doses, trying to keep the dough on the soft side.

TO PREPARE THE DOUGH IN A STAND MIXER: In the bowl of a stand mixer, combine the water with the honey and stir to dissolve, then sprinkle the yeast over the top. Attach the bowl to the mixer stand and fit it with the paddle attachment.

Add the eggs and the ¼ cup (60 ml) oil to the water-yeast mixture and beat until frothy and well blended. Add 2 cups (260 g) flour and the salt and continue beating until a smooth batter forms. Switch to the dough hook, add 2¼ cups (290 g) flour, and knead until a smooth, elastic dough forms, 4 to 5 minutes.

Dust the work surface with some of the remaining ¼ cup (30 g) flour and turn out the dough. Knead five or six times, until soft.

FOR EITHER METHOD: Shape the dough into a ball by folding the edges underneath and

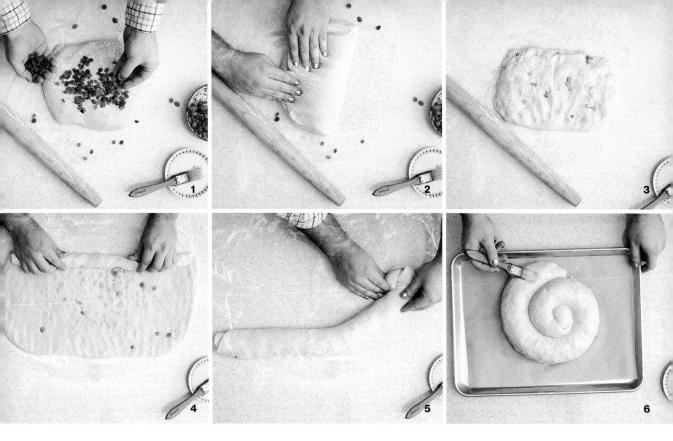

stretching the top surface of the dough. Put the remaining 1 tablespoon oil in a large bowl and spread it over the interior with your hands. Place the ball of dough upside down in the bowl to coat with oil and then invert it. Cover the bowl with plastic wrap and allow the dough to rise in a warm place until doubled in bulk, about 1 hour and 45 minutes.

Remove the plastic wrap and gently punch down the dough with your fist to deflate it to its original size. Re-cover the bowl and let sit for 15 minutes.

Line a baking sheet with parchment paper. Lightly flour the work surface. **1.** Turn out the dough, sprinkle the raisins over it, and knead lightly to incorporate them. **2.** Fold the dough in half to enclose the raisins. **3.** Pat it out with your palms, or roll with a rolling pin, into a rectangle about 12 by 16 inches (30 by 40 cm). Poke any stray raisins back into the dough.

4. Starting from a long side, roll up the dough like a jelly roll to form a log about 18 inches (45 cm) long and 2½ inches (6.25 cm) in diameter. **5.** Starting at one end, curl the log into itself to form a turban or snail shape and transfer to the baking sheet. Tuck the tail end of the coil underneath the dough to secure it. Cover with a clean towel and let rise in a warm place until doubled in bulk, 45 minutes to 1 hour.

Place a rack in the center of the oven and preheat the oven to 400°F (205°C).

6. Brush the entire surface of the dough with the egg wash. Bake the loaf until the surface begins to brown, about 20 minutes. Reduce the oven temperature to 350°F (175°C) and continue baking until the challah is a deep brown and sounds hollow when you tap the bottom, 15 to 20 minutes. Remove the challah from the oven, transfer to a wire rack, and allow to cool completely before serving.

Chopped Liver

The ingredient that makes chopped liver taste distinctly Jewish arguably isn't the livers but the onions. The backbone flavor of so many Jewish dishes, onions are added to this recipe twice: first chopped and sautéed with the liver and then grated raw just before serving. If you don't like raw onions, you can simply leave them out or replace them with fried onions.

Mitchell's mother, Sondra, used to chop the livers in a wooden bowl with a one-handed mezzaluna she called "the chopper," but a sharp knife and a cutting board work just as well.

MAKES 3 cups (585 g)

1½ pounds (675 g) chicken livers

2 large eggs

6 to 8 tablespoons (90 to 120 ml) chicken schmaltz or vegetable oil, or more to taste

1 pound (450 g) yellow onions (about 3 medium), one peeled and left whole, with the root end still intact, the others finely chopped

2½ teaspoons kosher salt

1 teaspoon freshly ground black pepper

1 tablespoon grainy mustard, plus more for serving

1 tablespoon prepared horseradish

Chopped fresh flat-leaf parsley for garnish (optional)

Dark bread or crackers for serving

Whole-grain mustard for serving

To clean the livers, first rinse them under cold running water. With a sharp paring knife, separate the two lobes of each liver. Cut away any visible fat, membranes, veins, or green patches and drain the livers in a strainer.

Put the eggs in a small saucepan, cover with cold water by about 1 inch (2.5 cm), and bring to a boil. Cook for 9 minutes from the moment the water boils, then remove the pan from the heat and run cold water over the eggs for a few minutes. Let the eggs cool completely, then peel and chop them; cover and set aside.

Meanwhile, heat the schmaltz in a 10- to 12-inch (25 to 30 cm) heavy skillet over medium-high heat. Add the chopped onions and sauté, stirring frequently, until soft and translucent, 7 to 8 minutes; don't let them brown. Reduce the heat to medium, add the livers, and sauté gently until they are cooked through and any liquid they release has evaporated, 15 to 20 minutes; they should still be rosy in the center. Season with the salt and pepper, remove from the heat, and let cool.

If using a wooden chopping bowl (see headnote), transfer the cooked livers and onions to it. Add the mustard and horseradish and, using a mezzaluna (metal chopping blade), chop the livers into small dice. (Some of the livers will break up to mush; others will hold their shape. The goal is to obtain a spreadable combination of small pieces and paste.) If not using a chopping bowl, transfer the liver mixture to a cutting board and chop using a very sharp knife, then transfer to a medium bowl and fold in the mustard and horseradish.

Add the chopped eggs to the liver and mix gently but well, then taste and adjust the seasoning with more salt and pepper if necessary. If you like, add more schmaltz to smooth out the flavor and texture of the liver.

The chopped liver can be made up to 2 days in advance to this point and refrigerated, covered. Before serving, remove the liver from the refrigerator and let sit at room temperature for a few minutes, taste, and adjust the seasoning if necessary, as it may have changed after chilling.

To serve, using a handheld box grater and holding on to the root end of the whole onion, grate as much of the onion as you like onto the chopped liver. Mix well, taste, and adjust the seasoning, if necessary. Sprinkle with parsley, if you like.

Serve with bread or crackers and mustard on the side.

Matzah Ball Soup

Mitchell's matzah balls are pillowy and tender and served in broth deeply infused with the taste of chicken. One way to help ensure a rich flavor is to use a stewing hen, so ask the butcher if they can order you one. Adding chicken necks and/or feet also helps, and gives the broth body.

Making the broth at least a day ahead allows time for the fat to rise to the top so you can easily spoon it off, but be sure to leave some of it for flavor. You can also make the broth up to a few months ahead and freeze it. The recipe makes more broth than you'll use for one meal, but the leftovers are excellent to have on hand. If you have any remaining matzah balls, refrigerate them separately from the broth.

MAKES 6 to 8 servings

FOR THE BROTH

One 4½-pound (2 kg) stewing hen or roasting chicken, quartered and rinsed

2 or 3 chicken necks or chicken feet, claws removed (optional)

2 pounds (900 g) yellow onions (about 4 large), roughly chopped

1 pound (450 g) celery stalks with leaves (about 8 medium), roughly chopped

8 ounces (225 g) parsley roots with tops, cleaned and roughly chopped, or about 10 flat-leaf parsley sprigs

1½ pounds (675 g) carrots (about 8 medium), peeled and halved crosswise

8 ounces (225 g) turnips (about 2 medium), peeled and cut into chunks

8 ounces (225 g) parsnips (about 2 medium), peeled and cut into chunks

1 tablespoon whole black peppercorns

1 small star anise point

2 tablespoons kosher salt

5 quarts (5 L) cold water

6 dill sprigs

FOR THE MATZAH BALLS

5 large eggs

1 teaspoon kosher salt

¼ cup (60 ml) melted chicken schmaltz, at room temperature

¼ cup (60 ml) hot broth (from above)

1 cup plus 2 tablespoons (130 g) matzah meal

FOR THE VEGETABLE GARNISH

8 ounces (225 g) carrots (about 2 large), peeled and sliced ⅛ inch (3 mm) thick

8 ounces (225 g) turnips (about 2 medium), peeled and cut into ⅓-inch (8 mm) dice

4 ounces (115 g) celery (2 medium stalks), cut into ¼-inch (6 mm) slices

1½ teaspoons chopped fresh dill

MAKE THE BROTH: Put the quartered hen, necks or feet (if using), onions, celery, parsley roots, carrots, turnips, parsnips, peppercorns, star anise, and salt in a very large (at least 12-quart/ 12 L) stockpot. Add the water and bring to a boil over high heat.

Reduce the heat to a simmer, partially cover the pot, and cook for 2 hours, skimming off any scum that rises to the surface with a large spoon.

Add the dill sprigs and simmer for another 45 minutes. Turn off the heat and allow the broth to cool.

Ladle the cooled broth through a fine-mesh sieve into storage containers. Refrigerate overnight.

recipe continues

The next day, remove any fat that congealed on the top of the broth. Refrigerate the broth for up to 2 days, or freeze for up to 3 months.

MAKE THE MATZAH BALLS: Combine the eggs, salt, schmaltz, and the ¼ cup (60 ml) broth in a medium bowl and whisk until blended.

Using a fork, stir in the matzah meal, mixing until smooth. Cover and chill in the refrigerator until the matzah meal has absorbed the liquid and the mixture feels almost firm, about 30 minutes.

In a large pot, bring 2 quarts (2 L) of the chicken broth to a low simmer. In a separate pot, bring about 5 quarts (5 L) water to a boil with 2 tablespoons kosher salt.

Remove the matzah ball mixture from the fridge. Wet your hands with cold water, scoop up a heaping tablespoonful of the mixture, and shape it into a ball by gently rolling it between your palms. (Rolling too tightly will prevent it from achieving its puffiest consistency.) Drop the matzah ball into the boiling water and repeat with the remaining mixture, cleaning and wetting your hands as necessary to keep the matzah balls from sticking to them. Be careful not to crowd the pot, or the matzah balls will not cook through fully; cook in batches or in two pots, if necessary.

Bring the water back to a full boil, then cover tightly, adjust the heat to a simmer, and cook until the matzah balls have risen from the bottom of the pot and expanded to about twice their size, 35 to 40 minutes. Occasionally a matzah ball might stick to the bottom of the pot; if so, just give it a nudge with a spoon to release it.

WHILE THE MATZAH BALLS COOK, MAKE THE VEGETABLE GARNISH: Add the sliced carrots and diced turnips to the pot of broth and simmer for 30 minutes. Add the sliced celery and continue cooking until all of the vegetables are tender, about 15 more minutes. Add the chopped dill and taste the soup for seasoning, adding more salt if needed. Keep warm until ready to serve.

Using a slotted spoon, remove the matzah balls from the boiling water and place them in the simmering soup. (If your matzah balls are done before your soup is ready, let them sit on a tray, then reheat them in the soup.)

To serve, transfer the matzah balls to bowls and ladle the broth and vegetables over the top. Start with one or two matzah balls per person, inviting guests to come back for seconds of soup and/or matzah balls.

Carrot and Sweet Potato Tzimmes

A sweet carrot dish made with or without meat, tzimmes is a staple of many traditional Ashkenazi homes. It's served on Shabbat, Sukkot, and often Rosh Hashanah, when sweet foods are eaten to help usher in the new year. Like Mitchell's brisket (page 54) and kasha varnishkes (page 52), this is a great make-ahead recipe. You can assemble it up to 2 days in advance, cover the baking dish, and refrigerate. The baking dish can go straight from the fridge to the oven, though you may need to add a few minutes to the cooking time. *(Pictured on page 40)*

MAKES 6 to 8 servings

1½ pounds (675 g) sweet potatoes (about 2 medium), peeled and cut into 1-inch (2.5 cm) chunks

1 pound (450 g) carrots (about 5 medium), peeled and cut into 1-inch (2.5 cm) chunks

8 ounces (225 g) sweet onion, such as Vidalia or Maui (1 small), cut into 1-inch (2.5 cm) chunks

¾ cup (115 g) pitted prunes, halved

2 tablespoons honey

¾ cup (180 ml) orange juice or ¼ cup (60 ml) frozen orange juice concentrate

4 tablespoons (60 g) unsalted butter or nondairy butter

Two 2-inch (5 cm) cinnamon sticks

1 or 2 star anise points

1½ teaspoons kosher salt

Pinch of freshly ground white pepper

Preheat the oven to 375°F (190°C).

In a 3-quart (3 L) baking dish (a 9-by-13-inch/ 23 by 33 cm dish works well), combine the sweet potatoes, carrots, onion, prunes, honey, orange juice, butter, cinnamon sticks, star anise, salt, and white pepper and toss everything around a few times to make sure the ingredients are evenly distributed.

Roast uncovered until the vegetables are tender and lightly browned and most of the liquid has been absorbed, about 1½ hours, giving the vegetables a stir about halfway through for even cooking. Taste and adjust the seasoning with more salt and white pepper if needed.

Remove and discard the cinnamon sticks and star anise and serve.

Gefilte Fish

One of the most iconic Jewish foods, gefilte fish takes its name from the Yiddish word *gefilte*, meaning "stuffed." Traditionally, ground raw fish was mixed with matzah meal or breadcrumbs and seasonings and tucked into the skin of a whole fish before it was roasted or poached and then served in slices. Over the years, stuffing a whole fish (see Sasha Shor's recipe on page 208) became less common, and more families started to make quenelles from the fish mixture and poach them. Jarred gefilte fish also became popular in the mid-to-late twentieth century. If that is the only gefilte you've encountered, know that the homemade version is entirely different—delicate, flavorful, and worth the effort.

Some fishmongers will grind fish for you, but you can also grind fresh skinless fillets yourself. Make sure the fish is very cold, and chill the blade of the food processor before grinding. You'll also want to use the pulse function so that you can stop chopping the fish before it turns into a paste.

MAKES 6 to 12 servings

FOR THE POACHING LIQUID

1 pound (450 g) bones from freshwater fish, without heads (optional)

3 medium yellow onions (about 1 pound/450 g), sliced

2 celery stalks with leaves (about 4 ounces/115 g), cut into chunks

3 large carrots (about 9 ounces/250 g), scrubbed and cut into chunks

1 tablespoon kosher salt

1 tablespoon sugar

1 teaspoon whole black peppercorns

3 quarts (3 L) cold water

FOR THE FISH MIXTURE

2 pounds (900 g) ground freshwater fish fillets (see headnote)—whitefish, pike, or perch, or a combination

2 large eggs, beaten

3 large carrots (about 8 ounces/225 g), peeled, 1 grated, the other 2 thinly sliced into coins

2 medium yellow onions (about 8 ounces/225 g), grated

½ cup (120 ml) cold water

¼ cup (30 g) matzah meal

1 tablespoon sugar

1 tablespoon kosher salt

½ teaspoon freshly ground white or black pepper

Vegetable oil

Iceberg lettuce leaves for serving

Beet horseradish for serving

MAKE THE POACHING LIQUID: In a wide stockpot, combine the fish bones (if using), onions, celery, carrots, salt, sugar, and peppercorns. Add the water and bring to a boil over high heat. Reduce the heat to low, cover, and simmer for about 1 hour, while you prepare the fish. When the broth is ready, remove the solids and discard; keep the liquid at a simmer, covered.

PREPARE THE FISH MIXTURE: In a large bowl or, more traditionally, in a wooden chopping bowl, combine the fish, eggs, grated carrot, grated onion, cold water, matzah meal, sugar, salt, and pepper and mix well to ensure all the ingredients are evenly distributed. To test the seasoning, shape a scant tablespoon or so of the fish mixture into a patty. Heat a splash of oil in a small sauté pan and fry your test patty. Once it has cooled, taste and adjust the seasoning as necessary, remembering that when the mixture is chilled, the flavors will be less pronounced.

SHAPE AND COOK THE GEFILTE FISH: Place the fish mixture near the pot of simmering poaching liquid. Wet your hands with cold water. Scoop up about ½ cup (4 ounces/115 g) of the mixture and shape it between your palms into an oblong puck, somewhere between an egg and a quenelle, then let it roll off your palm into the simmering liquid. Repeat with the remaining mixture, wetting and cleaning your hands regularly to keep the mixture from sticking. You should get about 12 patties of gefilte fish.

Add the sliced carrots to the pot and bring to a gentle boil. Turn down the heat to a very gentle simmer, cover, and cook for about 50 minutes,

until the gefilte fish is white and firm and the carrots are tender. Turn off the heat and let cool to room temperature.

Using a slotted spoon, transfer the gefilte fish and carrots to a storage container. Strain the cooking liquid over the top to cover, and chill until ready to serve.

To serve, place each gefilte patty in an iceberg lettuce cup and garnish with a boiled carrot coin. Serve with beet horseradish.

Kasha Varnishkes with Onions and Mushrooms

A helping of kasha varnishkes was Sondra's dying wish. "We made it for her on her deathbed," Mitchell recalls. He's already told his husband, Nate, that he needs to learn how to make the recipe, since Mitchell knows it will be one of his own last wishes.

The Davis family kasha varnishkes is loaded with onions, mushrooms, and butter—though it can be made with olive oil. You can make it up to 2 days ahead of time and store it in a covered baking dish in the refrigerator.

MAKES 6 to 8 servings

2 cups (480 ml) homemade or store-bought low-sodium chicken broth, broth from Matzah Ball Soup (page 47), or water, plus additional broth or water for reheating

Kosher salt

1 cup (175 g) uncooked kasha

1 large egg, beaten

Freshly ground black pepper

8 tablespoons (1 stick/115 g) butter or extra-virgin olive oil

1 pound (450 g) yellow onions (about 2 large), chopped

12 ounces (340 g) assorted fresh mushrooms, such as cremini and oyster, trimmed and roughly chopped

½ ounce (15 g) assorted dried mushrooms, such as porcini and chanterelle, soaked in hot water to cover until soft, drained, and finely chopped

8 ounces (225 g) bowtie pasta (farfalle) or egg noodles

Put the broth in a small saucepan, add a generous pinch of salt, and bring to a boil over medium-high heat. Reduce the heat and keep very warm.

Put the kasha in a wide saucepan or skillet, add the beaten egg, and stir to mix well; the kasha will clump together, but that's okay. Set the pan over medium-high heat and stir the kasha constantly to toast it. As it heats, the clumps will break apart into separate grains and the kasha will give off a distinct buckwheat aroma. It may start to stick to the bottom of the pan because of the egg, but it will release as it continues to toast. Once the kasha has browned slightly and has a strong toasted aroma, 7 to 8 minutes, pour in the hot broth. Add a generous amount of pepper, cover the pan, reduce the heat to very low, and simmer until all of the liquid has been absorbed and the kasha has plumped, 8 to 12 minutes. Remove from the heat and fluff the kasha with a fork. Set aside, uncovered.

Meanwhile, prepare the onions and mushrooms: Heat the butter in a large saucepan or large skillet over medium-high heat. Add the onions and sauté until translucent, 7 to 8 minutes. Add the fresh mushrooms, 2 teaspoons salt, and ¾ teaspoon pepper and cook, stirring often, until the mushrooms have given off most of their moisture and the moisture has evaporated, about 15 minutes.

Add the rehydrated dried mushrooms and cook for another 5 minutes or so to concentrate the flavors of the mixture. Taste and adjust the seasoning as necessary; the mixture should be highly seasoned at this point, almost too salty and peppery. Remove from the heat.

Bring a large pot of salted water to a boil (about 4 quarts/4 L water and 2 tablespoons salt). Add the pasta and cook until just past al dente, following the package instructions; the noodles should be tender.

Drain the pasta and return to the pot or transfer to a large bowl. Add the mushroom mixture and toss well, then add the kasha and toss again. Taste and adjust the seasoning with more salt and pepper if needed.

Serve immediately, or transfer to a 2- or 3-quart (2 or 3 L) baking dish. (The kasha can be covered and refrigerated for up to 2 days at this point.)

To finish the dish, preheat the oven to 325°F (160°C).

Spoon ½ to 1 cup (120 to 240 ml) broth (even better would be brisket pan juices, if you have them) over the kasha, cover with foil, and bake for 25 minutes.

Remove the foil, increase the heat to 375°F (190°C), and bake for another 15 to 20 minutes, until the top begins to brown. Serve piping hot.

Pickled Cucumber Salad

Everyone in Mitchell's family loves sour things, but if the vinegar in this quick pickle is too powerful for you, he suggests adding a tablespoon or two of sugar. You can also peel or not peel the cucumbers—a decision Mitchell makes depending on whether he wants to add color to the plate or on his "degree of laziness at the time of preparation," he jokes. *(Pictured on page 41)*

MAKES 8 servings

2 English (seedless) cucumbers (about 1¾ pounds/790 g), peeled if desired

2 tablespoons kosher salt

8 ounces (225 g) yellow or white onions (2 small), very thinly sliced

1 cup (240 ml) white vinegar (5% acidity)

1 cup (240 ml) cold water

1 to 2 tablespoons sugar, to taste (optional)

Using a food processor fitted with the slicing blade or a mandoline, thinly slice the cucumbers and transfer to a large bowl. Sprinkle the cucumber slices with the salt, tossing the slices to distribute the salt evenly.

Place a plate on top of the cucumbers to weight them down and let sit at room temperature for at least 1 hour but no more than 2 hours, until the cucumbers have given up a lot of their water and become soft.

Drain the cucumbers in a colander, rinse under cold water, and drain again. Transfer to a bowl and add the sliced onions.

Combine the vinegar and cold water and pour over the cucumbers. If using sugar, dissolve it in a little hot water and add to the cucumbers.

Pack the cucumbers and the brine into a 1-quart (1 L) glass jar or other nonreactive container and refrigerate until ready to serve. The cucumbers can be eaten right away, but they are best after they have sat for a day or two. They will keep for about 2 weeks in the refrigerator.

Brisket with Onions

Mitchell's family adopted this sweetly spiced brisket recipe from his friend's mom, Maxine Rapoport. On its own, brisket is a tough cut of meat, but when braised, as it is here, it turns meltingly tender. A whole brisket has two sections, the "point" (also called the deckle), which is smaller and thicker and contains large sections of fat, and the "flat," which is leaner and larger. Some meat departments sell only the flat, which is fine for this recipe, but use a whole brisket if you can to get a nice mix of fattier and leaner pieces.

This recipe takes several hours to make, but fortunately the brisket is even better the next day. *(Pictured on pages 40–41)*

MAKES 6 to 8 servings, with plenty of leftovers

5 tablespoons (75 ml) peanut or vegetable oil

One 5- to 7-pound (2.3 to 3.2 kg) whole beef brisket, trimmed of excess fat

Kosher salt and freshly ground black pepper

1 pound (450 g) onions (about 2 large), coarsely chopped

2 or 3 garlic cloves, minced

2 tablespoons dark brown sugar

2 tablespoons Worcestershire sauce

1 tablespoon dry mustard powder

1 tablespoon white vinegar

1 teaspoon chili powder

½ teaspoon sweet paprika

One 14-ounce (414 ml) bottle tomato ketchup

1¼ cups (300 ml) water

2 or 3 bay leaves

Preheat the oven to 325°F (160°C).

Heat the oil in a very large skillet over high heat. Place the brisket fat side down in the pan and cook until the first side is browned, 5 to 7 minutes. Season the exposed side of the brisket with ½ teaspoon salt and ¼ teaspoon pepper. (Because this is a large cut of meat, you may not be able to fit it in your skillet. The solution is to brown the brisket in the skillet in sections, letting half the brisket extend over the edges of the skillet and then turning it around to brown the other half, or to brown it in your roasting pan, set over two burners.) Turn the brisket over and brown the other side. Season the newly exposed side with another ½ teaspoon salt and ¼ teaspoon pepper. Remove from the heat.

In a large bowl, combine the onions, garlic, brown sugar, Worcestershire, mustard, vinegar, chili powder, paprika, 1 teaspoon salt, ½ teaspoon black pepper, the ketchup, and water (use some of the measured water to rinse out the ketchup bottle and pour that liquid into the bowl). Stir until well blended.

Transfer the brisket to a roasting pan or Dutch oven big enough to hold it with about an inch (2.5 cm) of space around it. Place the bay leaves on top of the meat and pour the ketchup mixture over. Cover the roasting pan (use aluminum foil if the pan doesn't have a cover) and cook for 2 hours.

Remove the brisket from the oven and uncover. Spoon off any visible fat, if you like, and let cool briefly. (Leave the oven on.)

When the brisket is cool enough to handle, scrape off the cooking liquid clinging to it and transfer the meat to a cutting board. Cut the brisket on an angle against the grain into thin slices, less than ¼ inch (6 mm) thick. As you slice the meat, transfer the slices back to the roasting pan, arranging them neatly in the cooking liquid.

When all of the meat is sliced, pour any juices on the cutting board back into the roasting pan, re-cover it, and return it to the oven. Continue cooking until the meat is tender enough to cut with a fork and the cooking liquid has thickened enough to form a nice gravy, another 1½ to 2½ hours. Remove from the oven and remove the bay leaves.

Serve the brisket immediately, with the gravy, or let it cool. Lift the meat out of the gravy and store the meat and gravy separately in the refrigerator for up to 2 days.

To reheat the brisket if made ahead, arrange the sliced meat in a roasting pan, cover with the gravy, and heat in a 325°F (160°C) oven until warm, 30 to 45 minutes.

Honey Walnut Cake

This easy-to-make sheet cake is excellent for entertaining—it uses just one saucepan (and the food processor), and the flavor and texture improve overnight as it soaks up the lemon-honey syrup. If you're short on time, the cake is also delicious on its own, without the syrup.

MAKES 24 squares

FOR THE CAKE

8 ounces (2 sticks/225 g) unsalted butter or nondairy butter, plus more for the pan

4 cups (400 g) walnut halves

1 cup (200 g) sugar

2 cups (480 ml) water

1 cup (340 g) light honey, such as acacia or wildflower

1½ teaspoons ground cinnamon

½ teaspoon kosher salt

2½ cups (325 g) unbleached all-purpose flour

1 teaspoon baking powder

1 teaspoon baking soda

FOR THE SYRUP

⅔ cup (225 g) light honey, such as acacia or wildflower

⅓ cup (80 ml) water

2 teaspoons finely grated lemon zest

⅓ cup (80 ml) fresh lemon juice (from about 2 lemons)

Preheat the oven to 350°F (175°C). Grease a 9-by-13-inch (23 by 33 cm) baking pan with butter.

MAKE THE CAKE: Pick out 24 of the best-looking walnut halves and set them aside for garnish. Put the remaining walnut halves in the bowl of a food processor, add the sugar, and pulse until the nuts are ground to a coarse meal. Be careful not to overprocess the nuts to a paste.

In a large heavy saucepan (large enough to hold all the batter ingredients), combine the water, butter, honey, cinnamon, salt, and ground walnut mixture and cook over medium-high heat, stirring frequently, until the butter melts and the mixture is uniformly combined. Remove from the heat.

Put the flour, baking powder, and baking soda in a bowl and whisk until blended, then stir into the honey-walnut mixture until just blended.

Pour the batter into the prepared pan and arrange the reserved walnut halves in even rows on top of the cake. It's fine if they sink somewhat into the batter, but they should still be fully visible.

Bake the cake until the top is golden brown and firm to the touch and a skewer inserted in the center comes out clean, or an instant-read thermometer inserted in the center reads at least 185°F (85°C), 30 to 40 minutes. Place the pan on a wire rack and let the cake cool to lukewarm.

MEANWHILE, MAKE THE SYRUP: Combine the honey, water, and lemon zest in a small saucepan, bring to a simmer over medium-high heat, and cook until the mixture becomes syrupy, about 5 minutes. Remove from the heat and stir in the lemon juice.

While the cake is still warm, spoon the syrup evenly over the top, letting each addition sink in before you pour on the next spoonful. Let the cake sit for at least 4 hours, or, better yet, overnight, to absorb the syrup.

Cut the cake into squares (with a walnut half in the center of each). Leftovers can be stored tightly wrapped or in an airtight container for up to 5 days.

Finding a Link to India and Iraq in a London Kitchen

SHARED BY

Max Nye

May 10, 1964, the day my family moved to England, was the first time my mother, Esther, stepped onto a plane. She was eleven years old and had never left India before. Nearly a century earlier, in 1877, my great-great-grandfather—I believe—moved our family from Baghdad to Calcutta. There they joined a growing Jewish community, complete with synagogues, schools, and a unique cuisine that's a blend of Indian flavors, Iraqi recipes, and Jewish customs.

While growing up in North London, my senses were flooded with those aromas. A notorious insomniac, my mother would start cooking as early as 4 a.m., and I'd often wake up to the fragrance of her cooking. Her menu for Rosh Hashanah changed from year to year, but before the holiday, I might smell dishes like rice pilau with tomatoes, slow-cooked beef curry, and pantras (little parcels of turmeric-spiced meat wrapped in pancakes and deep-fried).

These recipes belonged not just to my mother but to generations of women before her. As the dishes were passed down, they became more delicious, but also more precious, as the population of Calcuttan Jews began to dwindle and disperse across the globe after the partition in 1947. By the 1990s, the very existence of the cuisine was under threat.

FAMILY JOURNEY

Baghdad → Calcutta (present-day Kolkata) → London

The wedding of Florence and Moses, Max's maternal grandparents,
at Beth El Synagogue, Calcutta, 1954

In my family, the recipes were nearly lost twice. Life in 1960s Britain was hard for Jewish immigrants like my grandmother, and many other things took priority over cooking traditional foods. When my mom was in her late twenties, though, her aunty Ruby called her out of the blue and told her it was time she learned the recipes of our community. That day marked the first of their many cooking lessons. When other aunties got wind of the news, they started to share their own recipes, and my mom built up a collection in a big brown jotter.

I grew up as an expert on eating this food, but it wasn't until I was an adult that I learned to cook it. One weekend, I asked my mother, quite flippantly, if she'd teach me the basics and maybe help me put together a cookbook we could share with others. She jumped straight in.

I could never have known then that this project would span half a decade, see contributions from family and friends across continents, and involve months of research that would tell me more about my own heritage than I had ever imagined. It's brought me closer to my own identity.

MAX NYE comes from a Jewish community that moved from Iraq and other parts of the Middle East to India starting in the eighteenth century. He's working to document the recipes of this community in a forthcoming cookbook.

MAX NYE'S ROSH HASHANAH

Pantras
Fried Crepes with Chicken
62

Beef Curry with Spiced Tomato Sauce
64

Lubia Meetha
Green Beans with Garlic and Spices
65

Roast Chicken with Masala
66

Tomato Pilau
Rice with Tomatoes and Dill
67

Spiced Walnut and Apricot Semolina Cake
68

—Serve with—

chopped salad,
round challah

Pantras

Fried Crepes with Chicken

On Rosh Hashanah, "If we were really lucky, we would get a dish called pantras," Max says. These savory bundles of tender chicken and herbs wrapped up in crepes and fried are fantastic, but they do involve a few steps and definitely qualify as "project cooking." To streamline the work, you can make the crepe batter and the chicken filling a day ahead, and then enlist family to gather in the kitchen and help cook the crepes, fill and fold the tender packets, and fry them.

MAKES about 25 pantras

5 tablespoons (75 ml) canola oil, plus more for shallow-frying

3 cups (450 g) chopped onions

One 1-inch (2.5 cm) piece fresh ginger, peeled

8 garlic cloves

Kosher salt

1 teaspoon ground turmeric

1 pound (450 g) ground chicken breast

¼ cup (8 g) roughly chopped fresh cilantro

7 large eggs

4 cups (1 L) water

3 cups (390 g) all-purpose flour

2½ cups (125 g) panko breadcrumbs

MAKE THE FILLING: Heat 3 tablespoons of the oil in a large skillet (with a lid) over low heat. Add the onions and sauté until very soft and translucent, about 15 minutes.

Meanwhile, grate the ginger and garlic using a Microplane-style grater, or pulse in a food processor until finely chopped. Set aside.

When the onions are ready, add the ginger, garlic, 2 teaspoons salt, and the turmeric and cook, stirring occasionally, for about 5 minutes, until the ginger and garlic are softened and fragrant.

Increase the heat to medium-high and add the chicken. Cook for 2 minutes, stirring frequently to thoroughly mix the chicken and onions. Cover the skillet, reduce the heat to low, and cook gently, stirring occasionally, until the chicken is cooked through, 30 to 40 minutes. If there is still liquid left in the pan, remove the lid, increase the heat to medium-high, and cook for 2 to 3 minutes to evaporate the liquid. Remove the chicken from the heat and fold in the cilantro.

WHILE THE CHICKEN COOKS, MAKE THE CREPES: In a large bowl, whisk 3 of the eggs, the remaining 2 tablespoons oil, and 2 teaspoons salt together. Add the water and whisk until completely blended. Slowly whisk in the flour, making sure to get rid of any lumps. The batter should be just a bit thicker than heavy cream, so whisk in up to another ½ cup (120 ml) water if necessary.

Lightly coat a medium nonstick skillet with nonstick cooking spray and heat over medium-high heat. When the pan is hot, give the batter a stir, scoop out ¼ cup (60 ml), and pour it into the pan. Immediately tilt and swirl the pan so the batter spreads out evenly into a crepe that's at least 6 inches (15 cm) in diameter; a bit bigger is okay too. When the batter has set a bit and starts to bubble, 30 seconds or so, slide a thin spatula under the crepe, flip it, and cook until the second side is set and lightly browned, another 20 to 30 seconds. Transfer the crepe to a plate.

Repeat the process to make a total of about 25 crepes, stacking them on top of each other. If the crepes are sticking to each other, separate them with parchment or wax paper.

ASSEMBLE THE PANTRAS: Line a baking sheet with parchment paper and line a large plate or tray with paper towels. Lay a crepe on the work surface and arrange 1 heaping tablespoon of chicken filling in a line about 1 inch (2.5 cm) from the edge closest to you. Fold the bottom of the crepe over the filling, then fold the sides over and roll up, completely encasing the filling. Transfer to the lined baking sheet and repeat until you've assembled all the pantras.

Whisk the remaining 4 eggs in a bowl. Spread the breadcrumbs on a large plate. Dip each pantras into the eggs, letting the excess drip off, and then into the breadcrumbs, making sure all sides are well covered with crumbs. Set back on the sheet.

In a large skillet, heat about ½ cup (120 ml) oil over medium heat until hot. Carefully add a few pantras, without crowding the pan, and fry, turning once, until crisp and golden brown on both sides, 2 to 3 minutes on each side. Transfer them to the paper towel–lined plate to drain, and repeat the process for the remaining pantras. The ½ cup (120 ml) oil should be enough for about 12 pantras, so top it up as necessary, letting the new oil get hot before adding more pantras.

Arrange the pantras on a platter and serve immediately.

Beef Curry with Spiced Tomato Sauce

Dried curry leaves add a citrus-like note to this richly spiced beef dish. They're available at South Asian markets and online, and they keep well in an airtight container, much like bay leaves. If you can find fresh curry leaves, use them, but cut the quantity in half, since they are generally more potent. Serve this curry with Max's tomato pilau (page 67) or plain basmati rice to soak up the sauce.

MAKES 6 servings

3 tablespoons vegetable oil

2 pounds (900 g) boneless beef chuck, cut into 1-inch (2.5 cm) cubes

1 pound (450 g) yellow onions (about 3 medium), thinly sliced

8 dried curry leaves (see headnote)

3 bay leaves

1 tablespoon spicy Indian curry paste

1 tablespoon mild or hot curry powder

1 tablespoon ground coriander

2 teaspoons ground cumin

2 teaspoons garam masala

2 teaspoons kosher salt

1¼ teaspoons ground turmeric

½ teaspoon freshly ground black pepper

1⅓ cups (320 ml) water

2 cups (500 g) tomato passata/strained tomatoes

5 tablespoons (75 g) tomato paste

In a Dutch oven or other large heavy-bottomed pot, heat the oil over medium-high heat. Add the beef and let cook undisturbed until the first side is nicely browned, about 1 minute. Turn the pieces and continue cooking, adjusting the heat if needed to prevent the pan juices from getting too dark, until the beef chunks are nicely browned on all sides, about 10 minutes. Transfer the beef to a bowl and set aside.

Return the pan to the stove and reduce the heat to medium. Add the onions, curry leaves, and bay leaves and sauté until the onions are soft, deep golden, and fragrant, 15 to 20 minutes.

Add the curry paste, curry powder, coriander, cumin, garam masala, salt, turmeric, pepper, and ⅓ cup (80 ml) of the water to the onions and stir to blend well, then simmer the mixture for about 2 minutes.

Add the browned beef and stir to coat it with the onion-spice mixture. Add the tomato passata and tomato paste and stir to dissolve the tomato paste, then stir in the remaining 1 cup (240 ml) water. Bring the curry to a boil, cover the pot, and immediately reduce the heat so the liquid just simmers gently. Simmer until the beef is beautifully tender and the sauce is rich and flavorful, 2 to 3 hours.

When the curry is done, remove the lid, increase the heat a bit, and cook at a lively simmer for a couple of minutes to thicken the sauce. Taste and add more salt if needed.

Serve hot.

Lubia Meetha
Green Beans with Garlic and Spices

The cooking of Max's community is a blend of Middle Eastern and Indian flavors. This dish takes part of its name from the Hindi word *meetha*, meaning "sweet." Tomato paste adds a touch of fruitiness, while the spice blend garam masala brings a sweet-spicy complexity. The exact mix of spices in garam masala varies from cook to cook and among commercial blends, but most include coriander, cardamom, cumin, cloves, cinnamon, nutmeg, and black pepper. *(Pictured on page 61)*

MAKES 6 to 8 servings

3 tablespoons canola oil
1¾ cups (250 g) chopped onion
6 garlic cloves
One 1¼-inch (3 cm) piece fresh ginger, peeled
1 teaspoon kosher salt
1½ teaspoons garam masala
1 teaspoon ground turmeric
½ teaspoon freshly ground black pepper
¼ teaspoon cayenne pepper
One 6-ounce (170 g) can tomato paste (about ½ cup plus 2 tablespoons)
⅔ cup (160 ml) water
1½ pounds (675 g) green beans, trimmed and cut into 1½-inch (3.75 cm) pieces or in half

Heat the oil in a large wok or skillet over medium heat. Add the onions and sauté until soft and golden, about 12 minutes.

Meanwhile, put the garlic and ginger in a food processor and pulse until very fine, or chop as fine as you can with a sharp knife.

When the onions are ready, add the garlic-ginger mixture, salt, garam masala, turmeric, black pepper, and cayenne and fry for 1 to 2 minutes, until fragrant. Add the tomato paste and water, increase the heat to medium-high and cook for about 2 minutes, stirring constantly, to thicken the mixture slightly.

Add the green beans, reduce the heat to low, and cover the pan. Cook, stirring occasionally and adding a bit of water if the mixture looks dry, until the beans are meltingly tender and the sauce is deeply flavored, 30 to 45 minutes depending on the maturity of your beans.

Remove the lid, increase the heat to high, and cook, stirring constantly, to evaporate any excess liquid and concentrate the sauce. Taste the beans and adjust the seasoning with more salt, black pepper, and cayenne if needed. Serve hot.

Roast Chicken with Masala

In this easy-to-prepare main dish, sliced onions cook down with fragrant garlic, ginger, and spices into a sort of compote while the chicken breasts roast and their skin turns crisp. Skin-on chicken breasts on the bone aren't always easy to find, but don't be tempted to use boneless, skinless chicken—bone-in chicken thighs would be a fine substitute. The skin and bones add flavor and keep the meat moist during roasting. On-the-bone chicken breasts are often large, weighing in at 1 pound (450 g) or more, so rather than serve one per person, present the chicken on a platter and slice off portions for each guest. *(Pictured on pages 60–61)*

MAKES 6 to 8 servings

4 pounds (1.8 kg) bone-in, skin-on chicken breasts

Kosher salt

¼ cup (60 ml) vegetable oil

2 pounds (900 g) yellow onions
(3 or 4 large), sliced

3 tablespoons finely chopped peeled fresh ginger

2 tablespoons finely chopped garlic

4 teaspoons ground coriander

2 teaspoons ground turmeric

2 teaspoons ground cumin

¼ teaspoon freshly ground black pepper

¼ cup (60 ml) water

Finely chopped fresh flat-leaf parsley for garnish

Preheat the oven to 350°F (175°C).

Season the chicken breasts lightly with salt. Heat 1 tablespoon of the oil in a large skillet over medium-high heat. Arrange the chicken breasts skin side down in the pan and cook until golden brown on the bottom, about 5 minutes. Transfer the chicken to a plate (no need to brown the second side) and reduce the heat to medium-low.

Add the remaining 3 tablespoons oil to the skillet. Add the onions and sauté until soft and light golden, scraping up any browned bits from the bottom of the pan, 12 to 15 minutes.

Add the ginger, garlic, 2 teaspoons salt, the coriander, turmeric, cumin, and pepper and stir to blend. Stir in the water, bring to a simmer, and cook the onion mixture until slightly thickened and aromatic, about 2 minutes.

Transfer the onion mixture to a rimmed baking sheet or roasting pan, arranging it in the center and making sure to scrape out the skillet, then nestle the chicken breasts on top of the onions in one layer, skin side up. Spoon some of the onion mixture on top of the chicken breasts, but don't smother them.

Roast the chicken until it is cooked through, the skin is golden brown, and the internal temperature reaches 165°F (74°C), 45 minutes to 1 hour and 15 minutes, depending on the size of the pieces (if using thighs, the internal temperature should reach 175°F/80°C). Check the onions a couple of times during cooking; if they are getting dark around the edges, stir them and scoot them closer to the pieces of chicken so they're protected from the heat. Remove from the oven.

Transfer the onions and chicken to a serving platter, garnish with parsley, and serve.

Tomato Pilau

Rice with Tomatoes and Dill

Almost every Indian meal includes rice in some form, and this flavorful pilau from Max's family adds a festive touch to the holiday menu. To bring out the exceptional qualities of basmati rice—long, slender grains that stay separate and fluffy when cooked—rinse the rice with cool water until the water runs clear to remove surface starch. *(Pictured on page 60)*

MAKES 6 to 8 servings

2 tablespoons canola oil

1 cup (150 g) finely chopped onion

2 cups (400 g) basmati rice, rinsed in a sieve under cold water until the water runs clear and drained

3 tablespoons finely chopped fresh dill, plus more for garnish

2 bay leaves

2½ teaspoons kosher salt

⅛ teaspoon ground turmeric

2 tablespoons tomato paste

3 cups (720 ml) boiling water

Heat the oil in a large saucepan (with a lid) over medium heat. Add the onions and sauté until very soft and golden, about 10 minutes; don't let the onions brown. Add the rice, dill, bay leaves, salt, and turmeric and stir constantly for 1 minute.

Stir in the tomato paste, followed by the boiling water, and stir to dissolve the tomato paste. Bring the rice to a boil, cover the saucepan with the lid, and reduce the heat to very low. Simmer the rice, covered, for 15 minutes.

Remove the pan from the heat and let the rice cook in the residual steam and heat for another 10 minutes. Uncover the pan, use a fork to fluff the rice, garnish with more dill, and serve hot.

Spiced Walnut and Apricot Semolina Cake

This moist fruit-and-nut cake from Max's cousin Sharon doesn't include much sugar. Instead, it gets its sweetness from raisins and dried apricots, as well as from a classic confectioners' sugar glaze.

To keep your serving plate tidy when you drizzle on the glaze, first slide strips of parchment or waxed paper under the edges of the cake. Glaze the cake, and once the glaze has set a bit, carefully slide the parchment out from under it.

6 whole cloves or ¼ teaspoon ground cloves

4 cardamom pods or ¼ teaspoon ground cardamom

2 teaspoons ground cinnamon

¼ teaspoon ground nutmeg

1¼ cups (125 g) toasted walnut halves and pieces

⅔ cup (100 g) golden raisins

¼ cup (60 g) lightly packed roughly chopped dried apricots

⅔ cup (150 g) unsalted butter, at room temperature, plus more for greasing the pan

¼ cup (50 g) lightly packed light brown muscovado or dark brown sugar

3 large eggs

¾ cup (120 g) semolina flour

Finely grated zest of 1 orange

1½ to 2 cups (170 to 225 g) confectioners' sugar

3 tablespoons warm water

¼ to ½ cup (30 to 60 g) roughly chopped roasted pistachios (optional)

If using whole cloves and cardamom, grind them to a fine powder in a spice grinder (pick out any bits of cardamom husk that may remain). Put the ground cloves, cardamom, cinnamon, and nutmeg in a small bowl and mix well. Set aside.

Put the walnuts, raisins, and apricots in a food processor and process until as finely chopped as possible. Transfer to a bowl and set aside.

In a large bowl, using a whisk or handheld mixer, cream the butter and brown sugar until blended and fluffy. Whisk in the eggs, one at a time. Sift the semolina flour into the mixture and, using the whisk or a rubber spatula, mix to combine.

Add the orange zest, fruit-and-nut mix, and spice mix and fold all the ingredients together thoroughly with a rubber spatula. Cover the bowl and let sit at room temperature for 1 hour so the dried fruit can rehydrate and the flavors can meld. The batter will be quite thick.

Preheat the oven to 350°F (175°C). Grease a 4-by-8-inch (10 by 20 cm) loaf pan with a bit of butter. (A 5-by-9-inch/12.5 by 22.5 cm pan will also work, but your cake will be a bit flatter.)

After the 1-hour rest, give the cake batter a stir and pour it into the loaf pan, smoothing the surface with a spatula. Bake the cake until a skewer inserted in the center comes out moist but with no visibly wet batter and the top is golden brown, 30 to 40 minutes. Cool the cake in the pan for about 1 hour.

Run a thin knife around the edges of the cake to release it from the pan, carefully remove the cake, and set it on a serving plate.

Put 1½ cups (170 g) of the confectioners' sugar in a medium bowl and stir in the warm water, mixing vigorously. Continue to add more of the remaining sugar a few tablespoons at a time until you have a smooth, thick glaze. Drizzle the glaze over the cake in a pretty pattern. Sprinkle the pistachios on top, if using, and set the cake aside to allow the glaze to set, about 20 minutes.

Cut the cake into thin slices and serve. The cake will keep nicely in an airtight container for up to 4 days.

A Tunisian Matriarch's Recipes Find a New Home in Buenos Aires

SHARED BY

Jessica Solnicki

I decided to marry my husband at a Rosh Hashanah dinner. It was my first time in Paris, my first time meeting his extended family—grandparents, cousins—and, most important, my second time meeting his mother, Aline. She had piercing blue eyes, blond hair, and an infectious warmth, doling out hugs to everyone. For dinner, she made pkaila, a long-cooked Tunisian spinach stew punctuated with white beans, and explained to me that the greens are tied to a blessing praying that in the year ahead our enemies will be defeated. I fell for her instantly and knew that I wanted to be part of her family.

All of my holiday celebrations growing up were spent at my grandmother Pola's table. After the Holocaust, she moved to Buenos Aires, and in her beautiful apartment she served matzah balls, gefilte fish, and kugel. I inherited her love of hosting and her recipes, but in truth, I'd always yearned for the Sephardi kitchen. It seemed like a secret that no one would tell me unless I learned it from the inside. Aline was happy to whisper it to me.

At first, though, I couldn't understand her. Her instructions were in French, a language I don't know. I couldn't make sense of her Arabic

---

FAMILY JOURNEY

Livorno, Italy → *Tunis, Tunisia* → *Paris* → *Buenos Aires, Argentina*

Jessica's mother-in-law, Aline, and Aline's sister Michèle eating bomboloni at
their grandmother Dora's house in Salambo, Tunisia

either. Spanish is my mother tongue. Finally, we settled on Italian—
close enough to Spanish for us to get by. Aline's recipes for pkaila, small
salads called kemia, and more went with her when she moved from
Tunis to Paris as a teenager in 1957. When I married her son, she started
to share two weeks' worth of menus with me at a time and we would
write them down together. Food became our shared language.

During the years when we lived an ocean apart—she in France, I in
Argentina—we would cook together across the distance on video calls.
Finally Aline moved to Buenos Aires; she always said it reminded her of
Tunisia. Her first year here, we hosted forty people for Rosh Hashanah
together, making her pkaila and reciting the same blessing.

Aline passed away five years later, but she is still at our family's
holiday tables—in the Tunisian silver platters she gave me, in the spices
she left behind that I still use, and in her recipes. But most of all, she is
with me in how I live. She taught me to be generous without counting, to
forgive quickly, to laugh at myself, and to love deeply.

Born into a Greek and Polish family in Buenos Aires, **JESSICA SOLNICKI**
grew up eating matzah balls and latkes on holidays. Today she celebrates with
Tunisian recipes adopted from her late mother-in-law, Aline Dora Darmon, which
she collected in a family cookbook called *La Tunisie d'Aline*.

JESSICA SOLNICKI'S ROSH HASHANAH

Kemia de Navos
Turnip and Orange Salad
74

Kemia de Remolachas
Beet Salad with Cumin
75

Hinojos al Limón
*Braised Fennel Salad
with Lemon*
75

Pkaila
*Spinach, Beef, and
White Bean Stew*
76

Couscous
77

—Serve with—

round challah,
pickled turnips, harissa,
fresh pomegranates,
apples with honey and
sesame seeds

Kemia de Navos
Turnip and Orange Salad

Jessica refers to this bright salad—along with her beets with cumin and her fennel with lemon (both opposite)—as kemia, wonderful salads and cooked vegetable dishes served like mezze. If you've only eaten cooked turnips, this is an opportunity to try the delicious raw form of this humble root vegetable. A bit like a radish with a bold, earthy side, raw turnip brings a fresh crunch and delicate spiciness to this salad. Look for turnips that are smooth-skinned and firm, and be sure to slice them very thin with a mandoline.

MAKES 6 to 8 servings

¼ cup (60 ml) fresh lemon juice

1 teaspoon harissa, or more to taste

½ teaspoon kosher salt

⅛ teaspoon freshly ground black pepper

2 tablespoons extra-virgin olive oil

2 navel oranges

2 large turnips (about 1 pound/450 g), peeled, quartered lengthwise, and very thinly sliced on a mandoline

In a small bowl, stir the lemon juice, harissa, salt, pepper, and olive oil until combined into a dressing.

With a sharp paring knife, cut away the peels from the oranges, removing as much of the white pith as possible. Working over a large bowl to catch the juices, remove the orange segments by slicing between the membranes, letting the segments drop into the bowl. Discard the membranes.

Add the turnips to the bowl with the orange segments and juices. Add the dressing and toss gently but thoroughly to coat. Taste and adjust the seasoning with more harissa, salt, and pepper if necessary.

Serve the salad right away, at room temperature.

Kemia de Remolachas
Beet Salad with Cumin

Deeply flavored cumin-scented beet salads like this one are a staple on many North African tables. Beets range in size depending on the maturity and variety, so be sure to adjust the cooking time in this recipe according to the beets you buy. Smaller beets from the farmers' market can cook in less than 30 minutes, while larger mature ones may take over an hour. *(Pictured on page 73)*

MAKES 6 servings

1½ pounds (675 g) beets

Kosher salt

1½ tablespoons extra-virgin olive oil

2 teaspoons ground cumin, or more to taste

¼ teaspoon freshly ground black pepper

Put the beets in a small pot, add water to cover by about 1 inch (2.5 cm), and add 1 tablespoon salt. Bring to a boil over high heat, reduce the heat so the water is at an active simmer, and cook, partially covered, until the beets are completely tender when pierced with a paring knife or the tines of a fork; this will take 45 minutes to 1 hour and 15 minutes, depending on the size of your beets. Drain the beets.

When the beets are cool enough to handle, peel them with your fingers or a paring knife. Cut them into ¼-inch (6 mm) cubes.

Heat the olive oil in a large skillet over medium heat. Add the beets, along with the cumin, 1 teaspoon salt, and the pepper, and sauté until the seasonings are well distributed, about

3 minutes. Taste and adjust the seasoning with more cumin, salt, and pepper if necessary.

Transfer the beets to a bowl and serve warm or at room temperature.

Hinojos al Limón
Braised Fennel Salad with Lemon

This dish showcases fennel's ability to become silky-tender when gently cooked for a long time. The outer layer of a fennel bulb can be especially fibrous, but rather than pull it off and lose all that vegetable, you can simply peel the surface using a vegetable peeler if necessary. A drizzle of excellent extra-virgin olive oil makes a nice finishing touch to this dish. *(Pictured on page 73)*

MAKES 6 servings

3 large fennel bulbs (about 2 pounds/900 g)

¼ cup (60 ml) fresh lemon juice, or more to taste

3 tablespoons extra-virgin olive oil, plus more for drizzling

½ teaspoon kosher salt

2 cups (480 ml) water

Trim off the stalks and fronds from the fennel and trim the bases; if the bulbs look very fibrous, peel off the outer layer using a vegetable peeler. Cut the fennel bulbs lengthwise in half and then cut each half into narrow wedges; the widest part of the wedges should be about ½ inch (1.25 cm).

recipe continues

Arrange the fennel in an even layer in a wide deep skillet or a Dutch oven. Add the lemon juice, olive oil, salt, and water (the liquid should come about halfway up the fennel). Bring the liquid to a boil over medium-high heat, cover the pan, and reduce the heat so the liquid simmers gently. Cook the fennel until it is fork-tender and the liquid has reduced to just about ½ cup (120 ml), 1 to 1½ hours. (If the fennel is close to tender but you still have a lot of liquid, uncover the pan for the final few minutes of cooking.)

Taste a piece of fennel with some of the liquid and adjust the seasoning with more salt and lemon juice if you like. Gently turn the fennel so that it's bathed in the cooking liquid and let it cool.

Drizzle the braised fennel with olive oil and serve at room temperature or cold.

Pkaila
Spinach, Beef, and White Bean Stew

In many Sephardi and Mizrahi homes, Rosh Hashanah dinner commences with a Seder, a series of blessings over foods such as pomegranates, dates, and greens—including spinach, the dominant ingredient in this hearty stew—that are tied to wishes for the year to come. In Jessica's family, they eat fried spinach with honey as well as this classic Tunisian Jewish stew in the hopes that in the year ahead their enemies will be defeated.

The process for this recipe is easy, but it requires a few hours. The spinach is first cooked in a dry pan, without any oil or liquid, to let the water cook out of the leaves; then, the oil is added and the spinach is cooked for two more hours. To streamline your time in the kitchen, make the spinach mixture ahead, cool it to room temperature, and store it in the refrigerator, covered, for up to 1 day, or freeze it in an airtight container for up to 1 month. To use, defrost it at room temperature, reheat over medium-low heat, and continue with the recipe.

Serve the pkaila with Jessica's couscous (opposite). *(Pictured on page 72)*

MAKES 6 to 8 servings

2 pounds (900 g) fresh spinach, rinsed thoroughly, stemmed, and finely chopped

1¼ cups (300 ml) extra-virgin olive oil

1¾ cups (260 g) grated onion (about 1 large onion)

12 garlic cloves, grated on a fine grater, such as a Microplane, or finely minced

2 pounds (900 g) beef stew meat (such as chuck), cut into 1-inch (2.5 cm) pieces

1 cup (30 g) lightly packed finely chopped fresh flat-leaf parsley

1 cup (30 g) lightly packed finely chopped fresh cilantro

½ cup (15 g) lightly packed finely chopped fresh mint

1¾ cups (360 g) dried cannellini or white navy beans, soaked overnight in water to cover and drained

One 2-inch (5 cm) cinnamon stick

¼ teaspoon ground nutmeg

1 tablespoon kosher salt

1 teaspoon freshly ground black pepper

6 cups (1.5 L) water

Put the spinach in a Dutch oven or other large heavy-bottomed pot (big enough to eventually hold all the stew ingredients), set over medium heat, and cook until most of the water the spinach releases has evaporated, stirring and scraping the bottom of the pot frequently, 30 to 45 minutes.

Reduce the heat to low and add the olive oil. Cook the spinach for 2 more hours, occasionally scraping the bottom of the pot with a wooden spoon or spatula. It's fine if some of the spinach sticks to the bottom of the pot, but don't let it burn. It will become deep green (almost black), the oil will also be deep green, and the mixture will develop an intriguing nutty aroma.

Add the onion and garlic to the spinach and cook, stirring frequently, until slightly softened, about 10 minutes. Add the beef, parsley, cilantro, mint, drained beans, cinnamon stick, nutmeg, salt, and pepper. Add the water, increase the heat to high, and bring to a boil, then immediately cover the pot and reduce the heat to low. Cook the stew at a low simmer until the meat is fork-tender, the beans are fully tender, and the liquid has thickened slightly, about 3 hours. The oil will form a black layer on the surface. Remove the cinnamon stick, if you like. Taste and adjust the seasoning with more salt and pepper as necessary.

Serve the pkaila hot.

Couscous

Couscous is an essential part of cooking from the Maghreb, and Jews have been making it in the region for nearly one thousand years. Savory preparations are often at the heart of Shabbat meals and enjoyed on holiday tables like this one. In some Moroccan Jewish homes, a sweet version (page 275) is served at Mimouna, a celebration held at the end of Passover.

Making hand-rolled couscous may seem like a lot of work, especially since "instant" couscous is readily available. But the superior texture and flavor of homemade makes it worth the effort. You will need a special large-mesh sieve, which you can find online or at a well-stocked Middle Eastern store. A traditional couscous steamer, or couscoussier, is the ideal cooking vessel, but a wide steamer basket with a lid and a large pot or wok works nicely as well. *(Pictured on page 79)*

MAKES 6 to 8 servings

5 cups (2 pounds/900 g) semolina flour

1 tablespoon kosher salt

3 cups (720 ml) room-temperature water

½ cup (120 ml) vegetable oil

SPECIAL EQUIPMENT

Couscoussier or a large pot with a steamer basket

Couscous sieve or other flat sieve with ⅛-inch (3 mm) mesh

Put the semolina and salt in a very large, wide bowl and mix with your fingers to combine. Measure out 1 cup (240 ml) of the water and set it next to the bowl; set another cup with the oil next to it.

recipe continues

1. Dip your fingertips into the water and sprinkle some water droplets over the semolina and salt mixture; repeat with another round of water. 2. Start working the mixture with your hands, rubbing it gently between your palms. Continue adding droplets of water a few splashes at a time and keep working the mixture with your hands until all the water is well incorporated into the semolina. (It is best to add the water a little at a time to prevent any large clumps.) 3. At this point, small to medium balls should have formed in the bowl. Using the same technique as for the water, add the oil a few droplets at a time, stirring and pressing the semolina mixture between your palms. Once all the oil is incorporated, there should be many medium-sized balls.

4. Place the couscous sieve over another very large bowl. Pour half of the semolina mixture into the sieve. Shake the sieve to sift the semolina mixture into tiny granules; use your palms to gently press the semolina mixture through the sieve in a circular motion until all of it has been sifted through. If there are any large clumps that will not pass through the sieve, discard them. Add the remaining semolina mixture to the sieve and repeat the sifting process until all the semolina has passed through the sieve.

STEAM THE COUSCOUS: Fill the bottom pot of the couscoussier (or the bottom of another large pot) with water, cover, and bring to a boil over medium heat.

Remove the lid from the bottom of the couscoussier pot and place the steamer extension (or steamer basket) over the pot. 5. Transfer the sifted semolina mixture to the steamer. 6. Poke about 6 holes in the semolina with the handle of a wooden spoon to allow steam to pass through it. Place the lid on the couscoussier and steam the couscous for 45 minutes.

Transfer the steamed couscous to a large bowl and immediately pour ¼ cup (60 ml) room-temperature water over it; use a fork to stir and fluff the couscous. Keep adding water (up to 2 cups/480 ml) until the couscous is moist but not wet. Set aside for 30 minutes. This step ensures that the couscous will be tender at the end of the cooking process.

Transfer the couscous back to the steamer (no need to poke holes through the couscous this time), cover with the lid, and steam for another 20 minutes. Transfer the couscous to a very large bowl and set aside to cool completely.

Sift the cooled couscous through the sieve into another large bowl; you should have fairly even tiny couscous granules.

To serve, mound the couscous in a large serving bowl or individual bowls. Serve warm.

Yom Kippur

TEN DAYS AFTER Rosh Hashanah comes Yom Kippur, the holiest day of the year, traditionally marked with prayers of atonement, fasting, and the blowing of a ram's horn called a shofar. The period between the holidays is a time of reflection known as the Days of Awe, or Yamim Noraim in Hebrew, when we ask for forgiveness from others before asking the same of God on Yom Kippur.

In Israel, everything comes to a halt for the holiday. Businesses close, cities go quiet, and highways are empty—except for kids riding their bicycles. It's as if someone turned the volume to mute in one of the noisiest corners of the world. Whether you're religious or secular, it is a day like no other. But I remember that on my first Yom Kippur in New York, the city was bustling as it always is. There were no pockets of quiet, and as I left Trader Joe's, where I had picked up goods for a break-fast meal, I had to sort out what it means to honor Yom Kippur as a secular Jew outside of Israel. I've come to see it as an invitation to be Jewish however one likes. I use the time to think about my relationship with the world, my community, my family and friends—in essence, how I can do better.

For some families, the meals that bookend the fast are a deeply meaningful part of the holiday. In Kathy Berrie's home in New Jersey, Moroccan saffron-lemon chicken (page 86) is always served before the fast starts. When Erez Pinhas was little, his family would break the fast in the Israeli town of Rehovot with zom, a Yemenite yogurt soup (page 92) served with a spicy sauce called schug (page 93) and the bread salouf (page 95). These dishes offer a connection to the homelands their families left long ago.

In many Ashkenazi homes in the U.S., bagels, cream cheese, and lox picked up at delis or traditional appetizing shops are served at the break-fast meal. But gravlax, which can be cured before the holiday, is a wonderful way to add something homemade to the spread. For Devra Ferst, not only was gravlax her grandmother's signature recipe, it is the dish that changed their relationship forever (see page 96).

A Moroccan Lemon Chicken to Ask Forgiveness With

SHARED BY
Kathy Berrie

I was born in 1936 in Morocco in the most beautiful home. It was a wonderful life, but we didn't have what we have today. We didn't have a television and we didn't go to the theater. Our entertainment was our family and the meals in our home. We always had guests over, and my mother, Fiby, would make a rich dish layered with potatoes and meat and spiced with nutmeg and saffron, along with salads like one with peeled tomatoes with capers, while our Arab housekeeper rolled couscous by hand and baked fresh bread every day in the communal oven with flour from my father, Meir's, milling company.

That all changed when the war started. We could feel the anxiety in the air. My father's company was nationalized, making flour and fresh bread a rare thing in our home. My mother would listen to the news on the radio all day long and tell us what was going on. I was only five, but I remember seeing members of the Gestapo and their motorcycles from the playground where my nanny took me after Shabbat lunches. And, nearly eighty years later, I can still hear the shouts that echoed in late 1942: "The Americans are here! The Americans are here!"

FAMILY JOURNEY

Marrakech, Morocco → Casablanca, Morocco → Montreal → Westchester, NY → Queens, NY → Englewood, NJ

Kathy Berrie, circa 1950

During the war, the Jews of Morocco were nearly deported, but the king saved us. Still, our comfort and security weren't stable for long, and I felt betrayed by my country. At seventeen, I set out for Canada alone, crossing the Atlantic by boat. When I arrived in Montreal, I struggled. I told my mother I wanted to come back home, but she said there was no point, as everyone was leaving. Two years later, she and my sister joined me.

I never did move back to Morocco. Still, when I raised my children in New Jersey, I wanted them to know that they come from a proud Moroccan family, but they're American, with all the freedoms I never had. I spoke French and Arabic around them and made trips to Montreal, where I would pick up argan oil, wormwood for tea, and my mother's pastries. I continue to cook the same recipes my mother did when I was growing up. Every Yom Kippur, I make her saffron-lemon chicken with egg noodles and zucchini as our last meal before the fast. My son Scott is madly in love with the dish. He also makes it for the holiday for his family, but he tells me it's never the same. I have to admit, it takes patience and a special touch.

Born in Morocco, **KATHY BERRIE** was a little girl when
the Vichy Regime took control of the country during World War II.
While Moroccan Jews weren't deported, the war profoundly
shaped many of their lives.

KATHY BERRIE'S
YOM KIPPPUR

Saffron-Lemon Chicken
86

Sautéed Zucchini
87

—*Serve with*—

a selection of salads,
such as Moroccan carrots,
marinated beets,
matbucha, and challah

Saffron-Lemon Chicken

The key to this dish is the silky, sunny-yellow saffron sauce, so seek out the best-quality saffron you can afford; saffron threads are always preferable to powder. To preserve the intense fragrance and flavor of saffron, keep your supply tightly wrapped in the freezer.

This sauce is enriched and thickened with egg yolks, so take your time when you get to that step. If the heat gets too high, the eggs will set and curdle; if it's too low, the sauce won't thicken to the proper consistency. Using an instant-read thermometer will help you keep your temperature in the correct range. *(Pictured on pages 84–85)*

MAKES 6 to 8 servings

FOR THE CHICKEN

About 1½ teaspoons (0.5 g) saffron threads

1½ cups (360 ml) boiling water

One 4½-pound (2 kg) chicken, cut into 6 to 8 pieces, or 6 to 8 chicken pieces—bone-in breasts, thighs, and/or drumsticks

Kosher salt

3 tablespoons vegetable oil

1 head garlic, cloves separated and peeled

5 large egg yolks

⅔ cup (160 ml) fresh lemon juice (from about 4 lemons), or more to taste

FOR SERVING

1 pound (450 g) wide egg noodles

Finely chopped fresh flat-leaf parsley (optional)

MAKE THE CHICKEN: Put the saffron threads in a small bowl and pour the boiling water over them. Let cool, stirring once or twice, then set aside.

Season the chicken pieces generously with salt.

Heat the oil in a large heavy-bottomed skillet or Dutch oven over medium heat. Add the chicken and cook, turning occasionally, until the pieces are nicely browned on all sides, 10 to 15 minutes. (You may need to do this in batches to avoid crowding the skillet.)

Add the garlic and saffron water to the pan, cover, and adjust the heat to a low simmer. Cook the chicken until it's very tender, almost falling off the bone, 1 to 1½ hours. Remove the skillet from the heat and let the chicken cool for about 15 minutes.

Meanwhile, bring a large pot of water to a boil, season well with salt, cover the pot, and then reduce the heat slightly so the water stays hot and almost ready to cook the noodles once the chicken is finished.

In a small bowl, whisk together the egg yolks and lemon juice until well blended.

Pour the egg and lemon mixture into the chicken cooking liquid. Lift the pan and swirl several times until the sauce comes together and is blended.

Return the skillet to low heat and cook gently, swirling the pan or stirring with a silicone spatula, until the sauce reaches 175°F (80°C) and thickens slightly. You can test for doneness by dipping a large spoon in the sauce and running your finger across the coated spoon; if your finger leaves a clear track that doesn't instantly run back together, the sauce is ready. Taste the sauce and adjust the flavors with more salt and lemon juice if necessary; keep warm while you cook the noodles.

Bring the pot of salted water back to a boil. Add the egg noodles and cook according to the package instructions. Drain well.

Serve the chicken with the egg noodles, ladling the sauce and garlic cloves over the chicken. Sprinkle with parsley, if using.

Sautéed Zucchini

If you can find heirloom zucchini or other summer squash, this dish would be a nice destination for them. Look for golden varieties, such as Butterstick, or the slightly ridged light green Costata Romanesco, which is nicely dense and nutty. Whichever variety you use, choose small slender, firm ones, which will have fewer seeds and a nicer texture.

Serve this with the Saffron-Lemon Chicken (opposite). *(Pictured on page 85)*

MAKES 6 to 8 servings

3 tablespoons extra-virgin olive oil

1½ pounds (675 g) zucchini (about 6 small to medium zucchini), sliced into ½-inch (1.25 cm) half-moons

1 teaspoon kosher salt

¼ teaspoon freshly ground black pepper

Heat the olive oil in a large skillet (with a lid) over medium heat. Add the zucchini, season with the salt and pepper, and sauté, stirring occasionally, for about 5 minutes, until the zucchini is light golden brown.

Add about 1 tablespoon water to the skillet, cover, and cook the zucchini until golden and tender, another 10 to 15 minutes, flipping and turning it as needed. The goal is to get the zucchini fully tender but not mushy.

Taste the zucchini and season with more salt and pepper if needed. Serve hot.

The Child Who Rode Through the Desert on a Camel

SHARED BY
Erez Pinhas

In Yemen, my family always yearned for Zion. My mother made her way here as a child in a sack hanging on the side of a camel. To balance out the load, her brother sat in another sack on the opposite side, and their mom and uncle walked beside them through the desert. Part of my father's family practically hitchhiked onto a British naval ship that sailed from Mocha, at the bottom of the Red Sea, to Jaffa in 1932, while other relatives followed with Operation Magic Carpet, which brought nearly fifty thousand Jews from Yemen to Israel just after the state's founding.

In the early years, our community was deeply tied to customs from Yemen, from the music we played on tin buckets to how we prayed. The first generation knew the Torah by heart. In Yemen, study rooms with Jewish books weren't allowed, but they operated in secret, so my grandfather learned to read from every angle, even upside down, as he and other boys crowded around the few books available.

By the time I was growing up, our family wasn't just Yemenite, we were also Israeli. On Yom Kippur, we walked past the small home where a group kept strictly to the traditions of the old country to arrive at the

FAMILY JOURNEY

Rejam and Taiz, Yemen → *Tel Aviv* → *Yokne'am and Rehovot, Israel* → *Tel Aviv*

Erez's parents, Yosef and Tzidka, in Rehovot, Israel, 1960

"new" Yemenite synagogue. My friends and I would join in for the most important prayers and in between ride homemade skateboards up and down the empty streets. At the end of the day, my family would break the fast with the Yemenite yogurt soup zom, fresh vegetables, and a flatbread called salouf.

Over the generations, our community has scattered and adopted a more Western style of living, with lots of recipes from our neighbors. But we've kept our food and the tradition of eating together too. Although my father is nearly ninety, when I visit him, he cooks for the two of us. He knows that I come for the food I grew up on, which we both love. He makes dishes like zom and salouf and we celebrate.

After a career as a chef and restaurateur in the U.S., **EREZ PINHAS** returned to Israel, where he is now the chef of the restaurant at Asif: Culinary Institute of Israel, a partner organization of the Jewish Food Society in Tel Aviv. His family is from the Yemenite Jewish community, one of the oldest in the world.

**EREZ PINHAS'S
YOM KIPPUR**

Zom
Warm Yogurt Soup
92

Schug
Green Hot Sauce
93

Salouf
Yemenite Flatbread
95

—*Serve with*—

fresh vegetables and herbs,
grated tomato,
hilbeh (fenugreek sauce),
Yemenite spice mix, chile flakes

Zom
Warm Yogurt Soup

When Erez was growing up, his family often broke the Yom Kippur fast with bowls of this comforting Yemenite yogurt soup, which comes together quickly when everyone is hungry. Zom, which has Ottoman roots, is served in Yemen to new mothers and those with a cold or the flu, since it's believed to support a person's immune system, Moshe David writes in *Disappearing Flavors of the South (Yemen)*.

Serve the soup with the schug (opposite) and salouf (page 95).

MAKES 6 to 8 servings

1 quart (900 g) plain whole-milk yogurt

2 cups (450 g) sour cream

½ cup (60 g) all-purpose flour

1 tablespoon kosher salt

1 quart (1 L) water

1 tablespoon za'atar, or more to taste

1 teaspoon ground red chile, or more to taste

½ cup (100 g) small pieces challah (optional)

¼ cup (60 ml) fresh lemon juice, or more to taste

Heat the yogurt and sour cream in a large saucepan over medium heat, whisking, until warm and blended, about 5 minutes.

Combine the flour and salt in a medium bowl, then slowly stream in the water and whisk until it becomes a thin paste (a slurry). Whisk the slurry into the yogurt mixture, reduce the heat to low, and cook, stirring frequently, until the mixture is thickened but still light in texture, 10 to 14 minutes. Do not let it boil, or it could curdle.

Add the za'atar, ground chile, and challah (if using) and cook, stirring, for about 5 minutes, to blend the flavors.

Remove the zom from the heat and stir in the lemon juice. Taste and adjust the flavors with more salt, za'atar, chile, and lemon if needed.

Schug

Green Hot Sauce

A fiery and herby condiment, Yemenite schug is a staple in Israel and has gained popularity in the U.S. in recent years. You can use it like hot sauce. But schug isn't just about heat—cilantro and cardamom add another layer of complexity. Erez's family also includes cloves in the mix, a tradition he says they've maintained since they lived in Yemen.

Serve the schug on the side of the zom (opposite) or Rinat Tzadok's marak temani (page 252) so everyone can add as much (or as little) heat as they like. The schug can be made ahead and stored in the refrigerator for up to a week. *(Pictured on page 91)*

MAKES 2 cups (460 g)

15 small dried red chiles (about ½ ounce/ 15 g), such as chiles de árbol, stems and seeds removed

12 to 14 jalapeños (about 13 ounces/375 g), cored, seeded, and cut into chunks

6 garlic cloves

1 large bunch cilantro (140 g), any wilted leaves removed

1¾ teaspoons kosher salt

¾ teaspoon ground cumin

¼ teaspoon ground cardamom

¼ teaspoon freshly ground black pepper

Pinch of ground cloves

Put the dried chiles in a large bowl, cover with hot water, and soak until soft, about 20 minutes. Drain well.

Put the jalapeños, garlic, cilantro, and drained chiles in a food processor and blend until smooth, about 4 minutes. Add the salt, cumin, cardamom, pepper, and cloves and blend for another 2 minutes. Taste and adjust the seasoning with more salt if needed.

Salouf
Yemenite Flatbread

The Yemenite Jewish kitchen is famous for its breads, like flaky malawach and the rich Shabbat breads kubaneh and jachnun. Salouf are tender but chewy on the inside, delicately puffed and crisp on the outside, making them a perfect companion to Erez's zom (page 92). The play on textures comes from baking them on a hot stone or pan in a very hot oven, so be sure your oven is fully preheated before you bake the breads.

MAKES eight 6-inch (15 cm) flatbreads

3 cups (390 g) all-purpose flour

1 tablespoon (8 g) active dry yeast

1 tablespoon plus ¼ teaspoon sugar

1¼ cups (300 ml) lukewarm water

2 tablespoons canola oil, plus more for the baking sheet

1 tablespoon plus 2 teaspoons kosher salt

Put the flour, yeast, sugar, and water in a large bowl and, with a wooden spoon or your hands, mix to combine. Add the oil and salt and stir until all the ingredients are well mixed, and then knead the dough right in the bowl until smooth. (The dough is quite wet, so it's easiest to knead it in the bowl rather than on the counter.) Cover the dough with a clean towel and let rise until doubled in size, 30 minutes to 1 hour.

Knead the dough again for a minute or so, then cover and let it rise until doubled in size again, another 30 minutes to 1 hour.

Knead the dough one more time, cover, and let it rest for 30 minutes.

Preheat the oven to 500°F (260°C). Place a cast-iron skillet or flat griddle, pizza stone, or inverted baking sheet on the middle rack to heat along with the oven.

Generously oil a large baking sheet or the work surface and scrape the dough out of the bowl onto the oiled surface. Knead the dough a couple of times, then cut it into 8 even pieces, about 3 ounces (85 g) each. Turn the pieces so they're coated with oil. Cover the dough pieces lightly with a cloth, then oil your hands, take one piece of dough, and flatten it into a round about ¾ inch (2 cm) thick.

Carefully place the shaped dough on the preheated pan (don't worry if the shape isn't perfect) and bake until the dough has risen and puffed slightly and the underside is deeply browned, 3 to 4 minutes. Flip the bread and bake for another 3 to 4 minutes, making sure the interior is fully cooked and fluffy, not doughy. (You can bake more than one bread at a time if you use more than one pan, but you'll need to work fast so the oven temperature doesn't drop.)

Remove the baked salouf from the pan and cover with a clean towel to keep warm. Repeat with the remaining dough rounds. Serve the salouf right away.

A Gravlax Recipe That Arrived by Mail

SHARED BY

Devra Ferst

There was always gravlax when my grandmother Marjorie Balick was around. Ribbons of it sprinkled with dill seemed to appear out of thin air. When she visited, she would tuck extra slices into the refrigerator. They were always gone by the next afternoon, eaten with cream cheese on the bialys from Kossar's that we kept in the basement freezer.

For most of my childhood, my relationship with Grammy was one of push (me) and pull (her). I was ebullient and loud, while she was sophisticated and somber, never fully recovering from losing her mother, her husband, and her daughter—my mother—in the span of a few years. When I lost my mom at thirteen, our relationship only became more strained. I became anxious and afraid of doing anything incorrectly— and in Grammy's eyes, there was always a right way to do something.

When I was in my early twenties, she would call weekly and we'd struggle through the conversation, keeping tabs on one another but never really connecting. Craving her gravlax one weekend, I called and asked her for the recipe. It arrived at my New York City apartment a couple of days later by mail, along with a note in her signature elegant handwriting: "Every chef in New York makes it somewhat differently, so don't get upset if you read, or learn, another way to make this."

FAMILY JOURNEY

Wilmington, DE → Philadelphia → Brooklyn, NY

Devra with her grandparents Marjorie and Sydney Balick, late 1980s

The encouragement was small, but it felt like a revelation. It opened a door to a friendship that shaped my life profoundly. As Grammy softened, I became less afraid of making mistakes, and through cooking, we found common ground. I started to call her regularly as I was walking to the grocery store on the weekends, seeking her guidance on what to cook during the week ahead. She taught me how to roast chicken and make cold soups for the summer. She sent me many recipes, notes of wisdom, and even poems in the years that followed.

When she died, I inherited her large metal recipe box with cards for among others, spinach kugel, Swedish meatballs, stuffed cabbage, and the sesame noodles she made on repeat toward the end of her life. Mixed in are lists of cocktail party ideas and notes with household tips like, "If you scratch a piece of wood, mix instant coffee and water or oil into a rag and rub it over the scratch." My grandfather owned a furniture store, so I imagine that one came in handy in her life—it has in mine, as I've moved from one apartment to another.

When I miss Grammy—or need her reassurance—I thumb through the well-worn cards and scraps of paper. They feel like letters she never had a chance to mail.

DEVRA FERST has been a food writer for fifteen years and was one of the first contributors to the Jewish Food Society. She is the editorial director for the Society's digital archive and a contributing writer to this book. She grew up in Philadelphia in an Ashkenazi American family who came to the U.S. around the turn of the twentieth century.

Juniper Gravlax
100

—Serve with—

bagels, rye bread,
cream cheese, tomato, onion,
capers, and any other bagel
toppings you like

Juniper Gravlax

Unlike the Nova sold in bagel and appetizing shops, which is smoked, gravlax is cured with a mixture of salt and sugar, giving it a more subtle flavor. When Devra's grandmother sent her this recipe in a letter, she reminded her that there are many ways to make gravlax and she shouldn't worry if she heard of another. Devra has used that as license to adapt the recipe over the years, adding juniper berries.

Gravlax is wonderfully easy to make and a perfect fit for Yom Kippur break-fast, since it doesn't require any day-of cooking; just be sure to start the curing process early enough (at least 36 hours ahead). Serve the gravlax with bagels, cream cheese, thinly sliced red onion, capers (if you like), and plenty of dill.

Buy the freshest fish possible. Removing any pin bones that run down the center of the salmon fillet will make slicing your gravlax much easier. Ask your fishmonger to do this, or do it yourself: Run your finger along the salmon fillet until you feel a small bone. Using a clean pair of needle-nose pliers or heavy-duty tweezers, pull out the bone, pressing gently on the salmon around the bone as you pull so you don't tear the flesh. Repeat to remove any remaining bones.

SERVES 6 to 8

⅔ cup (130 g) sugar

⅓ cup (45 g) kosher salt

1 tablespoon juniper berries, toasted and crushed into a coarse powder

1 teaspoon freshly ground black pepper

1 large bunch (about 4 ounces/115 g) dill, plus 1 tablespoon chopped fresh dill for garnish

One 1½-pound (675 g) skin-on salmon fillet, cut from the thicker end, any pin bones removed

Combine the sugar, salt, crushed juniper berries, and pepper in a bowl and mix together.

Arrange about half the dill (stems included) in the center of a rimmed baking sheet or other shallow pan (make sure the pan will fit in your refrigerator), covering an area the size of your fillet.

Place the salmon skin side up on a cutting board and make 4 long but shallow cuts through the skin. Sprinkle about one-third of the sugar-salt mixture over the skin side of the fish, then place the fish skin side down on the bed of dill. Distribute another third of the sugar-salt mixture over the flesh side of the fish, then top with the remaining dill sprigs, making sure they cover the surface evenly. (Reserve the remaining salt mix.)

Wrap the fish and baking sheet tightly in plastic wrap and place a heavy pan on the fish to press it down, making sure the weight is evenly distributed. Refrigerate for 24 hours.

The next day, remove the fish from the refrigerator, unwrap, pull back the dill sprigs on the top (reserve them), and baste the fish with the juices that have accumulated in the pan. Sprinkle the top of the salmon with the remaining sugar-salt mixture and return the dill sprigs, arranging them neatly. Wrap with a fresh piece of plastic and place the heavy pan back on top. Return the salmon to the refrigerator for another 12 hours.

After 12 hours, remove the fish and gently rinse off the salt mixture with cool water, discarding the dill. Dry the salmon thoroughly by blotting it gently with paper towels. Keep tightly wrapped and refrigerated until ready to serve.

To serve, sprinkle the gravlax with the chopped dill, if using, and thinly slice the fillet at an angle, leaving the skin behind, slicing only as much as you plan to serve. Wrap any unsliced fish tightly in plastic wrap and keep in the refrigerator for up to 1 week.

Sukkot

THE FALL SEASON OF celebrations comes to a close with the holidays Sukkot and Simchat Torah (literally, "the joy of the Torah") the following day. In Hebrew, Sukkot is known as Chag ha'Asif, when the last fruits are collected before winter. In ancient Jerusalem, Sukkot was one of three pilgrimage festivals when Jews brought offerings to the Temple. It also recalls the forty years that the Israelites spent wandering in the desert from Egypt to the Promised Land. During the holiday, which lasts for a week in Israel and eight days elsewhere, meals are traditionally eaten alfresco in huts called sukkahs, which symbolize the temporary homes of the Israelites in the desert and of farmers during the harvest.

Unlike Rosh Hashanah or Passover, where I find the meaning of the holiday in the dishes on the table, at Sukkot I see it in the place that houses the table. Sukkahs are often festooned with paper chains and children's artwork, and the roofs are made from branches, bamboo poles, cornstalks, and the like, so diners can see the stars above them. In each, you'll find what are known as the four species—palm, myrtle, willow, and a citron called an etrog—which are traditionally shaken around the sukkah as a blessing is said. In some families, like Dr. Svetlana Davydov's Bukharian one, seasonal fruits like apples, pears, and pumpkins are also on display (see page 118).

Sukkot is centered around hosting and welcoming guests. With their temporary walls, sukkahs are a fitting metaphor for a space that's always open, like the table in the sukkah Ron Arazi's grandparents set up each year. Family, friends, and neighbors would stop by for a bowl of Moroccan fava bean soup with harissa and pita, made throughout the day so it was always fresh for the next visitor (see page 104).

The holiday is a powerful reminder at the start of the year to open up our own tables. By the time we take down our sukkahs, the new year is well on its way. We have a blank slate, our intentions are set, and wishes for the months to come have been made. Now is the time to bring them to life.

Fava Bean Soup for a Sukkah That's Always Open

SHARED BY
Ron Arazi

My grandparents had an open-door policy when it came to holiday celebrations in their tiny apartment. But there was something different about Sukkot, when that feeling of everyone being welcome seemed even richer.

They were very enthusiastic Zionists and moved from Morocco to Israel when my mom was little, settling in Be'er Sheva, where my grandfather Aharon worked as a mechanic. He kept the pieces of our family sukkah in the garage alongside his tools for all but one week of the year, when the metal poles and bright green tarp were set up in the front garden and decorated with an etrog, pomegranates, fresh yellow dates, and art my cousins and I made.

I have a lot of cousins: My mom is one of eight children, six sisters and two brothers, one of whom passed away in the Six-Day War. All of us would converge in the sukkah for the multiday open house my grandparents hosted. We were also there for my grandmother Rachel's cooking. She was very traditional, and each holiday had its own unique menu, with recipes she'd inherited from her mother and her mother's

---

FAMILY JOURNEY

Mogador, Morocco → Be'er Sheva, Israel → Brooklyn, NY

From right to left: Leetal's grandmother Rika and her two sisters, Corrina and Zali, at Leetal's dad's bar mitzvah celebration in Ramle, Israel, 1965

mother before that. For Sukkot, the menu started with an array of salads, but the heart of it was the fava bean soup that she topped with her homemade harissa cut with lemon and garlic.

For dipping into the soup, my grandfather made pita on a small electric grill throughout the day, so it would always be fresh for whoever stopped by. And it wasn't just family who joined in—neighbors and friends did as well. Back then, in Israel, neighbors were pretty much part of the family.

In Brooklyn, things are different. An open-house policy for our sukkah doesn't work so well, but we still invite guests over for meals in the backyard. We want to pass down the tradition to our kids, along with the family soup recipe and pita. As my wife, Leetal, likes to say, we're holding on to that with two hands.

RON ARAZI and his wife, Leetal, own the Middle Eastern provision company New York Shuk. Every year for Sukkot, they build a sukkah in their Brooklyn backyard.

**RON ARAZI'S
SUKKOT**

Pita

**Carrot Salad
with Cilantro**

**Charred Long
Hot Chile Peppers**

**Roasted Red
Pepper Salad**

**Tomato Salad
with Argan Oil**

**Fava Bean Soup
with Harissa**

—*Serve with*—

fresh fruit, olives,
and pistachios

Pita

Puffy, tender, and so much more delicious than store-bought, these pita are excellent partners for many of the dishes in this book. Ron's grandfather used to make them throughout the day during Sukkot so there were always fresh pita to dip into his wife's fava bean soup (page 117). Today Ron and Leetal make their pita in a wood-fired oven in their Brooklyn backyard, but a standard oven also works as long as you keep it hot—work quickly when you open it to bake the pita. *(Pictured on pages 108–109)*

MAKES 20 pita

7 cups (910 g) white bread flour, plus more for dusting

3 packets (2 tablespoons plus 1 teaspoon/21 g) active dry yeast

3 tablespoons sugar

2 teaspoons dried sage (optional)

1½ teaspoons kosher salt

3 cups (720 ml) water

In a large bowl, mix the flour, yeast, sugar, sage (if using), and salt. Add the water and mix until a sticky dough forms.

Turn out the dough onto a lightly floured board and knead until it is somewhat smoother, about 3 minutes; it will still be quite wet and sticky.

Transfer the dough to a lightly oiled bowl, turn to coat with oil, and cover with a clean towel or plastic wrap. Let rise until almost doubled in volume, around 1 hour.

Turn the dough out onto a lightly floured work surface and cut into 20 golf ball–sized (80 g) pieces. Shape each piece into a rough ball. Arrange on a lightly floured board or baking sheet and cover lightly with plastic wrap. Let the pita rise, covered, until a slight dimple remains when you poke a piece with your finger, about 15 minutes.

Preheat the oven to 475°F (245°C) and place a baking sheet upside down in the oven to preheat along with the oven.

On a lightly floured surface, with a rolling pin, roll one ball into a round about 6 inches (15 cm) in diameter and ⅛ inch (3 mm) thick. If the dough seems too elastic as you roll it, let the round rest for a few minutes to relax the gluten, then roll again. Be careful not to roll with too much pressure over the edges, as this could prevent the pita from properly puffing in the oven. Repeat with a second dough ball.

Working quickly, open the oven door and, using kitchen mitts, carefully pull out the hot baking sheet and put 2 dough rounds on it. (Don't worry if the dough rounds wrinkle a bit; the goal is to keep the oven as hot as possible by working fast.) Slide the sheet back into the oven and bake until the pita start to puff, about 2 minutes; ideally the dough will fully puff, like a balloon, but it's okay if only sections of the dough puff up.

Carefully flip the pita with tongs or a spatula and continue baking until they are pale brown and fully baked, another 1 to 2 minutes. Transfer to a wire rack and continue baking the remaining pita. As you get more comfortable with the process, you may be able to bake more than 2 at a time.

Serve the pita warm.

Carrot Salad with Cilantro

There are many ways to prepare a Moroccan carrot salad. Ron and Leetal like to roast the carrots, intensifying their sweet, earthy flavor, which plays nicely with the harissa, especially the one their company, New York Shuk, produces. Made from a variety of dried and/or roasted hot chiles, harissa is typically flavored with garlic and spices such as cumin and caraway. Be sure to taste your harissa, since heat levels and flavor profiles can vary, and adjust accordingly. *(Pictured on page 106)*

MAKES 6 to 8 servings

6 large carrots (about 1½ pounds/675 g), peeled and trimmed

¼ cup (60 ml) extra-virgin olive oil, or more to taste

1 teaspoon kosher salt

1 to 2 tablespoons harissa

1 tablespoon fresh lemon juice, or more to taste

2 tablespoons finely chopped fresh cilantro

Preheat the oven to 400°F (205°C).

Put the carrots on a rimmed baking sheet, drizzle with 2 tablespoons of the olive oil, sprinkle with the salt, and toss to coat. Cover the baking sheet with foil and bake until the carrots are very tender when pierced with a fork, 30 to 40 minutes.

Remove from the oven and let the carrots cool until you're able to handle them, then slice them into ¼-inch (6 mm) rounds.

Put the carrot slices in a bowl and add about 1 tablespoon of the harissa, the lemon juice, and the remaining 2 tablespoons olive oil. Toss well, taste, and adjust the seasoning with more harissa, lemon juice, olive oil, and salt.

Add the cilantro and toss once again. Serve right away, at room temperature, or refrigerate the salad and serve chilled.

Charred Long Hot Chile Peppers

Ron and Leetal like to use a long hot pepper for this super simple dish, which they serve as part of their salatim, or mezze, spread, but use whatever variety you have in your market. Anaheim chiles are a good, though milder, substitute. *(Pictured on pages 106–107)*

MAKES 6 to 8 servings

6 to 8 long hot green chiles
(or more if the chiles are small)

Extra-virgin olive oil for drizzling

Coarse sea salt or flaky salt

If you have a gas stove, char the chiles over a burner: Turn the burner on to high heat, set a chile directly on the burner, and cook, turning frequently, until it's blackened on all sides. Transfer to a bowl and repeat with the other chiles. Alternatively, char the chiles on a baking sheet under a hot broiler, turning frequently to blacken them on all sides.

Cover the charred chiles with plastic wrap or put them in a container with a tight-fitting lid and let them rest until cool enough to handle.

Scrape or peel the charred skin from the peppers; remove and discard the stems and seeds.

Transfer the chiles to a bowl, drizzle generously with olive oil, and sprinkle with salt. Serve warm or at room temperature.

Roasted Red Pepper Salad

Roasting peppers results in a smoky-sweet mellow flavor and a silky texture. Ron and Leetal prepare their peppers over a live fire, but a broiler is also a great option. Make sure to cook the peppers long enough to not just char the skin but to actually cook the flesh; they should collapse slightly and give off some juices. Don't rinse the peppers when you peel them and remove the seeds, since that would wash away much of their flavor. If you need to, moisten your fingertips with water to help brush away the sometimes pesky seeds.

6 red bell peppers

1 or 2 garlic cloves, finely chopped

2 tablespoons extra-virgin olive oil

1 tablespoon preserved lemon paste,
finely chopped preserved lemon rind,
or finely grated zest and juice of ½ lemon

1 teaspoon apple cider vinegar or
white vinegar

½ teaspoon kosher salt

Heat the broiler. Put the peppers on a
baking sheet and place them about 4 inches
(10 cm) from the heating element. Broil, turning
frequently, until the skins are blackened on all
sides and the peppers are soft. (If you don't have
a broiler, roast the peppers on a baking sheet in
a 475°F/245°C oven, turning them occasionally,
until the skins have blackened and the peppers
have collapsed slightly, about 40 minutes.)

Transfer the peppers to a bowl, cover with
plastic wrap, and let sit for 15 to 20 minutes.

Once the peppers are cool enough to handle,
peel or scrape off the skin; discard the cores
and seeds.

Slice the peppers into ¼-inch (6 mm) strips
and put them in a bowl. Add the garlic, olive oil,
preserved lemon, vinegar, and salt and mix well.
Taste and adjust the seasoning as needed.

Serve the salad at room temperature, or
refrigerate and serve chilled.

Tomato Salad with Argan Oil

Argan oil, which comes from the argan tree, is
used in Moroccan cuisine, more as a seasoning
than a cooking oil. The oil has a distinctive
nuttiness that plays well with spicy harissa and
bright fruity tomatoes. If you can't find argan oil,
use a full-flavored extra-virgin olive oil. *(Pictured
on page 107)*

MAKES 6 to 8 servings

6 large tomatoes (about 2 pounds/900 g)

½ teaspoon kosher salt

1 to 2 tablespoons harissa, or more to taste

¼ cup (60 ml) argan oil

To peel the tomatoes, bring a large pot of water
to a boil and fill a large bowl with ice water.

With a sharp paring knife, cut a small X in the
bottom of each tomato; this will allow the skin
to release easily from the tomato flesh.

Put the tomatoes in the boiling water and then
remove them as soon as you can see that the
skins are loosening, usually 30 to 45 seconds;
riper tomatoes will take less time than firmer
ones. Transfer the tomatoes to the ice water
and let cool completely, then remove them from
the water and pull off the skins with your fingers
or a paring knife. Cut out the cores, halve the
tomatoes, and scoop out most of the seeds
with your fingers and discard them.

Cut the tomatoes into ¼- to ½-inch (6 to 12 mm)
dice and place in a bowl. Add the salt, harissa,
and argan oil and mix well. Taste and add more
salt and harissa if you like. Serve the salad
right away.

Fava Bean Soup with Harissa

In Ron's family, Sukkot was always defined by this comforting fava bean soup, which his grandmother called talachsa. It's substantial enough for a meal, especially when paired with freshly baked pita and Moroccan salads. Fava beans are mild, but the soup gets a garlicky harissa-based topping that you add to each bowl just before serving.

Dried split fava beans are nutty-tasting and quick-cooking, since their outer skin has already been removed. Don't confuse them with whole dried fava beans, which take much longer to cook, require peeling, and won't yield the creamy consistency you want for this soup.

MAKES 6 to 8 servings

1 tablespoon extra-virgin olive oil

1 teaspoon ground turmeric

5 tablespoons (50 g) finely chopped garlic

3 cups (18 ounces/510 g) dried split fava beans, rinsed

7 cups (1.7 L) water

3 tablespoons harissa

2 tablespoons canola oil

2 teaspoons fresh lemon juice

Kosher salt

Heat the olive oil in a Dutch oven or other large heavy-bottomed pot over medium-high heat. Add the turmeric and 2 tablespoons of the garlic and cook until aromatic, about 1 minute. Add the fava beans and water and bring to a boil. Cover the pot, reduce the heat to low, and simmer, covered, until the beans are completely tender, 30 to 35 minutes.

Meanwhile, in a small bowl, stir together the harissa, canola oil, lemon juice, the remaining 3 tablespoons garlic, and 2 teaspoons salt; set aside.

Transfer the beans and the cooking liquid to a blender, add 1 tablespoon salt, and puree the soup until smooth; you may need to do this in batches.

Return the soup to the pot, taste, and add more salt, if you like.

Serve the soup in individual bowls, garnishing each one with a spoonful of the harissa topping. To make ahead, store the soup and the harissa topping separately in the refrigerator for up to 2 days and reheat the soup before serving.

A Bukharian Grandma on YouTube

SHARED BY

Dr. Svetlana Davydov

It was illegal to celebrate Jewish holidays when I was growing up in Tashkent under Soviet rule, but my grandfather was a Bukharian rabbi, so each year we built a sukkah outside in our big yard despite the prohibition. We would cover the walls and floors with rugs and my father would decorate the sukkah with fresh fruits that were in season. We would eat there, enjoying stuffed vegetables and meat-filled pastries called samsa, fried carp with garlic and cilantro, and rice dishes like plov and bakhsh.

We stopped celebrating the holidays as a family after my grandfather died, but I always knew I was a Jew. That fact startled some people, including the head of the medical school I attended. When I took the entrance exam, I received a top score; as he reviewed my paper and learned of my background, he announced in shock that I was a young Bukharian Jewish woman. Most of the time, though, I kept that private. When I was a doctor, I would walk to work on Yom Kippur and make it through the day without writing prescriptions.

FAMILY JOURNEY

Tashkent, Uzbekistan → *Santa Severa, Italy* → *Queens, NY* → *Long Island, NY*

Svetlana and her husband, Ilya, at their marriage
registration at city hall in Tashkent, Uzbekistan, 1968

When the Soviet Union fell, we moved as refugees to the United States, where my daughters married and I helped raise my six grandchildren the way I was raised, with our family's old traditions, including seeing one another almost every day. My grandchildren are nearly adults now, but we still cook together and joke around; they're always pushing me to do something new. I'm in my seventies and I play Nintendo and basketball. They've even produced YouTube videos featuring me cooking plov and stuffed vegetables, which Elena's friends love. They're growing up in a different society, in a place with a new mentality. Here, Elena says, she doesn't want to hide her Bukharian identity, she celebrates it with pride; she says she has nothing to be shy about.

The Bukharian Jewish community is more than two thousand years old.
Rooted in Central Asia, its cooking reflects the many cultures that moved through
the region along the Silk Road, coming from as far away as East Asia.
DR. SVETLANA DAVYDOV, who grew up in this community, shared
this story with the help of her granddaughter Elena Katan.

DR. SVETLANA DAVYDOV'S
SUKKOT

**Stuffed Vegetables
and Grape Leaves**
122

Samsa
Pastries with Beef and Squash
123

**Fried Carp with
Garlic and Cilantro**
124

Plov
*Rice Pilaf with Beef,
Carrots, and Cumin*
126

Bakhsh
Rice with Beef and Herbs
127

—Serve with—

chopped salad,
lemons, cilantro

Stuffed Vegetables and Grape Leaves

Vegetables stuffed with rice and/or meat—including stuffed cabbage, grape leaves, onions, and more—are popular in Jewish kitchens around the world. The flavorings vary by community, but in many, it's customary to serve them at the harvest holiday Sukkot as a nod to an abundant harvest. *(Pictured on pages 120–121)*

MAKES 6 to 8 servings

3 large zucchini (about 2 pounds/900 g)

1 pound (450 g) ground beef

1 bunch cilantro, leaves and tender stems finely chopped

1 medium tomato, cored, peeled, seeded, and finely chopped

1 cup (150 g) finely chopped sweet onion, such as Vidalia or Walla Walla, or yellow onion, plus 1 large sweet or yellow onion, thinly sliced

½ cup (100 g) medium-grain rice, rinsed and drained

Kosher salt and freshly ground black pepper

⅓ cup (80 ml) water

3 red or green bell peppers, tops cut off and seeds and inner ribs removed

6 to 8 canned or jarred grape leaves, rinsed and drained

½ cup (120 ml) extra-virgin olive oil

½ cup (120 ml) passata/strained tomatoes

Cut each zucchini crosswise into 3 pieces and hollow out the insides with a melon baller or small spoon. Finely chop the zucchini flesh and set aside in a bowl.

Put the ground beef, cilantro, tomatoes, chopped onion, rice, 1½ teaspoons salt, ¼ teaspoon pepper, and the water in a large bowl. Mix the filling ingredients with your hands or a wooden spoon until well combined. If you want to check the seasoning, fry a small spoonful of the filling and taste; adjust with more salt and pepper if needed.

STUFF THE VEGETABLES: Stuff the zucchini pieces and the bell peppers with the filling (the center pieces of the zucchini will be open on both ends, so just pack the filling tightly). One at a time, lay the grape leaves flat on the work surface and spoon about 2 tablespoons of filling onto the middle of the lower half of the leaf. Fold the sides over the filling and roll up the leaf from the bottom, tucking in the left and right sides as you go; the result should look like a small burrito or spring roll.

Heat the olive oil in a Dutch oven or other large heavy-bottomed pot over medium heat. Add the sliced onion and cook until nearly translucent, 8 to 10 minutes; don't let the onion brown. Add the reserved chopped zucchini flesh, the passata, and 1 teaspoon salt, bring to a simmer, and cook, stirring constantly, until the sauce is slightly reduced and thickened, 2 to 4 minutes. Taste and adjust the seasoning with more salt if needed.

Reduce the heat to low and carefully layer in the stuffed vegetables, tucking the grape leaves around the zucchini and peppers. Stir 1 teaspoon salt into ¼ cup (60 ml) water and pour it over the vegetables. Place an upside-down plate on top of the stuffed vegetables; alternatively, cut a round of parchment paper to fit and lay it over the vegetables.

Cover the pot and simmer the stuffed vegetables until completely tender, 1 to 1½ hours. Carefully transfer the vegetables and grape leaves to a large platter.

Taste the sauce and adjust the seasoning with more salt and pepper if necessary, then spoon it around the vegetables. To serve, carefully cut the peppers in half, and give everyone at least one portion of zucchini, pepper, and stuffed grape leaf, along with some of the sauce.

Samsa
Pastries with Beef and Squash

Part of the family of stuffed savory pastries that includes Indian samosas and Middle Eastern sambusak (page 195), samsa are enjoyed across Central Asia and are a staple in Svetlana's family. She makes two fillings, both straightforward and easy to prepare. Mini puff pastry squares need only a few minutes to thaw, but if you're using larger puff pastry sheets, be sure to allow time to defrost them, ideally overnight in the refrigerator. *(Pictured on page 124)*

MAKES 32 samsa (16 of each type)

FOR THE SQUASH FILLING

2 cups (about 8 ounces/225 g) diced butternut squash

1 tablespoon extra-virgin olive oil

¼ cup (40 g) very finely chopped yellow onion

½ teaspoon kosher salt

⅛ teaspoon freshly ground black pepper

FOR THE BEEF FILLING

8 ounces (225 g) beef chuck, excess fat trimmed, finely chopped (aim for ⅙-inch/ 4 mm pieces)

¼ cup (40 g) very finely chopped yellow onion

½ teaspoon kosher salt

⅛ teaspoon freshly ground black pepper

All-purpose flour for dusting

1 package frozen nondairy mini puff pastry squares (3 inches/7.5 cm) or 2 large sheets (about 9 inches/22.5 cm) frozen nondairy puff pastry, such as Pepperidge Farm

1 large egg, beaten, for egg wash

Position the racks in the upper and lower thirds of the oven and preheat the oven to 400°F (205°C).

MAKE THE SQUASH FILLING: Put the squash on a rimmed baking sheet and drizzle with the olive oil. Toss to coat the squash with the oil and then spread it into an even layer. Roast until very tender and browned around the edges, 20 to 25 minutes; don't let the squash roast to the point of drying out. Remove from the oven, transfer to a medium bowl, and let cool slightly.

WHILE THE SQUASH IS ROASTING, MAKE THE BEEF FILLING: Put the beef, onion, salt, and pepper in a bowl and mix well. Refrigerate until ready to use.

When the squash is cool enough to handle, mash it with a fork to a smooth consistency (it's fine if it's a little bit chunky). Stir in the onion, salt, and pepper, then taste and adjust the salt and pepper if necessary; the filling should be highly seasoned.

Line two baking sheets with parchment paper. Lightly dust your work surface with flour and lay out 16 of the puff pastry squares. Or, if using larger sheets of pastry, roll one sheet out into a 12-inch (30 cm) square and cut it into sixteen 3-inch (7.5 cm) squares.

Place about 1 tablespoon of the squash filling on the center of each square. Bring the top two corners of the square downward to the center so they meet and cover most of the filling. Bring the lower part of the pastry square up and over

baking sheets top to bottom and front to back and continue baking until the samsa are nicely browned all over, 25 to 30 minutes.

Transfer the samsa to a wire rack and let them cool for at least a few minutes. Serve hot or warm.

Fried Carp with Garlic and Cilantro

Bukharian Jews historically lived in landlocked areas, such as what is modern-day Uzbekistan, so the fish in the community's recipes are typically freshwater varieties like carp. Fried fish in garlic sauce has been a staple of the Bukharian Shabbat table since the time of the Talmud, writes Amnun Kimyagarov in *Classic Central Asian (Bukharian) Jewish Cuisine and Customs*. In Svetlana's family, this version is served on special occasions and on holidays such as Sukkot.

If you can't find carp, striped bass steaks work well here.

MAKES 6 to 8 servings

2½ pounds (1.1 kg) carp or striped bass, cut into ¾-inch (2 cm) steaks

Kosher salt

5 garlic cloves, finely chopped

½ bunch cilantro, leaves and tender stems finely chopped

1¼ cups (300 ml) boiling water

1 cup (240 ml) extra-virgin olive oil

the filling, almost like you're making a triangular paper hat. Wrap any extending pastry points around the samsa to make a nice tight package and pinch the seams to seal.

Place the samsa seam side down on one of the baking sheets, leaving about 1 inch (2.5 cm) between them. Brush the samsa with the beaten egg.

Repeat with the remaining puff pastry and the beef filling to make 16 more samsa; you may have a bit of beef filling left over, depending on how much fat you needed to trim off the meat. Arrange them on the second baking sheet and brush with the egg.

Reduce the oven temperature to 375°F (190°C). Slide the baking sheets into the oven and bake the samsa for about 15 minutes, then rotate the

Season the fish steaks on both sides with
2 teaspoons salt.

Combine the garlic, cilantro, 2½ teaspoons salt,
and boiling water in a wide dish and stir
to dissolve the salt; set aside.

Heat the olive oil in a wide skillet over
medium heat until hot. Add the fish and fry,
turning once, until lightly golden brown,

about 4 minutes per side. (You may need to fry
in batches to avoid crowding the skillet.)

When the fish is done, immediately dip each
piece into the garlic sauce, turning to coat, and
arrange on a serving platter. Let cool to room
temperature.

When ready to serve, drizzle each piece of fish
with a few spoonfuls of the sauce to moisten.

Plov

Rice Pilaf with Beef, Carrots, and Cumin

A rich pilaf studded with meat, plov is the national dish of Uzbekistan and an important part of the Bukharian kitchen. In Svetlana's family, the word is pronounced "plof," and when she and her granddaughter Elena launched a YouTube channel together, this was the first dish they filmed. It gets its distinctive flavor from a generous amount of cumin seeds, whose earthiness complements the sweetness of the carrots.

MAKES 6 to 8 servings

3 large carrots (about 12 ounces/340 g), peeled and cut into julienne strips

1 tablespoon cumin seeds

¼ cup (60 ml) vegetable oil

1 pound (450 g) beef chuck, cut into 1-inch (2.5 cm) pieces

1 large yellow onion, thinly sliced

Kosher salt

2 cups (480 ml) boiling water, or more as needed

3 cups (600 g) medium-grain rice, rinsed and drained

Put about 1 cup (115 g) of the julienned carrots in a small bowl and set aside. Put the remaining carrots into another bowl, add the cumin seeds, and mix well.

Heat the oil in a large Dutch oven over medium-high heat until very hot. Add the beef and fry, without stirring, until the bottoms of the pieces have browned. Stir the meat and continue cooking, turning occasionally, until all sides are nicely browned.

Add the onion and 2 teaspoons salt to the beef, stir, and cook until the onion is starting to get soft and translucent, about 5 minutes. With a spatula, scoot the beef and onion to the sides of the pot, clearing a space in the middle. Add the reserved 1 cup (115 g) carrots to the center of the pot and cook until they're starting to get tender, about 5 minutes, then stir them into the beef and onions.

Spread the remaining carrots in one layer on top of the beef and season with 1 teaspoon salt. Add the boiling water, cover the pot, and bring everything to a boil, then reduce the heat to medium.

Uncover the pot, spread the rice over the carrots in an even layer, and sprinkle with 1 tablespoon salt. If necessary, add more boiling water to cover the rice by about ¼ inch (6 mm). Adjust the heat to maintain a lively simmer and cook the plov until the water has started to evaporate, about 5 minutes. Using a spatula, push the rice into the center of the pot to form a mound. Use the handle of a spatula or large spoon to make 6 deep holes in the rice mixture. Place a shallow heatproof bowl or plate over the plov; alternatively, cut a circle of parchment paper to fit and place it over the plov. Drape a clean dish towel over the pot and cover with the lid, tying up the loose ends of the towel so they don't hang over the burner.

Reduce the heat to low and cook the plov until the rice is fully tender and all the water has evaporated, about 40 minutes. Remove from the heat.

To serve the plov, spoon the rice and top layer of carrots onto a serving platter and top with the beef mixture. Serve hot.

Bakhsh
Rice with Beef and Herbs

A staple of Bukharian Shabbat tables, this herby rice is also wonderful for a meal in a Sukkah. In some homes, it's cooked in a cloth bag that's submerged in a pot of water on the stove, but it can also be prepared more simply in the oven, as it is here. The generous amount of cilantro gives the dish a delicious freshness. A small quantity of chicken livers adds an earthy richness, but you can leave them out if you don't like liver. *(Pictured on page 121)*

MAKES 6 to 8 servings

8 ounces (225 g) beef chuck, finely chopped (aim for ⅙-inch/4 mm pieces)

4 ounces (115 g) chicken livers, trimmed and finely chopped (aim for ⅙-inch/ 4 mm pieces)

2 cups (60 g) finely chopped fresh cilantro leaves

5 scallions, white and light green parts, finely chopped

1 tablespoon kosher salt

½ teaspoon freshly ground black pepper

2 cups (400 g) medium-grain rice, such as Arborio or Valencia

2⅓ cups (560 ml) water

½ cup (120 ml) extra-virgin olive oil

Preheat the oven to 400°F (205°C).

Put the beef, chicken livers, cilantro, scallions, salt, and pepper in a large ovenproof pot with a lid, such as a Dutch oven. Stir to combine. Add the rice, water, and olive oil and stir again to combine well.

Cover the pot and bake the bakhsh for 40 minutes. Remove the pot from the oven and gently fluff the contents with a fork.

Reduce the oven temperature to 350°F (175°C), cover the pot and return to the oven, and bake the bakhsh, covered, for 30 more minutes.

Remove the pot from the oven, give everything another stir, and serve the bakhsh hot.

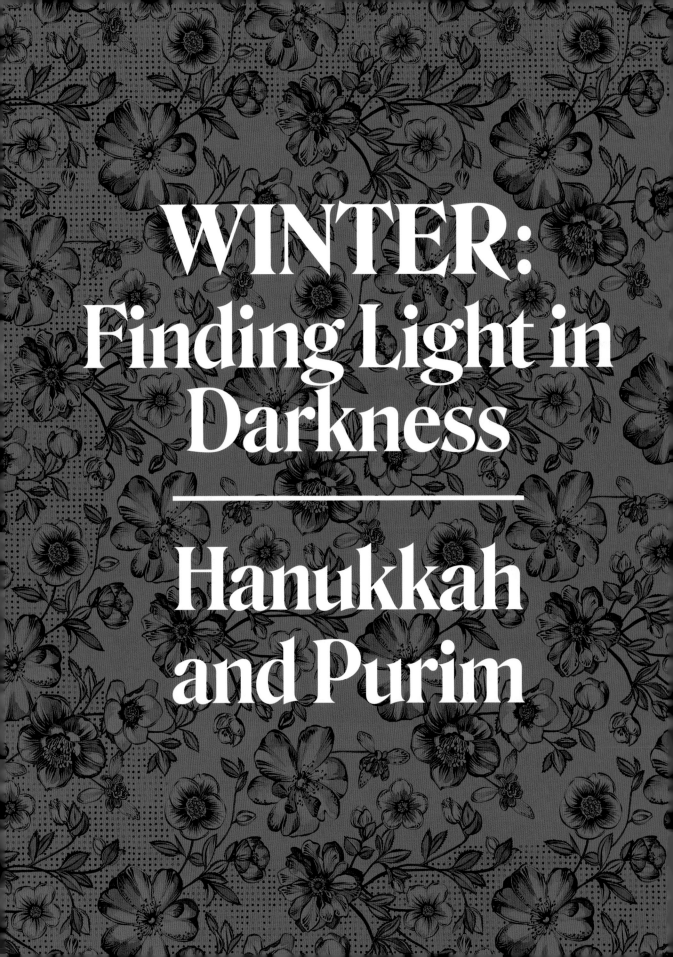

WINTER:
Finding Light in
Darkness

Hanukkah
and Purim

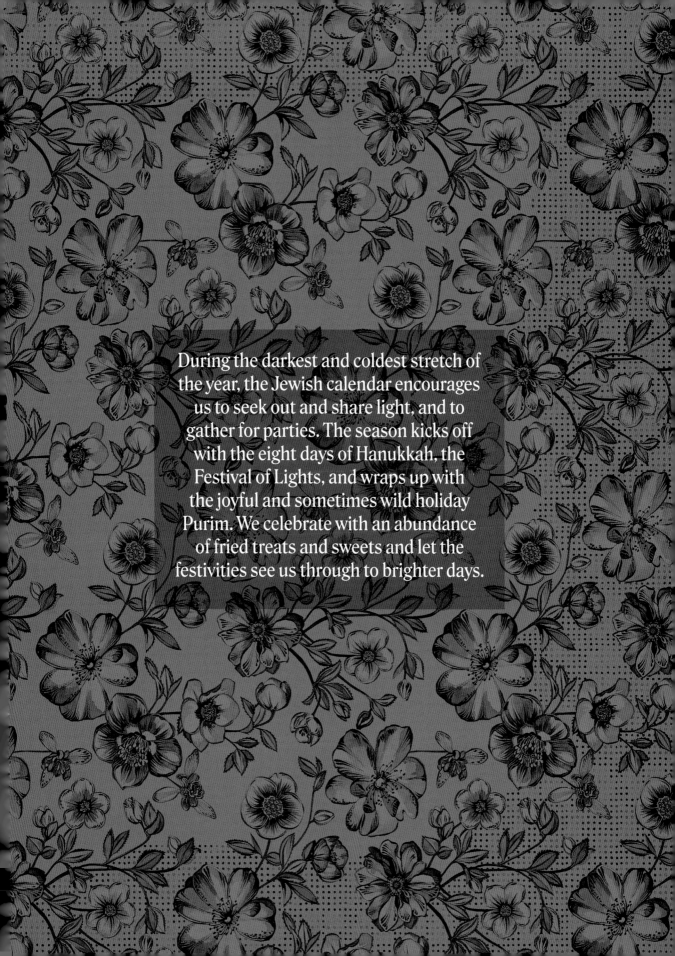

During the darkest and coldest stretch of the year, the Jewish calendar encourages us to seek out and share light, and to gather for parties. The season kicks off with the eight days of Hanukkah, the Festival of Lights, and wraps up with the joyful and sometimes wild holiday Purim. We celebrate with an abundance of fried treats and sweets and let the festivities see us through to brighter days.

Hanukkah

IN DECEMBER, THE SCENT of pine and fir trees lingers on the street corners of New York City, and Christmas markets seem to sprout from the pavement. But as I walk around the Lower East Side, where I live, I like to seek out the sparkling lights of Hanukkiahs—or, as my American friends call them, menorahs—glowing in windows.

Most often, when we share the origin story of Hanukkah, we overlook the details of a military victory nearly 2,200 years ago, when the Maccabees recaptured the Temple in Jerusalem from the army of Emperor Antiochus, who had outlawed Judaism and tried to replace it with Hellenism. Instead, we tell the story of how just one vial of holy oil was found after the victory and how when it was lit to rededicate the Temple, it miraculously burned for eight nights though it should have lasted for only one.

In memory of the oil that burned in the Temple, we prepare fried foods like jam-filled doughnuts called sufganiyot and crispy potato latkes. For Elizaveta Vigonskaia (see page 158), latkes are a holiday staple, not only for Hanukkah. They are a reminder of desperate times in 1940s Ukraine when her mother fried latkes in fish oil to keep her family alive.

Jewish cooks around the world have long interpreted the tradition of frying for the holiday in their own ways. In Milan,

Lorenza Pintar grew up not knowing she was Jewish but enjoying apple fritters and sweet doughnuts topped with cinnamon and sugar every winter (see page 132). And chef Nir Mesika's Moroccan grandmother would fry doughnuts called sfenj, while his Egyptian grandmother dropped small balls of dough into hot oil to make zalabia, a recipe she learned from a Muslim neighbor who made the sweet for Ramadan (see page 148).

Adopting and adapting culinary traditions from neighbors is a hallmark of Jewish cooking. In Copenhagen, when Margit Scheftelowitz was little, Christmas Eve was a special night for everyone in the city, including her Jewish family (see page 140). Her mother would prepare a rice pudding called risalamande, which Margit makes today along with sweet Danish doughnuts for her annual Hanukkah party in northern Israel.

For me, Hanukkah is the most social of all the Jewish holidays, with eight nights for parties. I keep the menu simple and ensure there is plenty to drink alongside the spread. While the adults enjoy "the bar," I head to the kitchen, open the windows wide, and finish frying the latkes.

Before we eat, we gather to light the candles in the Hanukkiahs, one for each child present. When they are all lit, they shine brightly for us and those who might see them through the window. They remind me of the children's song we sing in Israel on the holiday, "Banu Choshech L'Garesh." Its lyrics roughly translate as, "We are here to fight the darkness. . . . Every one of us is a tiny flicker, but together, we are a strong light."

A Secret Hanukkah in Italy

SHARED BY
Lorenza Pintar

In my family, certain traditions were repeated over and over. On Fridays, my great-grandmother Emma would polish a set of silver candleholders and place them next to one another on the credenza. She never lit candles, but the holders stood there until Saturday night, when she would move them to opposite edges of the credenza until the next Friday. And in December, we had a Christmas tree—my father is Christian—which we decorated with candles, lighting a new one each night for eight nights.

But most of our traditions took place at the table. Our year was marked by special recipes like wintertime doughnuts laced with cinnamon and raisins and latkes topped with thick stracchino that were served and then disappeared until the next year. When I was a child in Milan, no one told me where these traditions came from.

My parents also didn't tell me that during Mussolini's regime my grandmother was forced to wash her teacher's dishes every day after school and that my great-grandfather was hit in the street by the Blackshirts. They hid their identities for protection. What remained were the rituals and, most of all, the food.

FAMILY JOURNEY

Milan → Brooklyn, NY

Lorenza's grandmother Aurelia in Northern Italy, 1965

When I was a young adult and my mother finally told me we were Jewish, I immediately felt at ease, with a sense of comfort and belonging. That was the start of us reclaiming our history. My mother, born Magdalena, also adopted the Hebrew name Yael, and I began learning about Jewish customs.

After my sister passed away, my mom set out to research our family, finding names of our relatives on Inquisition documents from Sicily and discovering that we have Ashkenazi roots as well. She started to write down our family recipes, putting them into a cookbook we called *Rebelot*, a Milanese word for something that is all mixed up. The process was very healing for her and helped me understand how important it is to be rooted.

In Brooklyn, where I live now, I make latkes for Hanukkah and light candles for eight nights on a menorah instead of a Christmas tree. And on Fridays, I do what my great-grandmother couldn't—I place her candleholders together and light candles for Shabbat.

LORENZA PINTAR is a yoga instructor and beauty care entrepreneur based in Brooklyn. Her great-grandparents lived in Italy under Fascist dictator Benito Mussolini. Starting in 1938, his government enacted the Leggi Razziali, or racial laws, a series of anti-Semitic measures that outlawed marriage between Italian Jews and non-Jews, banned Jews from educational institutions, and imposed numerous other restrictions.

**Latkes with
Stracchino**
136

Cassola
Italian Cheesecake
137

Frittole Dolci
*Italian Cinnamon
and Raisin Doughnuts*
138

Apple Fritters
139

—*Serve with*—

candied orange peel,
walnut-stuffed dates

Latkes with Stracchino

The key to crispy latkes is to remove as much liquid from the shredded potatoes and onions as possible before you mix in the other ingredients. Wrapping the grated onion and potatoes in a clean dishcloth and using it to wring out the liquid is a helpful technique.

Lorenza's family serves their latkes with stracchino, an Italian cow's-milk cheese with a creamy texture. If you can't find it, a good substitute would be Taleggio, which has a slightly more assertive flavor but an equally soft and buttery texture. *(Pictured on pages 134–135)*

MAKES 6 to 8 servings; about 30 latkes

1 large yellow onion (about 8 ounces/225 g)

2 large russet potatoes (about 1½ pounds/675 g), peeled

½ cup (65 g) all-purpose flour

1 large egg

1½ teaspoons kosher salt

½ teaspoon freshly ground black pepper

Vegetable or sunflower oil or other neutral oil for deep-frying

8 ounces (225 g) stracchino cheese for serving

Grate the onion and then the potatoes on the large holes of a box grater or in a food processor fitted with the shredding blade.

Put the onion and potatoes in the center of a clean dish towel, wrap them in the towel, and twist the towel over a bowl to squeeze out the excess liquid. Transfer the onion and potatoes to a large bowl and set aside.

After about 5 minutes, pour off the water from the onion-potato liquid, leaving the potato starch that has settled on the bottom of the bowl behind, then scrape the starch into the bowl with the onion and potatoes. Add the flour, egg, salt, and pepper and mix until well combined.

Line a tray with paper towels and set near the stove. Heat 1 inch (2.5 cm) of oil in a large skillet over medium-high heat. To check whether the oil is hot enough to begin frying, drop a few shreds of potato into the oil: If they sizzle briskly, the oil is ready; if not, keep heating it. (If you try to fry the latkes in oil that's not hot enough, they will be heavy and greasy.)

Once the oil is hot, scoop out a tablespoon of the latke mixture and carefully slide it into the oil. Use the spoon to pat down the potatoes into a flat disk. Add about 5 more latkes to the oil and fry, turning once, until golden brown on both sides, 3 to 5 minutes per side. Transfer the latkes to the paper towel–lined tray and continue frying the remaining latkes in batches.

Serve the latkes hot, with a dollop of stracchino on each one.

Cassola
Italian Cheesecake

Lorenza grew up in Milan eating ricotta cheesecake around Hanukkah, but it's most often thought of as a treat from Rome, where it's customarily served for Shavuot in Jewish homes and on Christmas in Catholic ones. It likely arrived in the Eternal City via Sephardi Jews who fled Sicily during the Spanish Inquisition.

The lightly sweetened cake gets its flavor and tender texture from ricotta, so use the best-quality cheese you can find. Some artisan ricottas are sold still in their draining baskets, with a bit of whey in the bottom of the container; be sure to drain the cheese for a few minutes before using in the recipe.

MAKES 6 to 8 servings

Butter and breadcrumbs for the pan

½ cup (75 g) raisins

1½ tablespoons Cognac or Marsala

1½ cups (350 g) ricotta cheese, drained

½ cup (100 g) granulated sugar

1 teaspoon ground cinnamon

Finely grated zest of 1 lemon

Pinch of kosher salt

3 large eggs

Confectioners' sugar for dusting

Preheat the oven to 350°F (175°C). Grease an 8-inch (20 cm) round cake pan with butter and sprinkle generously with breadcrumbs to coat the entire surface; tap to shake out any excess crumbs.

Put the raisins in a small bowl and add the Cognac and enough warm water to cover. Soak the raisins until they're softened and have absorbed some flavor, about 20 minutes. Drain well and set aside.

In a large bowl, combine the ricotta, granulated sugar, cinnamon, lemon zest, and salt, stirring vigorously with a spoon to blend and aerate the mixture. Add the eggs one at a time, stirring to incorporate each egg before adding the next one. When the batter is nicely creamy, fold in the raisins.

Pour the batter into the prepared pan and bake until the cake is lightly puffed and browned on top and the edges are pulling away from the sides of the pan, 35 to 45 minutes. Remove from the oven and let cool on a wire rack.

Dust the top of the cassola with confectioners' sugar, cut into slices, and serve.

Frittole Dolci

Italian Cinnamon and Raisin Doughnuts

Jewish families around the world celebrate Hanukkah with fried sweets, but these vary widely by community. In Moroccan homes, you might find sfenj (page 156); in Egyptian families, zalabia (page 152); and in Israel, sufganiyot filled with jam. Lorenza's family makes these yeasted fritters that are studded with plump raisins and flavored with grappa.

MAKES about 2 dozen doughnuts

½ cup (75 g) raisins

1½ cups (360 ml) warm whole milk

1½ cups (360 ml) lukewarm water

1 tablespoon (8 g) active dry yeast

¼ cup (50 g) plus 1 teaspoon sugar

2 tablespoons grappa or Cognac

3½ cups (455 g) all-purpose flour

Finely grated zest of ½ lemon

½ teaspoon kosher salt

Sunflower or other neutral oil for deep-frying

FOR THE CINNAMON SUGAR

¾ cup (150 g) sugar

¼ cup (20 g) cinnamon

In a small bowl, soak the raisins in ¼ cup (60 ml) of the warm milk until plump and tender, about 15 minutes. Drain the raisins, reserving the milk.

Pour ¼ cup (60 ml) of the lukewarm water into a small bowl, add the yeast, the 1 teaspoon sugar, and the grappa, and stir to combine.

In a large bowl, combine the flour, the remaining ¼ cup (50 g) sugar, the lemon zest, and salt and whisk until well mixed. Pour in the yeast mixture and stir until well blended.

Add the raisins and the reserved soaking milk along with the remaining 1¼ cups (300 ml) milk and 1¼ cups (300 ml) water and mix until you have a smooth, loose batter. Cover the bowl with plastic wrap and let the batter rise at room temperature for about 4 hours, giving it a gentle stir after the first hour and again after 3 hours.

Line a tray with paper towels and set it near the stove. Put the sugar and cinnamon in a large wide bowl, stir to mix, and set it near the stove.

Add about 4 inches (10 cm) oil to a medium pot (the pot should be tall enough that the oil won't overflow when you add the batter) and heat over medium-high heat (you can also use a deep fryer) to 350°F (175°C). When the oil is hot, scoop up 1 heaping tablespoon of the batter and carefully drop it into the oil. Add a few more doughnuts to the hot oil, but don't crowd the pot, or the temperature will drop too much. Fry the frittole, turning once, until they puff up and are golden on both sides, 3 to 5 minutes per side. Transfer to the paper towel–lined tray and continue cooking the frittole in small batches. (As you work, give the batter a stir from time to time to be sure the raisins are well distributed so you get a few in each frittole.) Once you've fried several frittole, put them in the bowl of cinnamon sugar and roll until well coated, then transfer them to a plate and keep warm until serving.

Apple Fritters

Another fried treat for Hanukkah, these simple batter-coated apple slices, dusted with cinnamon sugar, are best eaten hot from the stove. *(Pictured on page 135)*

MAKES about 16 fritters

1½ cups (195 g) all-purpose flour

3 tablespoons granulated sugar

⅛ teaspoon kosher salt

1½ cups (360 ml) milk or water

Peanut or sunflower oil for deep-frying

4 tart apples, such as Granny Smith, peeled, cored, and sliced into ½-inch (1.25 cm) rings

FOR THE CINNAMON SUGAR

2 tablespoons confectioners' sugar

1 tablespoon ground cinnamon

In a large bowl, whisk the flour, granulated sugar, and salt to blend. Slowly pour in the milk, whisking constantly, until you have a smooth batter; don't worry about a few little lumps.

Line a baking sheet with paper towels and set it near the stove. Heat about 2 inches (5 cm) of oil in a medium deep pot or a deep-fryer; the pot should be tall enough that the oil won't overflow when you add the apples.

When the oil reaches 350°F (175°C), dip an apple ring in the batter until well coated and carefully slide it into the oil; repeat with 2 more slices. Fry the apple rings, turning once, until golden brown, about 3 minutes on each side. Transfer to the paper towel–lined sheet and continue frying the remaining apples, a few at a time. Scoop out any little bits of batter from the oil so they don't burn.

Stir the confectioners' sugar and cinnamon together in a small cup and generously dust the fried apples with the sugar and spice. Serve immediately.

Danish Christmas Sweets for a Very Merry Hanukkah

SHARED BY

Margit Scheftelowitz

A special atmosphere would settle across all of Copenhagen at Christmastime when I was growing up. There were Christmas lights and carol singers, and shops sold holiday treats like little round doughnuts called aebleskiver.

Our family didn't have a Christmas tree, but we did celebrate Christmas Eve with a special dinner and presents. We would drive to my grandparents' house to pick them up and bring them back to our home for a dinner of my mother, Hilde's, wonderful chicken soup with lokshen noodles, followed by roasted duck with potatoes and red cabbage.

Keeping with Danish Christmas tradition, we'd have a rice pudding called risalamande for dessert. My mother would hide a whole almond in the pudding, and whoever found it (often me, much to my sister's disappointment) received a special gift as a reward—shops all over Denmark sell such gifts just for this tradition.

In Israel, the atmosphere, of course, is quite different. You don't feel Christmas unless you live among Christian Arab communities—but Hanukkah is everywhere. I moved here in 1961 and have hosted a

FAMILY JOURNEY

Copenhagen, Denmark → Kfar Vradim, Israel

Margit's children, from right to left: Eli, Dina, and Uri,
with friend Razi Arad, at Hanukkah, 1970

Hanukkah party for my family every year since, keeping a few traditions
from Christmas in Copenhagen with me.

Today we have the party on the Shabbat during Hanukkah, when
my children and grandchildren can come to visit. We always start in
the afternoon with coffee, latkes, and aebleskiver made in a pan that
belonged to my grandmother. Since everyone loves these doughnuts best,
I hide the almond in the batter instead of the rice pudding, and everyone
devours them in hopes of finding the lucky one.

MARGIT SCHEFTELOWITZ and her husband, Moritz, moved to Israel from
Denmark in 1961, but they kept many of their Danish traditions alive for their children,
like dressing nicely for dinner, formally introducing friends to one's parents, and searching
for a hidden almond in a Christmas dessert—at a Hanukkah party. Their son Uri Scheft,
who cofounded Breads Bakery in New York City and is the chef and owner of Lehamim
Bakery in Tel Aviv, is known for his challah (page 313), among other things.

MARGIT SCHEFTELOWITZ'S
HANUKKAH

Aebleskiver
Danish Doughnuts
144

Risalamande
Danish Rice Pudding
146

Aebleskiver
Danish Doughnuts

Margit serves these sweet treats that are somewhere between a doughnut and a pancake at her annual Hanukkah party. Borrowing from a custom associated with risalamande, a Danish Christmas rice pudding (page 146), she hides an almond in one of the aebleskiver. Whoever finds it receives a special present from her.

Margit uses a cast-iron aebleskiver pan, but you can find various types of aebleskiver pans, including electric ones, online. She also uses a knitting needle as a tool to flip the doughnuts in the pan, but you can use a wooden skewer or chopstick. To streamline your workflow, you can make the batter up to 12 hours ahead; store it, well sealed, in the refrigerator.

MAKES 25 to 30 doughnuts

1½ cups (360 ml) lukewarm whole milk

1½ tablespoons (2 packets/14 g) active dry yeast

3 tablespoons granulated sugar

3 large eggs

1¾ cups (225 g) all-purpose flour, sifted

¼ teaspoon kosher salt

1 Granny Smith apple

8 ounces (2 sticks/225 g) unsalted butter

1 whole blanched almond

1 cup (115 g) confectioners' sugar for dusting

Berry jam of your choice for serving

SPECIAL EQUIPMENT

Aebleskiver pan

MAKE THE BATTER: Put the milk, yeast, and sugar in the bowl of a stand mixer fitted with the paddle attachment and mix on medium speed until thoroughly combined. (You can also make the batter by hand using a whisk.) Reduce the mixer speed and add the eggs one at a time, waiting until each egg is well incorporated before adding the next. Add the flour and salt and mix until the batter is smooth, scraping down the sides of the mixer bowl as needed.

Remove the bowl from the mixer stand, cover with a towel, and let the batter rise in a warm place until doubled in volume, about 1 hour. After the batter has risen, transfer it to a large pitcher and set aside.

MEANWHILE, PREPARE THE APPLES: Line a baking sheet with paper towels.

Peel and core the apple and cut it crosswise into ⅛-inch (3 mm) slices. Cut the apple slices into small squares, about ½ inch (1.25 cm); they don't need to be perfectly uniform. Put the apples and ¼ cup (60 ml) water in a small saucepan, bring to a simmer over medium heat, and cook, partially covered, until the apples are tender, about 15 minutes. Using a slotted spoon, transfer the apples to the prepared baking sheet to drain and let cool.

Melt the butter in a small saucepan over low heat. Remove from the heat and let sit for a few minutes, until the milk solids and water settle on the bottom of the pan. Spoon or pour off the clear melted butter fat and set aside; discard the milky layer.

FRY THE DOUGHNUTS: Line a baking sheet or tray with paper towels. Heat the aebleskiver pan over medium heat (electric pans will just have one setting). **1.** After a few minutes, when the pan is quite hot, pour about 1 teaspoon of clarified butter into each hollow of the pan.

2. Pour 1 generous tablespoon of the batter into each hollow; the batter should reach the rim.

3. Add a few pieces of apple to the center of each doughnut, slipping the almond into the center of one. After 1 to 2 minutes, the edges of the doughnuts should be golden brown and most of the batter should be set, though the centers may still be loose. **4.** Poke a knitting needle or wooden skewer into the side of one

doughnut and carefully flip it over to cook the other side; repeat with the rest of the doughnuts. Keep cooking the doughnuts, turning them occasionally, until all surfaces are browned and the doughnuts are cooked through, about 7 minutes. Using the knitting needle, carefully transfer the fried doughnuts to the paper towel–lined baking sheet.

When all the doughnuts are fried, dust them generously with the confectioners' sugar. Serve with your favorite berry jam alongside.

Risalamande
Danish Rice Pudding

When Margit was growing up in Copenhagen, her mother cooked a special dinner on Christmas Eve with this rice pudding for dessert. The pudding, cooked apples, and cherry sauce can be prepared one day ahead and refrigerated separately. Bring the pudding and sauce back up to room temperature and whip the cream and fold it into the pudding right before serving to give it a lighter texture. If you like, you can follow a Danish custom of hiding an almond in the dessert. Be sure to have a prize on hand for whoever finds it.

MAKES 6 to 8 servings

FOR THE RICE PUDDING

1 cup (200 g) short-grain rice, such as Arborio

½ cup (120 ml) water

4 cups (1 L) whole milk

Seeds scraped from 1 large vanilla bean or 1½ teaspoons vanilla extract

FOR THE APPLES

1 large Granny Smith apple

FOR THE CHERRY SAUCE

2 cups (500 g) pitted sour cherries in syrup

2 tablespoons cornstarch

2 tablespoons water

2 tablespoons sugar

FOR THE WHIPPED CREAM

1 cup (240 ml) heavy cream

1½ tablespoons sugar

MAKE THE RICE PUDDING: Put the rice in a medium saucepan, add the water, and bring to a simmer over medium-high heat. Add the milk and vanilla seeds, if using, and stir to mix well.

As soon as the milk begins to simmer, reduce the heat to low, partially cover the pan, and cook, stirring occasionally, until the liquid is absorbed and the rice pudding is thick, about 45 minutes. Toward the end of cooking, stir the mixture more often to keep it from sticking or burning on the bottom of the pot. If using vanilla extract, add it at this point.

Transfer the rice pudding to a large bowl, cover, and set aside to cool, about 30 minutes.

MEANWHILE, PREPARE THE APPLES: Line a baking sheet with paper towels.

Peel and core the apple, cut it crosswise into ⅛-inch (3 mm) slices, then cut the slices into small squares, about ½ inch (1.25 cm); they don't need to be perfectly uniform. Put the apples and ¼ cup (60 ml) water in a small saucepan, bring to a simmer over medium heat, and cook, partially covered, until the apples are tender, about 15 minutes. Using a slotted spoon, transfer the apples to the prepared baking sheet to drain and cool.

MAKE THE CHERRY SAUCE: Put the cherries and their syrup in a small saucepan and heat over medium heat. Meanwhile, in a small bowl, mix the cornstarch with the water until smooth (your finger is the best tool for this; this mixture is called a slurry). When the cherry syrup begins to simmer, add the cornstarch slurry, lower the heat, and simmer the sauce, stirring constantly, until glossy and thick, 1 to 3 minutes.

Remove the pan from the heat and sprinkle the sugar over the surface of the sauce to prevent a film from forming. Set the sauce aside to cool to room temperature.

Just before serving, put the cream and sugar in a large bowl and beat with a handheld electric mixer or a whisk until the cream doubles in volume and forms soft peaks, 3 to 4 minutes.

Fold the cooled apple slices into the rice pudding and then gently fold in the whipped cream until well combined, keeping as much volume of the whipped cream as possible.

Serve the rice pudding in individual bowls with about 2 tablespoons of the cherry sauce spooned over each portion.

An Egyptian-Moroccan Doughnut Duel

SHARED BY

Nir Mesika

I am half Moroccan and half Egyptian, and both sides of my family lived in the kitchen when I was growing up. In Sephardi Jewish culture, there's friendly competition between cooks to see who makes better food. It was that way with my grandmother Mazal, who was born in Morocco, and Rubi, my Egyptian grandmother. They lived close by, only a few minutes from our home, and on every Shabbat, of course, we had to see both for a meal.

As the Egyptian side of my family was very liberal, sometimes the Shabbat meal was a barbecue after I'd come back from surfing at a nearby beach and my grandfather had returned from fishing. The Moroccan side was the opposite, religious and spiritual, so we often joined them for lunch after synagogue, when my grandmother Mazal would host up to fifty people.

During Hanukkah, naturally, the competition continued, with dueling fried treats. One night was spent at Mazal's home, where we ate the light doughnuts called sfenj, which she most likely learned from her mother, along with very sweet mint tea. Another of the eight evenings was spent

---

FAMILY JOURNEY

Alexandria, Egypt → *Kiryat Ha'im, Israel* → *New York City* → *Tel Aviv*

Casablanca, Morocco → *Afula, Israel* → *Kiryat Bialik, Israel* → *New York City* → *Tel Aviv*

Nir's grandparents Mazal and Itzhak Ben David, 1990

at Rubi's home, where she fried zalabia, small round fritters she'd learned to make from a Muslim neighbor in Alexandria who prepared them for Ramadan.

I should add that the competition was in good fun. My grandmothers had a nice connection and would talk about food whenever they saw each other. And both of their Hanukkah treats have lived on. My spin on the zalabia with orange blossom syrup was on the menu at my restaurant for a time, and I make the sfenj at home every year for Hanukkah.

NIR MESIKA is the chef of Timna, a restaurant that first opened in New York City and later relocated to Tel Aviv. His family traces their roots through North Africa back to the Iberian Peninsula before the Inquisition.

NIR MESIKA'S HANUKKAH

Zalabia
Doughnuts with
Orange Blossom Syrup
152

Sfenj
Moroccan Doughnuts
156

—*Serve with*—

fresh citrus,
Jordan almonds

Zalabia

Doughnuts with Orange Blossom Syrup

Nir's grandmother Rubi learned to make zalabia from a Muslim neighbor in Alexandria, who fried them for Ramadan. Nir's updated her recipe over the years, making the doughnuts a bit larger and swapping in orange blossom water for rosewater in the aromatic syrup.

MAKES about 2 dozen doughnuts

FOR THE DOUGHNUTS

1 packet (2¼ teaspoons/7 g) active dry yeast

1½ cups (360 ml) warm water

2¼ cups plus 2 tablespoons (305 g) all-purpose flour

1 tablespoon sugar

2 tablespoons canola oil, plus more for deep-frying

¼ teaspoon kosher salt

FOR THE SYRUP

½ cup (170 g) honey

2 tablespoons orange blossom water

1 teaspoon grated lemon zest

2 tablespoons fresh lemon juice

MAKE THE DOUGH: In a small bowl, stir together the yeast and warm water.

Sift the flour into a large bowl and whisk in the sugar. Add the yeast mixture and whisk to combine (the dough will be on the wet side). Whisk or stir in the oil and salt.

Cover the bowl with plastic wrap and set aside to rise until the dough has doubled in size and bubbles have started forming on the top, about 1 hour.

MEANWHILE, MAKE THE SYRUP: Combine the honey, orange blossom water, lemon zest, and lemon juice in a medium bowl and stir to blend. Set aside.

FRY THE ZALABIA: Set the bowl of syrup near the stove, along with a plate or platter for the finished zalabia. Fill a medium, tall pot (tall enough that the oil won't overflow when you add the zalabia) with 3 to 4 inches (7.5 to 10 cm) canola oil. Heat the oil over high heat until it reaches 365°F (185°C); the oil is hot enough when a few small pieces of dough sizzle and brown quickly when added to it.

Using two tablespoons, scoop up a heaping spoonful of dough with one spoon and gently lower it into the hot oil, using the other spoon to scrape the dough into the oil. The dough should puff up instantly. Add one or two more portions of dough to the pot, but don't crowd it, or the oil temperature will drop too much and your zalabia will be greasy.

Fry the doughnuts, flipping occasionally, until puffed, crisp, and golden brown, about 2 minutes on each side. Make sure to monitor the heat, turning it down if necessary so that the outsides of the zalabia don't cook too quickly, leaving the insides undercooked. Remove the doughnuts from the oil with a slotted spoon, letting the excess oil drip back into the pot, and place in the bowl of syrup. Toss to coat and then transfer to the serving plate. Repeat with the remaining dough.

Drizzle the zalabia with more syrup, if you like, and serve immediately.

Sfenj
Moroccan Doughnuts

Nir's Moroccan grandmother, Mazal, used to fry fresh sfenj for Hanukkah, but it was his mom, Yaffa, who taught him to make them. Today Nir keeps the holiday tradition going, pairing the doughnuts with rosewater pastry cream for a festive touch. To streamline the process, make the pastry cream up to one day ahead.

MAKES about 1 dozen doughnuts

FOR THE DOUGHNUTS

2½ cups (325 g) all-purpose flour

1½ teaspoons (4 g) active dry yeast

⅓ cup plus 1 tablespoon (85 g) sugar

¼ teaspoon kosher salt

1 cup (240 ml) lukewarm water

1 tablespoon arak, ouzo, or other anise-flavored spirit

⅓ cup (65 g) sugar

2 tablespoons ground cinnamon

Vegetable oil for deep-frying

FOR THE PASTRY CREAM

1 cup (240 ml) whole milk

¼ cup (50 g) sugar

½ vanilla bean, split lengthwise, or ½ teaspoon vanilla extract

2 large egg yolks

2 tablespoons cornstarch, whisked together with 2 tablespoons milk

1½ teaspoons rosewater

MAKE THE DOUGH: Put the flour, yeast, sugar, and salt in a large bowl and whisk to blend, then whisk in the water and arak. Mix until you have a sticky, uniform dough. Cover the bowl with plastic wrap and let rise at room temperature for about 1 hour; the dough should almost double in size.

MAKE THE PASTRY CREAM: Put the milk, sugar, and vanilla bean, if using, in a small saucepan and bring to a gentle simmer over medium heat. Remove the vanilla bean, scrape the seeds into the milk, and return the bean to the hot milk. Keep warm over low heat, but don't let simmer.

In a large bowl, whisk together the egg yolks and cornstarch mixture. While whisking constantly, pour a little of the hot milk into the bowl. Gradually add the remaining hot milk in a thin stream, continuing to whisk.

Pour the mixture back into the saucepan and cook over medium heat, stirring constantly with a wooden spoon, until the mixture begins to boil and thicken, then boil, stirring constantly, for about 2 minutes. Remove from the heat.

Remove the vanilla bean and let the pastry cream cool slightly, then stir in the rosewater. If using the vanilla extract, add it at this point. Cover and set aside until ready to use; if it will be longer than 2 hours, store the pastry cream in the refrigerator.

FRY THE SFENJ: Mix the sugar and cinnamon in a shallow bowl and set near the stove. Line a large plate with paper towels and set it near the stove.

Heat about 3 inches (7.5 cm) of oil in a wide deep pot (deep enough that the oil won't overflow when you add the dough) over medium heat until it reaches 365°F (185°C). Grease your hands lightly with oil and pull off a piece of dough about the size of a Ping-Pong ball (45 g). Use your finger to make a hole in the center of the dough ball, stretching the hole slightly to make a ring; don't worry if the dough doesn't look like a perfect doughnut—it will be fine once it's fried.

Gently slide the doughnut into the hot oil. Repeat with a few more pieces of dough, but don't overcrowd the pot; keep an eye on the oil temperature so it doesn't get too low, which would make the doughnuts greasy.

Fry the doughnuts, turning once, until deep golden brown, 1½ to 2 minutes per side. Lift out each doughnut with a slotted spoon or tongs, letting the excess oil drip back into the pot, and transfer to the sugar-cinnamon bowl. Toss to coat evenly, then transfer the doughnut to the paper towel–lined plate. Repeat with the remaining dough.

To serve, transfer the pastry cream to a piping bag fitted with a small plain tip. (If the pastry cream is very stiff, whisk until light and fluffy before filling the bag.) Pipe a dollop of pastry cream into the center of each sfenj and serve.

The Latkes That Helped Our Ukrainian Family Survive

SHARED BY
Elizaveta Vigonskaia

My mom, Ester, was determined that we would survive. On June 22, 1941, German forces invaded the Soviet Union, and two days later, my father joined the Soviet Army. Before he left, he told my mother to stay in Kyiv. But she was smart and knew it was no longer safe. In September, she took my brother and me with her to the train station, where we caught the last train heading east to the Ural Mountains, deep in Russia. A week later, Nazi forces massacred nearly thirty-four thousand Jews at Babyn Yar on the outskirts of Kyiv. If my mom hadn't decided to run away, we might have been among them.

In 1945, we returned to Kyiv, where we were reunited with my father. Again, everything changed. There was no food anywhere, only famine. I was a small child then, but I remember people dying on the street from hunger. My mom would send me to pick up a loaf of bread and I would stand in line for three, four, sometimes even five hours. When she found a single potato, she would grind it up, add salt, and fry latkes in fish oil a doctor prescribed for nutrients. To this day, I cannot think about the smell of fish oil, it turns my stomach—but this is how we survived.

FAMILY JOURNEY

Kyiv, Ukraine → Long Beach, CA → Brooklyn, NY

Elizaveta and her brother Emil in Kyiv, 1939

As life became better and food less scarce, we no longer needed the fish oil. Every holiday, my mom would fry latkes in regular oil, topping them with roasted meat. This is absolutely delicious. Today I live near my children in Brooklyn and I am the one who makes this dish. It reminds me of my mother and this terrible time, but it also helps me appreciate that we have a good life in America.

ELIZAVETA VIGONSKAIA is a survivor. As a child, she narrowly escaped the atrocities of Babyn Yar and later endured a famine that struck Ukraine just after World War II. Selfhelp, an organization that supports elderly New Yorkers and provides services to Holocaust survivors, introduced Elizaveta to the Jewish Food Society team in 2020.

Latkes with Braised Short Ribs
162

—Serve with—

rye bread,
tossed salad

Latkes
with Braised
Short Ribs

If you make the short ribs the day before serving, it will simplify the workflow of this recipe, and the time in the fridge will allow the fat to float to the top and solidify, making it easy to skim off. *(Pictured on pages 160–161)*

MAKES 6 to 8 servings; about 24 latkes

FOR THE STEW

2 pounds (900 g) bone-in short ribs, cut across the bone into 2½-inch (6 cm) pieces

1½ tablespoons kosher salt

½ teaspoon freshly ground black pepper

2 tablespoons vegetable or grapeseed oil

1 large yellow onion (about 10 ounces/280 g), finely chopped

2 garlic cloves, finely chopped

5 whole allspice berries

Water for braising

FOR THE LATKES

1 medium yellow onion (about 6 ounces/170 g)

4 large russet potatoes (about 3 pounds/ 1.3 kg), peeled

1 tablespoon all-purpose flour

1 large egg

1 large egg yolk

1½ tablespoons kosher salt

½ teaspoon freshly ground black pepper

Vegetable oil for deep-frying

A few dill or parsley sprigs for garnish

MAKE THE SHORT RIBS: Season the short ribs with the salt and pepper. Heat the oil in a large heavy-bottomed pot, such as a Dutch oven, over medium-high heat. Once the oil is hot, carefully add the short ribs and cook, turning occasionally, until nicely browned on all sides, about 5 minutes per side. Transfer the meat to a plate and reduce the heat to medium.

Add the onion and garlic to the pot and sauté until soft and light gold but not browned, about 15 minutes.

Return the short ribs to the pot and add the allspice and enough water to come about three-quarters of the way up the sides of the pot. Bring to a boil, cover the pot, and reduce the heat to medium-low, adjusting it if necessary so the liquid simmers gently. Cook the short ribs for about 1½ hours and then, using a pair of tongs, carefully turn the short ribs.

Continue cooking the short ribs, partially covered, for another 1 to 1½ hours, until the meat is very tender and the liquid has reduced and thickened slightly. Remove from the heat.

Let the short ribs partially cool in their liquid and then spoon off the fat that rises to the surface. Once the short ribs are cool enough to handle, take them out, shred the meat, and discard the bones; set aside. If the cooking liquid seems watery, return it to the stove and simmer for a few minutes to thicken and concentrate the flavors. Taste and season with more salt and pepper if needed. (You can cook and shred the short ribs ahead of time, then refrigerate the meat and the cooking liquid separately. Just before serving, remove any remaining fat that's hardened on the cooking liquid, and gently reheat the meat in a bit of the liquid.)

MAKE THE LATKES: Grate the onion and then the potatoes on the large holes of a box grater or in a food processor fitted with the shredding blade. Put the grated onion and potatoes in the center of a clean dish towel, wrap them in the towel, and twist it over a large bowl to squeeze out as much liquid as possible, capturing the liquid in the bowl; set the bowl aside. Put the squeezed onion and potatoes into another large bowl.

After about 5 minutes, the potato starch in the liquid will have settled at the bottom of the bowl. Gently drain off the water, leaving the starch behind, then scrape the potato starch into the bowl with the onion and potatoes. Add the flour, whole egg, egg yolk, salt, and pepper and mix until well combined.

Preheat the oven to 350°F (175°C). Line a tray with paper towels.

Place a large skillet over medium-high heat, add about 1 inch (2.5 cm) of oil, and heat until hot. To check whether the oil is hot enough, drop a few shreds of potato into the oil. If they sizzle briskly, the oil is ready; if not, keep heating it. (If you try to fry the latkes in oil that's not hot enough, they will be heavy and greasy.)

Once the oil is hot enough, scoop out about 1½ tablespoons of the latke mix, put it in your palm, and shape it into a flat disk about 3 inches (7.5 cm) wide. Gently slide the latke into the oil. Repeat the process, adding 4 or 5 more latkes to the pan, taking care not to overcrowd the pan. Fry the latkes, turning once, until golden brown on both sides, about 5 minutes per side. Transfer to the paper towel–lined tray and continue frying the latkes in batches.

BAKE THE LATKES AND SHORT RIBS: Arrange the latkes in one layer in a couple of shallow baking dishes, such as 9-by-13-inch (23 by 33 cm) Pyrex dishes. Place a small mound of the shredded short ribs on each latke and spoon the short rib cooking liquid over the latkes.

Bake until the latkes have absorbed some of the cooking liquid and everything is nicely heated through, about 15 minutes.

Garnish the dish with dill sprigs and serve hot.

Purim

PURIM COMES JUST BEFORE spring, when a big party is what's needed to bring us out of winter's gloom. The most raucous day of the Jewish year, it's a holiday where no limits are placed on joy, when parties and sharing sweet gifts with friends are the rule.

The merriment commemorates the survival of the Jewish people in the Persian Empire long ago. As the story is told in the Book of Esther (Megillat Esther in Hebrew), an adviser to King Ahasuerus named Haman was plotting to kill the Jews of Persia, but his efforts were thwarted by Queen Esther and her guardian and cousin (sometimes called her uncle) Mordechai. The megillah is chanted aloud, and humorous plays and skits called spiels are acted out. It's customary to dress up in costumes, drink until one can no longer tell the difference between Haman and Mordechai, and celebrate until all hours.

In Ilana Isaac's family, there were always card games and pastries like cheese sambusak (page 195) and date-filled cookies called b'ebe be tamer (page 197) at their Purim parties. Celebrations often feature baked goods, which are a signature of the holiday and also offer an opportunity to use up flour before Passover, as Joan Nathan suggests in her *Jewish Holiday Cookbook*. When Stella Hanan Cohen was growing up in Rhodesia (present-day Zimbabwe), the mesas d'alegria, or Sephardi "tables of happiness" made for Purim and life-cycle events like weddings, were topped with medieval sweets like the orange cake called pan d'Espanya (page 170) and boulukunio, an almond and sesame seed brittle (page 172).

But Purim isn't just about parties. It's also a time to give to those in need; to enjoy a Purim seudah, or feast; and to exchange care packages called mishloach manot, filled with treats like candies, nuts, and hamantaschen. Today many people buy baskets to send to friends and family, but when Yonit Naftali was growing up in Israel, her mother would bake Hungarian pastries like multilayered fluden and beigli, a yeasted dough rolled up in a spiral with ground walnuts or poppy seeds, for their neighbors (see page 178).

Before Purim, I like to browse the Jewish Food Society archive and try new Purim treats with my daughter, Ella. I'll invite friends over for a late-night gathering with hamantaschen and sherry. The winter holidays remind me to hold those I love closer. Spending time with them is what sustains me through the cold gray months.

"Tables of Happiness" from Medieval Spain Live On in Zimbabwe

SHARED BY

Stella Hanan Cohen

There was a sort of magical atmosphere laden with spirituality and closeness in the kitchens where the women of my grandmother's and mother's generations gathered before weddings and holidays like Purim. They worked like alchemists in holy communion to make sweets like snow-white masapan, crunchy almond and sesame seed brittle, and date-filled cookies for the mesas d'alegria, or tables of happiness.

Each woman in the kitchen had her specialty, and she would never hand over her recipe. Instead, she turned her back so no one would see that little secret of extra mastic or how many drops of orange blossom water she added. But the real secret ingredients were the time and the love the women dedicated to create these magical treasures.

As they worked, there was a beautiful cacophony of Ladino, Spanish, Turkish, and Greek spoken in the kitchen, and they would sing old songs called romansos. They had such nostalgia for their homeland, for Spain, but none of them had ever lived there. My ancestors are Rodesli, who, following the expulsion from the Iberian Peninsula in 1492, resettled

FAMILY JOURNEY

Spain → Rhodes, Greece → Marmaris, Turkey → Élisabethville, Belgian Congo (present-day Lubumbashi, Democratic Republic of the Congo) → Salisbury, Rhodesia (present-day Harare, Zimbabwe)

Stella's father Sam (far right) and friends on a boat from Rhodes to Rhodesia, 1936

on the island of Rhodes in the Ottoman Empire. There they tenaciously clung to the Ladino language, customs, and recipes. And when part of our community, including my family, moved to southern and central Africa in the twentieth century, they brought that heritage with them.

We've been making these dishes in exile for five hundred years with the same recipes and love as our ancestors. Every mouthful is a piece of history, and we wouldn't have our history without the food. It's my raison d'être that they're not forgotten.

STELLA HANAN COHEN is the author of *Stella's Sephardic Table: Jewish Family Recipes from the Mediterranean Island of Rhodes* and the great-granddaughter of Yaacov Copouya, the rabbi of Rhodes in the early twentieth century. Her life's work is to preserve her community's culture and history.

STELLA HANAN COHEN'S PURIM

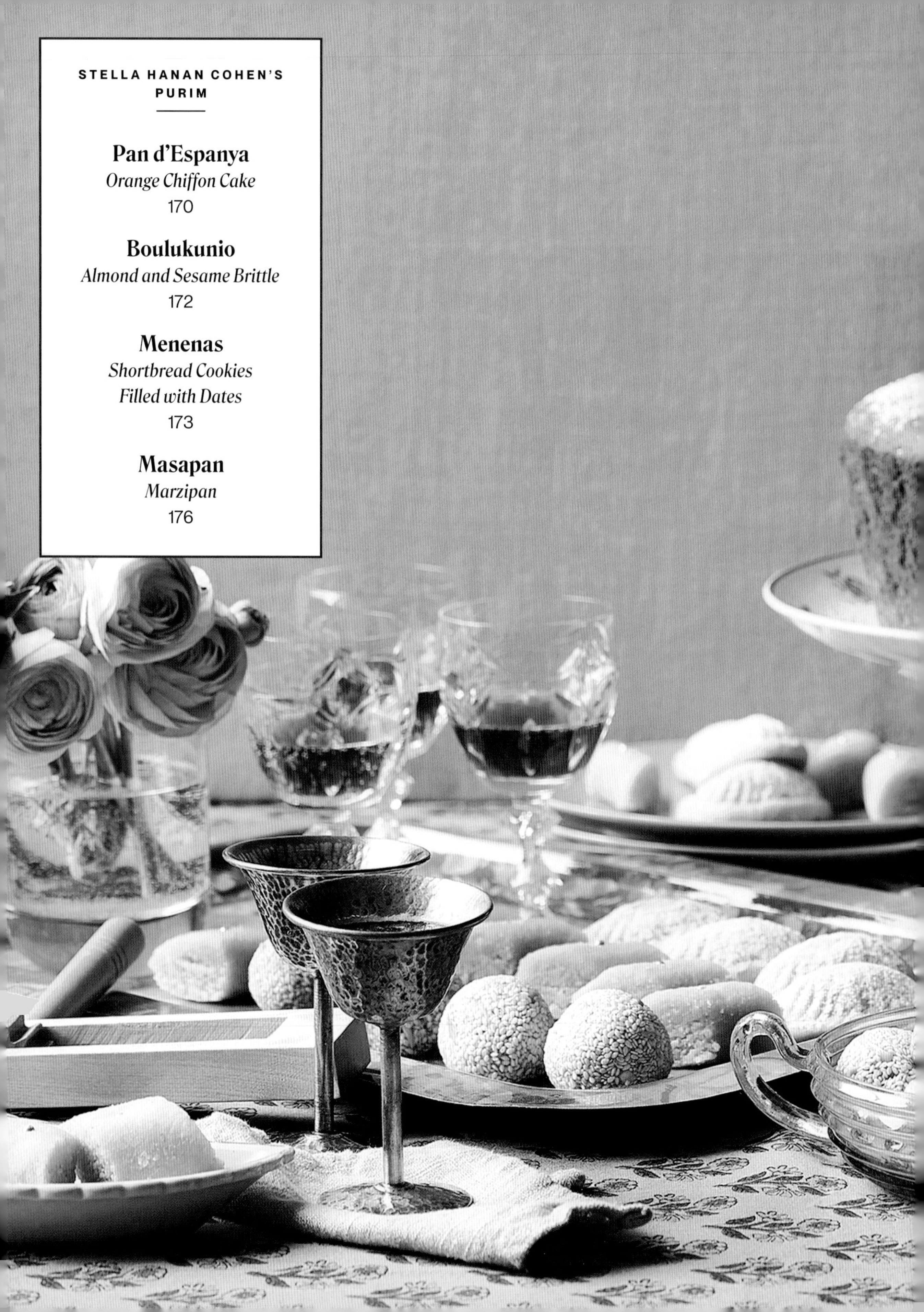

Pan d'Espanya
Orange Chiffon Cake

"Pan d'Espanya (called pan esponjado in Ladino, a Judeo-Spanish language derived from Old Spanish) is the iconic orange chiffon cake that has been made for generations by the Jews of Spain," explains Stella. It's traditionally made to break the Yom Kippur fast and as part of the sweets spread for celebrations like Purim and life-cycle events. But there doesn't need to be a special occasion to have it, she says. You can serve it as a teatime snack or as a finale to a meal, with berries and lightly whipped cream.

The delicate, moist cake gets its loft and light texture from whipped egg whites, so take care while you're working with them: make sure to not get any yolk in the whites and don't overwhip them. An egg white will have maximum expansion potential if whipped just barely to the firm peak stage; going beyond that, to the point at which the whites are stiff, can mean less volume in your cake.

MAKES one 10-inch (25 cm) cake

2 cups (235 g) cake flour, sifted

2 heaping teaspoons baking powder

⅛ teaspoon kosher salt

8 large eggs

1 cup (200 g) superfine sugar
(sometimes called baker's sugar)

½ cup (120 ml) vegetable or sunflower oil

2 teaspoons finely grated orange zest

¾ cup (180 ml) fresh orange juice
(from about 3 oranges)

1 teaspoon orange blossom water

¾ teaspoon cream of tartar (optional)

Confectioners' sugar for dusting (optional)

SPECIAL EQUIPMENT

A 10-inch (25 cm) 2-piece tube or angel food
cake pan

Preheat the oven to 350°F (175°C). Set out a
10-inch (25 cm) tube or angel food cake pan,
but do not grease it.

Put the cake flour, baking powder, and salt in a
medium bowl and whisk to blend; set aside.

Separate the eggs, putting 6 of the yolks in the
bowl of a stand mixer fitted with the paddle
attachment (or use a large bowl and a handheld
electric mixer); discard the other 2 yolks (or
reserve them for another use). Put all 8 egg
whites into a small bowl (or another large bowl
if you will be using a handheld mixer) and cover
with plastic wrap; set aside at room temperature.

Add the superfine sugar to the egg yolks and
beat at high speed until pale and creamy, about
2 minutes. Turn the mixer to low and beat in
the oil, orange zest, orange juice, and orange

blossom water. With the mixer still on low speed,
add the flour mixture, beating only until the
batter is combined, scraping down the sides of
the bowl as needed. Remove the bowl from the
mixer stand and set aside.

Put the egg whites in a clean mixer bowl, attach
it to the mixer stand, and fit the mixer with the
whisk attachment (or use the handheld mixer
with clean beaters). Beat the egg whites until soft
peaks form. Add the cream of tartar, if using, and
continue to beat the egg whites until they hold
firm peaks; take care that you don't beat them to
the point of becoming grainy. Remove the bowl
from the mixer stand.

With a large rubber spatula or a metal spoon,
scoop up about one-third of the egg whites
and gently fold them into the batter. Continue
with the rest of the egg whites, a third at a time,
folding gently until just combined with no white
streaks remaining.

Pour the batter into the ungreased tube pan and
smooth the surface with a spoon. Bake until the
cake is firm to the touch and a skewer inserted
in the center comes out clean, 40 to 50 minutes.
Immediately invert the cake pan onto a wire
rack and let the cake cool completely, about
1½ hours.

To remove the cake from the pan, loosen the
edges of the cake by running a long, thin knife
around the inside of the pan and the center tube.
Gently ease the cake out onto a wire rack and
separate the cake from the base of the pan. Flip
the cake back upright and lightly dust the top
with confectioners' sugar, if using.

Serve right away. Wrap any leftovers tightly in
plastic and store at room temperature.

Boulukunio

Almond and Sesame Brittle

"This version of almond and sesame seed brittle is an ancient recipe that dates back generations, to medieval Spain," Stella explains. While it is traditionally served on Purim and Hanukkah, "most households like to keep a stash of boulukunio in an airtight tin on standby." Layered between sheets of parchment paper, the chewy candy can be stored for up to 1 month.

Take your time when you toast the sesame seeds, aiming for a light, even toast with no burnt seeds, which would make the candy bitter. Adding a pinch of flour to each batch of seeds in your skillet helps absorb the oil that will be released as they toast, keeping the seeds separate and dry. A candy thermometer is essential for this recipe. *(Pictured on pages 174–175, bottom row)*

MAKES 35 candies

FOR THE CANDY

2 cups (280 g) hulled sesame seeds

About 1 teaspoon all-purpose flour

½ cup (65 g) blanched slivered almonds, lightly toasted

Vegetable oil for greasing the baking sheet

FOR THE SYRUP

½ cup (170 g) honey

½ cup (120 ml) water

1½ cups (300 g) sugar

SPECIAL EQUIPMENT

Candy thermometer

MAKE THE CANDY: Put 1 cup (140 g) of the sesame seeds in a large heavy-bottomed skillet over medium heat and sprinkle with a small pinch of flour. Toast the sesame seeds until lightly and evenly golden, stirring and shaking the pan often, about 4 minutes. Transfer the sesame seeds to a large heatproof bowl. Repeat this process with the remaining 1 cup (140 g) sesame seeds, adding another pinch of flour.

Add the almonds to the bowl of sesame seeds and stir to mix.

Generously grease a small rimmed baking sheet or heatproof shallow baking dish with vegetable oil; set aside. Line another baking sheet with parchment paper; set aside.

MAKE THE SYRUP: Put the honey, water, and sugar in a medium saucepan and bring to a boil over medium-high heat, stirring until the sugar is dissolved. Attach a candy thermometer to the side of the pan and boil, without stirring, until the syrup reaches 245°F (118°C), 20 to 30 minutes.

Remove the pan from the heat and immediately pour the mixture over the sesame seeds and almonds. (Note: The syrup is extremely hot, so use caution and don't use your hands to stir!) Stir the mixture vigorously with a wooden spoon or stiff silicone spatula and then pour the mixture onto the oiled baking sheet. Let the mixture cool until it's comfortable to touch.

Dampen your hands lightly in cold water, scoop up about 1 tablespoon of the mixture and roll it into a 1-inch (2.5 cm) ball, then set on the parchment-lined baking sheet. Repeat with the remaining mixture. Or, for an alternative shape, roll the mixture into 4 ropes, each about 1 inch (2.5 cm) thick. Cut diagonally into 1-inch (2.5 cm) sections using a sharp knife dipped into hot water between every few cuts.

Cool the candies at room temperature until firm; they will remain chewy.

Menenas

Shortbread Cookies Filled with Dates

Menenas, also known by their Arabic name, ma'amoul, are delicate cookies filled with nuts and/or dates. "Traditionally the Rhodesli womenfolk molded the menenas into oval shapes and decorated the tops with a feathery design by pinching the dough with a pair of tweezers," Stella writes in her cookbook *Stella's Sephardic Table: Jewish Family Recipes from the Mediterranean Island of Rhodes*. Wooden molds with ornate designs are an easier alternative and still produce beautiful cookies. You can find menenas or ma'amoul molds online or at well-equipped Middle Eastern shops, but any cookie mold that is deep enough to create a shallow dome shape with decorative impressions will work.

To streamline the process for this recipe, make the date filling up to 2 days ahead and keep it in an airtight container in the refrigerator. *(Pictured on pages 174–175, top row)*

MAKES 20 cookies

FOR THE FILLING

½ cup (60 g) walnuts

¾ cup (100 g) lightly packed finely chopped pitted dates

2 tablespoons hot water

2 tablespoons unsalted butter

¼ teaspoon ground cinnamon

⅛ teaspoon ground cloves

½ teaspoon finely grated orange zest

½ teaspoon orange blossom water

FOR THE DOUGH

2¼ cups (290 g) all-purpose flour, plus more for dusting

½ cup (80 g) fine semolina flour

½ teaspoon baking powder

2 tablespoons confectioners' sugar

8 ounces (2 sticks/225 g) unsalted butter, cut into small pieces, at room temperature

1 tablespoon whole milk

1 teaspoon vanilla extract

1 cup (115 g) confectioners' sugar for dusting

SPECIAL EQUIPMENT

An oval wooden cookie mold, about 2½ by 1¼ inches (6.25 by 3 cm)

PREPARE THE FILLING: Pulse the walnuts in a food processor until finely chopped (or finely chop them with a knife); set aside.

Put the dates, hot water, and butter in a large skillet and heat over medium heat, mixing and smashing the dates with a fork, until a soft paste-like mixture forms, about 2 minutes. Stir in the cinnamon, cloves, and orange zest. Remove from the heat, add the walnuts and orange blossom water, and stir until thoroughly combined.

Transfer the date paste to a plate and refrigerate it for 30 minutes, or until completely cool.

MEANWHILE, PREPARE THE DOUGH: Combine the all-purpose flour, semolina flour, baking powder, and confectioners' sugar in a large bowl. Add the butter and rub it into the flour with your fingertips until the mixture looks like coarse meal. Add the milk and vanilla and stir with a wooden spoon or spatula until the dough begins to hold together.

recipe continues on page 176

Transfer the dough to a lightly floured work surface and, using the palms of your hands, knead gently until it becomes smooth, about 1 minute. Shape the dough into a ball, wrap it in plastic wrap, and refrigerate for at least 15 minutes and up to 1 hour.

Remove the cooled date paste from the refrigerator and take 1 heaping teaspoon (about 10 g) and roll it between your palms into a ball. Set the date ball on a large plate and continue with the rest of the filling, making 20 balls total.

Arrange the oven racks in the lower and upper thirds of the oven and preheat the oven to 325°F (160°C). Line two baking sheets with parchment paper.

SHAPE THE COOKIES: Take the dough from the refrigerator and divide it into 20 walnut-sized pieces (about 1 ounce/30 g each). Roll each piece into a ball with your hands; the balls should be twice the diameter of the date balls.

Gently press your fingertip or the handle of a wooden spoon into one dough ball to create an indentation in the center. Carefully enlarge the indentation by cradling the dough ball in one palm and pinching the edges with the index finger and thumb of your other hand, working around the inside and outside of the dough to form a shell ¼ inch (6 mm) thick. Gently push a date paste ball into the dough shell and press the edges of the dough together over the top of it, gently pinching the dough to enclose and seal in the filling in an even layer of dough and reshaping the stuffed dough into a ball. Repeat with the remaining dough and filling.

Dust your cookie mold lightly with flour. With your palm, gently press a filled dough ball into the mold, unpinched side down. Flip the mold over and tap against the work surface until the menena pops out. Place the cookie decorated side up on one of the prepared baking sheets. Repeat with the rest of the filled dough balls, spacing them about ½ inch (1.25 cm) apart on the baking sheets.

Bake the menenas until they are firm and pale ivory, 20 to 30 minutes, rotating the baking sheets top to bottom and front to back about halfway through. The cookies should not brown, or they will be hard. Remove from the oven and let the cookies sit on the baking sheet for 1 minute, then carefully transfer them to a wire rack. Dust the cookies generously with confectioners' sugar while still warm and let cool to room temperature.

Masapan
Marzipan

Making masapan, or marzipan, is a treasured tradition in Stella's community. "We acquired the centuries-old skill from the nuns of the convents of Toledo, handcrafting freshly ground almonds with sugar syrup into orange blossom–scented masapan," she explains. Since it's made from scratch from ground whole blanched almonds, it has a slightly less refined texture than store-bought marzipan.

Whole blanched (skinned) almonds are sometimes available in the bulk or natural foods aisle of a grocery store and are easily sourced online. If you can't find them, slivered almonds will work fine. The masapan will keep for a week, but be sure to store it in an airtight container, as it can dry out quickly. *(Pictured on pages 174–175, center row)*

MAKES about 50 pieces

1 pound (450 g) blanched whole almonds

2 cups (480 ml) hot water

2 cups (400 g) sugar

1 teaspoon fresh lemon juice

FOR SHAPING

1 cup (240 ml) water

1 teaspoon orange blossom water

FOR DECORATING

Silver decorating balls (dragées)

Working in 3 batches, grind the almonds in a food processor until very finely ground and sandy in texture; use the pulse setting to ensure that the almonds don't turn into an oily paste. You should end up with about 4 cups (450 g) ground nuts.

Put the hot water and sugar in a large heavy-bottomed stainless steel saucepan and stir, off heat, until the sugar is completely dissolved. Then bring the syrup to a boil over high heat, without stirring (to prevent crystallization). Boil the syrup until it reaches 235°F (113°C), the soft-ball stage, about 30 minutes. If you don't have a thermometer, carefully take a small spoonful of the syrup and drop it into a glass of cold water. Let it cool for a few seconds, then feel the sugar; it should form a soft, pliable ball. If it doesn't quite hold together, cook for another minute or so and retest.

Remove the pan from the heat, add the ground almonds and lemon juice, and stir vigorously with a wooden spoon or stiff silicone spatula. Return the pan to low heat and, stirring constantly to avoid sticking or scorching, cook until the paste comes away from the sides of the pan, 2 to 3 minutes.

To test whether the marzipan is ready, roll a small amount of it—the size of a small marble—between your palms (be careful, the marzipan is hot). If it stays in a ball and does not stick to your hands, it's ready; remove the pan from the heat.

Transfer the marzipan to the bowl of a stand mixer fitted with the whisk attachment. Beat on medium speed until the marzipan is homogenous and increases in volume a bit, about 2 minutes, adding ½ teaspoon water at a time if needed to bring the mixture together.

SHAPE AND DECORATE THE MARZIPAN:

Put the water in a small bowl and add the orange blossom water. Dampen your hands with the scented water, scoop out a portion of marzipan, and roll it into a rope 1 inch (2.5 cm) thick; the length of the rope doesn't matter. With a sharp knife, cut the rope into 1½-inch (3.75 cm) diagonal pieces, measured from point to point. Repeat with the rest of the marzipan mixture.

Press a silver ball into the center of each piece of marzipan and arrange on a pretty serving plate.

Hungarian Purim Sweets to Take Pride In

Yonit Naftali

After the Holocaust, my grandmother Paula had next to nothing. From a family of ten brothers and sisters, she was one of only four to survive. There was nothing left, almost no one left. One of the few things that remained were her mother's recipes, which she knew by heart: yeasted doughnuts with brandy for Hanukkah, a nut torte layered with chocolate ganache for Passover, and semolina dumplings with cheese for Shavuot.

Years later, Paula wrote the recipes on pieces of paper and passed them on to my mother, Eva, who says they are all she has left from her family, from her tradition. She never changes a thing when she makes them—she won't even use a machine to grind the nuts. For Purim when I was little, my job was to grind them by hand in my grandmother's old grinder; I was also tasked with grating the lemon and mixing the poppy seeds for the layered Hungarian pastry fluden and for beigli, a swirled log filled with poppy seeds or walnuts.

We made these for mishloach manot and added a small bottle of wine, some chocolates, and a few sweets we'd bought to each package. It was my responsibility to take them to our neighbors. They weren't

FAMILY JOURNEY

Oradea, Hungary (present-day Romania) → *Nahariya, Israel* → *Jerusalem* → *Tel Aviv*

Yonit's grandparents Paula and Paul Gelberg with
their daughter, Eva Gelberg (Naftali), circa 1951

Hungarian or even Ashkenazi; most were Moroccan, and I remember
feeling embarrassed because our pastries were so different from the
ones they were baking in their homes. I always wanted my mother to
pack more of the store-bought treats and fewer of our pastries.

When I was ten, though, one of our neighbors, Shlomit, came to our
home the day after I'd delivered the package to return our plate. She
asked if there were any more pastries and told me she waited every year
for our mishloach manot. My embarrassment turned to pride in that
moment, pride in my mom and in our recipes.

On Purim, it's customary to give mishloach manot, small packages of sweets,
to friends, family, and neighbors. In food writer and content editor **YONIT NAFTALI**'s
family, the classic mishloach manot recipes come from her grandmother Paula,
who grew up in a Hungarian home in Oradea, a border town in Transylvania that
during the twentieth century was part of both Hungary and Romania.

Beigli
*Pastry Roulade Filled with
Poppy Seeds and Walnuts*
182

Fluden
*Layered Pastry with Poppy
Seeds, Walnuts, and Apples*
184

Hamantaschen with Chocolate Ganache and Poppy Seeds
186

Beigli

Pastry Roulade Filled with Poppy Seeds and Walnuts

Yonit's family fills these yeasted roulades with two types of filling: one with nutty-sweet poppy seeds and one with lemon-scented walnuts. It's customary to drink heavily on Purim, and Yonit's mother says that even the dough should be drunk, so there's a little wine added to it.

You can buy ground poppy seeds from a good baking supply store or buy whole seeds and grind them yourself in a spice grinder, after soaking them in very hot water for about 30 minutes and draining well. *(Pictured on page 181)*

MAKES two 11-inch (27.5 cm) roulades

FOR THE DOUGH

4⅓ cups plus 1 tablespoon all-purpose flour (570 g), plus more for dusting

Finely grated zest of 2 lemons

8 tablespoons (1 stick/115 g) unsalted butter, cut into small cubes, at room temperature

1 ounce (28 g) compressed fresh yeast or 1 tablespoon plus ½ teaspoon (10 g) active dry yeast

⅓ cup (80 ml) lukewarm whole milk

3 tablespoons sugar

⅓ cup (80 ml) dry white wine

1 large egg

1 large egg yolk

¼ teaspoon kosher salt

FOR THE POPPY SEED FILLING

1 cup (145 g) ground poppy seeds

¾ cup (180 ml) whole milk

¼ cup (50 g) sugar

1 teaspoon vanilla extract

1 large egg white, lightly beaten

FOR THE WALNUT FILLING

1 cup (120 g) walnuts

3 tablespoons whole milk

⅓ cup (65 g) sugar

Finely grated zest of 1 lemon

1 teaspoon vanilla extract

1 teaspoon brandy (optional)

1 large egg white, lightly beaten

FOR THE EGG WASH

1 large egg yolk, beaten with 1 tablespoon milk

MAKE THE DOUGH: Put the flour, lemon zest, and butter in the bowl of a stand mixer fitted with the dough hook. Mix on medium-low speed until the ingredients are well combined and the butter pieces are no larger than a small pea, 1 to 2 minutes.

In a small bowl, mix the yeast, milk, and sugar together, stirring until the yeast dissolves.

Add the yeast mixture to the flour mixture and mix on low speed until the liquid is incorporated, stopping the mixer and scraping the sides and bottom of the bowl as needed to ensure that all the flour is moistened. The dough will still be slightly dry and shaggy.

With the mixer running on low, gradually add the wine and mix until the dough absorbs the liquid, another minute or two. Add the egg, egg yolk, and salt and mix on medium-low speed until the dough is smooth and homogenous, 5 to 7 minutes.

Transfer the dough to a large bowl and cover with a towel. Set it in a warm place and let rise until doubled in size, 40 to 60 minutes.

WHILE THE DOUGH IS RISING, MAKE THE POPPY SEED FILLING: Combine the ground poppy seeds, milk, and sugar in a small saucepan and bring the mixture to a lively simmer over medium-high heat, then cook, stirring constantly, until the mixture becomes thick and spreadable, about 20 minutes. Remove the pan from the heat, stir in the vanilla, and set the filling aside to cool for about 10 minutes (if the filling is too warm, the egg white will set when you add it).

Add the egg white to the filling and stir to combine well. Set aside to cool completely, about 20 minutes.

MEANWHILE, MAKE THE WALNUT FILLING: Pulse the walnuts in a food processor until finely ground (don't grind so much that they become a paste). Transfer the walnuts to a medium bowl, add the milk, sugar, lemon zest, vanilla, brandy, if using, and egg white, and stir until combined into a spreadable paste. Set aside.

Line two baking sheets with parchment paper and set aside.

SHAPE THE BEIGLI: Once the dough has doubled in size, transfer it to a clean work surface. Knead it a few times and divide it into 2 equal pieces.

Roll out one piece of dough on a lightly floured surface with a rolling pin to a 14-by-11-inch (35 by 27.5 cm) rectangle. Turn the dough if necessary so a short end is in front of you. Spread the walnut filling evenly over the dough, leaving a ¾-inch (2 cm) border without filling on the long sides of the dough and a slightly larger border along the short end farthest from you. (The filling will be pushed toward the end as you roll up the dough, so this wider border will prevent it from leaking out when you shape the roulade.)

Fold the right and left sides of the dough inward about 1 inch (2.5 cm) over the filling. (This will prevent the filling from seeping out the sides of the beigli.) Starting at the end closest to you, roll up the dough into a log shape. Transfer the beigli to one of the prepared baking sheets, seam side down; set aside. Repeat the process with the second piece of dough and the poppy seed filling and place the poppy seed beigli on the second baking sheet. Let the pastries rest for 15 minutes.

Place the racks in the upper and lower thirds of the oven and preheat the oven to 400°F (205°C).

Brush the pastries with the egg wash and poke several holes along the tops and sides of the rolls with the tines of a fork. This will allow steam to escape during baking. Bake the pastries for 15 minutes, then reduce the oven temperature to 375°F (190°C). Rotate the pans front to back and top to bottom and continue baking until the pastries are a deep golden brown, 20 to 30 minutes. Take the beigli out of the oven and cool for at least 20 minutes, or until completely cool.

With a serrated knife, cut the beigli into 1-inch (2.5 cm) slices. Serve at room temperature.

Fluden

Layered Pastry with Poppy Seeds, Walnuts, and Apples

Fluden has a centuries-old history. Its name comes from a German word and before that the medieval Latin word *flado*, meaning "flat cake," explains András Koerner in *Jewish Cuisine in Hungary: A Cultural History with 83 Authentic Recipes*. Versions with multiple layers, called flódni, are more recent inventions, dating back to the second half of the nineteenth century. Since then, Koerner notes, the pastry's been a favorite in Hungarian homes for Purim.

The impressive pastry requires a few steps, but you can streamline the process by making the dough and the poppy seed and walnut fillings the day before; keep them all well wrapped in the fridge. The apple filling, though, is best made the day you bake the fluden.

MAKES one 9-inch (22.5 cm) square cake

FOR THE DOUGH

1 ounce (28 g) compressed fresh yeast or 1 tablespoon plus ½ teaspoon (10 g) active dry yeast

5 tablespoons (75 ml) dry white wine

1½ tablespoons brandy

4½ cups (585 g) all-purpose flour, plus more for dusting

11 ounces (2¾ sticks/300 g) cold unsalted butter, cut into cubes

2½ teaspoons finely grated lemon zest

¼ teaspoon kosher salt

2 large egg yolks

1 cup (200 g) sugar

FOR THE POPPY SEED FILLING

½ cup (70 g) ground poppy seeds (see headnote on page 182)

¾ cup (180 ml) whole milk

⅓ cup (65 g) sugar

1 teaspoon vanilla extract

FOR THE WALNUT FILLING

1¼ cups (150 g) walnuts

¼ cup (60 ml) whole milk

⅓ cup (65 g) sugar

2 teaspoons finely grated lemon zest

1 teaspoon vanilla extract

FOR THE APPLE FILLING

5 Granny Smith apples, peeled and grated

¼ cup (30 g) ground walnuts

¼ cup (50 g) sugar

1 tablespoon ground cinnamon

Softened butter for greasing the baking dish

FOR THE GLAZE

3 tablespoons apricot jam

1 tablespoon hot water

MAKE THE DOUGH: In a small bowl, mix the yeast with the wine and brandy until dissolved; set aside.

Put the flour, butter, lemon zest, and salt in the bowl of a stand mixer fitted with the dough hook and mix on low speed until well combined, with butter pieces no larger than a small pea, 3 to 5 minutes. Add the egg yolks and sugar and mix on medium-low speed until a shaggy dough forms, about 3 minutes.

With the mixer running, gradually pour in the yeast mixture. Once all the liquid is incorporated, increase the speed to medium and mix the dough until smooth and soft, 5 to 7 minutes.

Transfer the dough to a clean work surface and divide it into 4 equal pieces. Wrap each piece in plastic wrap and refrigerate for about 1½ hours.

MAKE THE POPPY SEED FILLING: Combine the ground poppy seeds, milk, and sugar in a small saucepan and bring the mixture to a lively simmer over medium-high heat, then cook, stirring constantly, until the mixture becomes thick and spreadable, about 20 minutes. Remove the pan from the heat, stir in the vanilla, and set the filling aside to cool completely, about 30 minutes, stirring occasionally.

MAKE THE WALNUT FILLING: Pulse the walnuts in a food processor until finely ground but not pasty. Transfer to a medium bowl, add the milk, sugar, lemon zest, and vanilla, and stir until combined. Set aside.

MAKE THE APPLE FILLING: Using your hands, squeeze the juices out of the grated apples and then put them in a colander set on a plate to drain any remaining liquid. Set aside.

Preheat the oven to 425°F (220°C). Butter a deep 9-inch (22.5 cm) square baking dish.

MAKE THE GLAZE: Stir the apricot jam with the hot water in a small bowl until the jam is dissolved. Set aside.

ASSEMBLE THE CAKE: Take one piece of dough from the refrigerator, lightly flour the work surface, and roll the dough out into a 10-inch (25 cm) square about ¼ inch (6 mm) thick. Measure the exact inside dimension of your baking dish and trim the dough square to that size. Gently roll the dough square up around your rolling pin, position it over the baking dish, and unroll it so it sits squarely in the bottom of the dish, trimming off any remaining excess dough if necessary. Reserve all the dough trimmings, covered loosely with plastic wrap so they don't dry out.

Spread the poppy seed filling in an even layer over the dough, making sure it comes all the way to the edges.

Roll out a second piece of dough in the same manner. Trim it as necessary (reserve the trimmings) and place the dough over the poppy seed filling. Spread the walnut filling in an even layer over the dough.

Repeat the rolling and trimming with a third piece of dough and place it over the walnut filling. Sprinkle the ground walnuts evenly over the dough. Give the grated apples one more squeeze to remove any remaining liquid and distribute them evenly over the walnuts. Sprinkle the sugar and cinnamon over the apples.

Roll and trim the last piece of dough and place it over the apple layer. Brush it with 2 tablespoons of the apricot glaze. Poke holes evenly all over the surface of the dough with a fork.

Gently press the reserved dough trimmings into a ball and knead a few times, until smooth. Roll out the dough to ¼ inch (6 mm) thick. Using a pastry wheel or a large knife, cut about 12 strips of dough that are about ½ inch (1.25 cm) wide and 11 inches (27.5 cm) long. Arrange the strips in a diagonal grid pattern over the top of the dough and trim the ends neatly. Brush the strips with the remaining apricot glaze.

Put the fluden in the preheated oven and immediately reduce the temperature to 375°F (190°C). Bake until the top is deep golden brown, 40 to 50 minutes. Remove from the oven and cool the fluden completely on a wire rack.

Run a sharp knife around the edges of the pastry to release it from the baking dish. Cut the fluden into 12 rectangular pieces. Use a small spatula to lift out the pieces; the first one might be a bit tricky. Serve the fluden at room temperature.

Hamantaschen with Chocolate Ganache and Poppy Seeds

Many Purim sweets, like hamantaschen, are shaped to represent the hat, ears, or another part of Haman, the villain of the holiday story. "By eating them, we symbolically erase Haman's name," according to Jewish culinary scholar Gil Marks. This recipe for hamantaschen from Yonit offers two different fillings: a traditional poppy seed one and a more modern chocolate ganache. To save time, you could fill the cookies with store-bought jam or chocolate spread. To ensure the best "three-cornered hat" shape, chill the filled and shaped cookies for about 20 minutes in the freezer before baking.

MAKES about 30 cookies

FOR THE DOUGH

3 cups plus 2 tablespoons (400 g) all-purpose flour, plus more for dusting

1½ teaspoons baking powder

½ teaspoon kosher salt

10 tablespoons (150 g) butter, at room temperature

¾ cup (150 g) sugar

1 large egg, at room temperature

1 large egg white, at room temperature

1 teaspoon vanilla extract

Finely grated zest of 1 lemon

FOR THE POPPY SEED FILLING

½ cup (70 g) ground poppy seeds (see headnote on page 182)

6 tablespoons (90 ml) whole milk

⅛ cup (25 g) sugar

½ teaspoon vanilla extract

1 large egg white, lightly beaten

FOR THE CHOCOLATE GANACHE FILLING

4 ounces (115 g) dark chocolate, chopped (about ¾ cup)

½ cup (120 ml) heavy cream

MAKE THE DOUGH: Whisk the flour, baking powder, and salt together in a medium bowl. Set aside.

Put the butter and sugar in the bowl of a stand mixer fitted with the paddle attachment and beat on medium speed until lighter in color and fluffy, about 2 minutes. Reduce the speed to low, add the egg, egg white, vanilla, and lemon zest, and mix until the ingredients are thoroughly combined, scraping down the sides of the bowl as needed. Add the flour mixture and continue mixing on low speed just until the dough comes together into a ball, about 1 minute, scraping

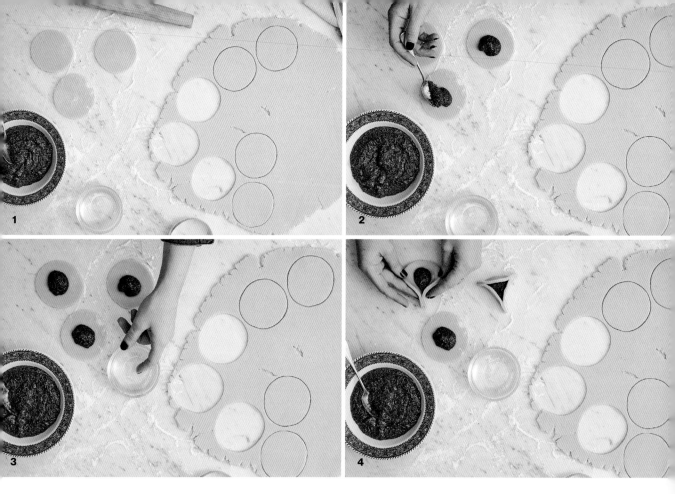

down the sides and to the bottom of the bowl to be sure all the flour gets incorporated.

Turn the dough out onto a piece of plastic wrap and shape it into a disk. Wrap tightly and refrigerate for at least 45 minutes and up to 1 day.

MEANWHILE, MAKE THE POPPY SEED FILLING: Combine the ground poppy seeds, milk, and sugar in a small saucepan and bring the mixture to a boil over medium-high heat, then reduce the heat to low and cook, stirring constantly, until the mixture becomes thick and spreadable, 5 to 10 minutes. Remove the pan from the heat, stir in the vanilla, and set the filling aside to cool for about 10 minutes (if the filling is too warm, the egg white will set when you add it).

Add the egg white and stir until well blended. Set aside to cool completely.

MAKE THE CHOCOLATE GANACHE FILLING: Put the chopped chocolate into a small metal bowl. Bring the cream to a simmer in a small saucepan over medium heat. Immediately remove the cream from the heat, pour it over the chocolate, and let sit for 30 seconds.

Stir the chocolate mixture with a heatproof spatula until it becomes a smooth, silky, and homogenous ganache. Set aside to cool to room temperature, stirring occasionally to speed the cooling.

Preheat the oven to 375°F (190°C). Line two baking sheets with parchment paper.

SHAPE AND FILL THE HAMANTASCHEN:
Divide the dough in half and keep one half wrapped in plastic while you roll out the other piece. **1.** Lightly flour a work surface and roll the dough portion out into a round that's just less than ¼ inch (6 mm) thick. The exact shape of the dough round isn't important, but it's important to get an even thickness. Using a 3-inch (7.5 cm) round cookie cutter, cut out as many circles as possible. Remove the scraps of dough, cover, and set aside.

Set a small bowl of cool water next to the work surface. **2.** Drop 2 teaspoons of the poppy seed filling onto the center of each circle of dough (you should have some filling left over, which you'll use when you roll the dough scraps to make a few more cookies). **3.** Working with one circle at a time, dip your finger into the water and lightly moisten the edge of a circle of dough. **4.** Gently pinch the edges of the dough together at three evenly spaced spots, creating three distinct points. Pinch the corners tightly,

and shape the sides up so they are neat and even and enclose but do not fully cover the filling, leaving some of it visible in the center. The cookies should look like three-cornered hats. Repeat with the rest of the dough circles, arranging the cookies about 2 inches (5 cm) apart on the prepared baking sheets as you work.

Repeat the process with the second piece of dough and the chocolate filling, reserving the dough scraps. Then press the dough scraps together, reroll, and repeat the shaping and filling process, making an even number of poppy seed and chocolate cookies.

Chill the cookies in the freezer for about 20 minutes.

Bake the cookies until the edges and undersides are light golden brown, 15 to 20 minutes, rotating the baking sheets top to bottom and front to back about halfway through baking. Remove from the oven and cool the cookies on a wire rack.

Bringing the Purim Party from Baghdad to Tel Aviv

SHARED BY

Ilana Isaac

After the establishment of Israel, life for the Jews of Baghdad became very difficult, so when I was nine years old, my family fled the city in the middle of the night. It was my mother's decision, and to this day, I don't know how she persuaded my father. We were already a family of six and my mother was pregnant. I remember every detail of that two-month journey. We took a boat, walked through an orchard, and took a bus and then a train to reach Tehran, where we stayed for a while with relatives. Finally we boarded a flight for Israel. To a child, it was very exciting, it felt like going on vacation—I didn't understand the danger.

It wasn't easy for my family to adjust to a new life in Israel in the early 1950s. My parents tried to cling to customs from the past whenever they could. One of our main traditions was celebrating Purim. In Baghdad, aunts and cousins would come by for weeks before the holiday to bake together, making treats like date-filled b'ebe be tamer, savory cheese sambusak, and coconut cookies. On Purim, we ate them with oranges and tea while we played cards, with a special table for the children and another for the grown-ups.

FAMILY JOURNEY

Baghdad → Akko, Israel → Tel Aviv

From left to right: Marcel, sister Nur, and sister-in-law Hana in Baghdad, 1947

In Israel, my mother saw to it that the tradition wasn't lost. Even before we had a house to live in, when we were still in an immigrant camp, the party continued.

ILANA ISAAC's mother, Marcel, never wrote down her recipes. Her granddaughter Ayelet Izraeli, who is Ilana's niece, was the one to ensure they were documented. "She had the recipes in her head and I had to fish them out," Ayelet says. She and her sister Dana are trying to keep the tradition of the family's Purim party alive.

ILANA ISAAC'S PURIM

Cheese Sambusak
Savory Cheese Pastries
195

B'ebe be Tamer
Date-Filled Cookies
197

Coconut Cookies
198

—*Serve with*—

fresh citrus,
fresh cucumber

Base Dough

Use this versatile rich yeasted dough to make the cheese sambusak or b'ebe be tamer cookies. If you're making both the sambusak and the cookies, simply double this recipe for enough dough. It can be made up to 1 day in advance.

MAKES enough for 1 recipe sambusak or b'ebe be tamer

1 tablespoon plus ½ teaspoon (10 g) active dry yeast (1½ packets)

½ cup plus 2 tablespoons (150 ml) lukewarm water

1 tablespoon sugar

2½ cups (325 g) all-purpose flour

1½ teaspoons kosher salt

3½ ounces (7 tablespoons/100 g) unsalted butter, melted and cooled but still pourable

¼ cup (60 ml) canola oil

Put the yeast, water, and sugar in the bowl of a stand mixer fitted with the dough hook and mix until combined. (If your dough hook doesn't reach the bottom of your bowl, use the paddle attachment.)

Add the flour and salt and mix on medium-low speed to incorporate them. With the mixer running, slowly add the butter and then the oil, mixing until the dough starts to come together. Increase the mixer speed to medium and knead until you have a smooth, soft dough, about 12 minutes. The dough will be quite oily.

Transfer the dough to a large bowl and cover with plastic wrap. Set aside in a warm place until the dough has almost doubled in size, 1 to 1¼ hours.

Transfer the risen dough to a clean work surface and lightly knead it for a few strokes, then continue with your chosen recipe. (Alternatively, wrap the dough tightly in plastic wrap and refrigerate for up to 24 hours. Let the dough come to cool room temperature before you continue with your recipe.)

Cheese Sambusak
Savory Cheese Pastries

Filled pastries have been made by Arab cooks for more than a thousand years; recipes for sanbusaj or sanbusa are found in the tenth-century Arab cookbook *Kitāb al-ṭabīkh*. There are several variations on the name, but in Mizrahi communities, they are most often known as sambusak. Fillings also vary, but for Purim, Ilana's mother, Marcel, stuffed them with cheese using the same dough to make the date-filled cookies called b'ebe be tamer (page 197).

The balance between crust and filling is important here, so be careful with the thickness of the dough and the amount of filling. The sambusak are best when still warm from the oven, but you can make them up to one day in advance and store the cooled pastries in an airtight container, then reheat them in a 425°F (220°C) oven for about 5 minutes. *(Pictured on page 192)*

MAKES 4 dozen sambusak

FOR THE FILLING

8 ounces (225 g) feta cheese, finely crumbled

2 large eggs

½ cup (120 g) ricotta cheese

½ teaspoon kosher salt

1 tablespoon all-purpose flour, plus more for dusting

1 recipe Base Dough (opposite)

FOR THE EGG WASH AND FINISHING

1 large egg, lightly beaten

½ cup (70 g) sesame seeds for sprinkling

Place the racks in the upper and lower thirds of the oven and preheat the oven to 350°F (175°C). Line two baking sheets with parchment paper.

MAKE THE FILLING: In a medium bowl, stir together the feta, eggs, ricotta, salt, and flour until well combined.

Divide the dough into 4 pieces. Cover 3 of the pieces with plastic wrap. On a lightly floured work surface, roll the remaining piece of dough out to a 12-inch (30 cm) round, lifting the dough from the work surface after every few strokes of the rolling pin so that it doesn't stick. The round doesn't need to be a perfect circle, but rolling to this size will ensure the correct thickness of the dough.

Using a 3-inch (7.5 cm) round cookie cutter or glass, punch out 12 rounds from the dough. Discard the scraps.

Put 1½ teaspoons (about 10 g) of the cheese filling in the center of each circle. Fold the dough in half over the filling, forming a half-moon shape, being careful not to create air pockets. Using a fork, press the edges of the sambusak together to seal them (and make them look pretty). Arrange the sambusak on one of the prepared baking sheets (they will not expand much during baking, so there should be some space in between them, but not too much is needed). Repeat with the rest of the dough and filling, arranging the second half of the sambusak on the second baking sheet. Lightly brush each sambusak with the egg wash and sprinkle with the sesame seeds.

Bake the sambusak, rotating the pans front to back and top to bottom halfway through, until golden brown, 20 to 24 minutes. Remove from the oven and let cool completely before serving.

B'ebe be Tamer
Date-Filled Cookies

When Ilana's family lived in Baghdad, relatives would gather in the weeks leading up to Purim to bake these date-filled cookies, along with cheese sambusak (page 195) and coconut cookies (page 198) for their annual Purim party. Today Ilana is passing along the baking tradition to her grandchildren in Israel, adding hamantaschen (page 186), which she calls by their Hebrew name, oznei Haman, to the menu.

The rich, buttery dough is slightly soft, so shaping the cookies might be a bit of a challenge at first. Once you've filled and shaped a few, however, you'll get the hang of it.

MAKES about 3 dozen cookies

1 cup (300 g) unsweetened date paste

2 tablespoons unsalted butter

1 recipe Base Dough (page 194)

Flour, for dusting the work surface

1 large egg, beaten, for egg wash

About ½ cup (70 g) sesame seeds for sprinkling

Place the racks in the upper and lower thirds of the oven and preheat the oven to 350°F (175°C). Line two baking sheets with parchment paper.

Put the date paste and butter in a medium bowl and microwave on low power until the paste has softened slightly and the butter has melted, or heat gently in a small saucepan over low heat.

Remove from the microwave or stovetop and mix until the filling is evenly combined and easy to work with.

Divide the dough into 4 pieces. Cover 3 of the pieces with plastic wrap. On a lightly floured work surface, roll out the remaining piece of dough into a rough round that is ⅛ inch (4 mm) thick, lifting the dough from the work surface after every few strokes of the rolling pin so that it doesn't stick. Using a 3-inch (7.5 cm) round cookie cutter or glass, stamp out 9 rounds from the dough.

Place 1½ teaspoons of the date mixture in the center of each round. Gather the edges of the dough over the center and pinch closed, making a small parcel. Flip the parcel so the seam is down and gently flatten it into a disk with the palm of your hand. Place on one of the prepared baking sheets, seam side down, and repeat with the remaining rounds. Then repeat with the remaining dough and filling, putting the second half of the pastries on the second baking sheet.

Lightly brush the cookies with the beaten egg and sprinkle them with the sesame seeds. Using the handle of a wooden spoon dipped in the egg wash, gently press 3 holes into each cookie, pushing the handle of the spoon all the way down to the baking sheet. This is decorative and also prevents air pockets from forming and making the cookies puff.

Bake the cookies, rotating the pans halfway through, until golden brown, 20 to 25 minutes. Remove from the oven and cool completely on a wire rack before serving.

Coconut Cookies

These simple coconut cookies are crunchy on the outside and slightly chewy on the inside. They are made without flour, meaning they are both kosher for Passover and gluten free. Make sure you choose unsweetened shredded coconut, which you can find at natural food stores and in some supermarkets.

MAKES about 2 dozen cookies

2½ cups (250 g) unsweetened shredded coconut, or more if needed

⅔ cup (130 g) sugar

3 large eggs, whisked

Place the racks in the upper and lower thirds of the oven and preheat the oven to 350°F (175°C). Line two baking sheets with parchment paper.

In a medium bowl, stir the coconut, sugar, and eggs together until evenly combined.

Scoop out just less than 2 tablespoons of the mixture, put it in your palm, and squeeze your hand into a fist around the mixture to create a small log with indentations from your fingers. If the mixture doesn't hold together, return it to the bowl and add another couple of tablespoons of coconut, then try another cookie. When the consistency is correct, the cookies will be quite delicate but will retain the indentations and stay intact as you place them on the baking sheet. Transfer the first cookie to one of the prepared baking sheets and repeat with the remaining mixture, placing the cookies about 2 inches (5 cm) apart on the baking sheets.

Bake the cookies until they are golden brown and lightly crisped, rotating the pans top to bottom and front to back halfway through, 20 to 25 minutes. Remove from the oven and transfer the cookies to a wire rack to cool completely. They will become crisper as they cool.

SPRING: A Bountiful Time for Jewish Hospitality

Passover and Shavuot

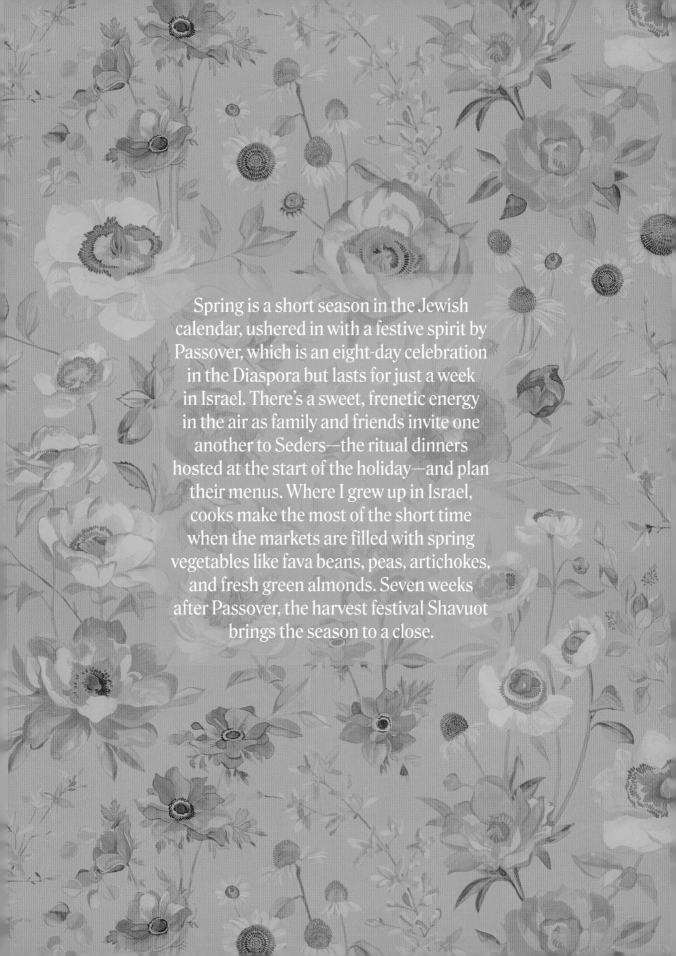

Spring is a short season in the Jewish calendar, ushered in with a festive spirit by Passover, which is an eight-day celebration in the Diaspora but lasts for just a week in Israel. There's a sweet, frenetic energy in the air as family and friends invite one another to Seders—the ritual dinners hosted at the start of the holiday—and plan their menus. Where I grew up in Israel, cooks make the most of the short time when the markets are filled with spring vegetables like fava beans, peas, artichokes, and fresh green almonds. Seven weeks after Passover, the harvest festival Shavuot brings the season to a close.

Passover

THERE'S AN EXCITEMENT, a sense of anticipation that sets in every spring in the lead-up to Passover. In early Judaism, this bountiful month, Nissan, marked the start of the Hebrew calendar. Nissan included the spring festival of Passover, which also commemorated the Exodus from slavery in ancient Egypt.

Today, the story of the Exodus is retold at Seders, the ritual meals that are as much feast as they are storytelling event. For me, Seder is the clearest expression I know of Jewish hospitality and of our community's gift for telling stories through food. At the start of the meal, we proclaim in Aramaic, "Kol dichpin yete ve'yechol," meaning, "All who are hungry, come and eat." The phrase has been interpreted in many ways, but I have always felt it literally. Seder is a time to open our homes and make sure everyone feels welcome. The menus in this chapter come from some of the most generous hosts I know, like my dear friend Rinat Tzadok (see page 244), who hosted one of the greatest Seders I've ever attended out of an Airbnb.

At Passover, more than any other Jewish holiday, food plays a vital role in the ritual, with the foods on the Seder plate serving as both symbols and guideposts for retelling the story. Among them are charoset, a sweet paste made of fruits and nuts that represents the mortar our ancestors used when they were slaves in Egypt;

salt water and bitter herbs to recall their tears and the bitterness of slavery; and an egg to represent spring, the cycle of life, and the festival offering in the Temple.

At the heart of the table is matzah. Also known as the bread of affliction, it stems from the Exodus itself, when there was no time to allow dough to rise before fleeing. This is why hametz (leavening) is forbidden during the holiday. The result is iconic Jewish dishes like matzah ball soup and the many riffs on it; Mexico City–born pastry chef Fany Gerson's features a chile-spiked broth finished with lime and avocado (page 229). Many Sephardi families, like Alexandra Zohn's (see page 264), use matzah to make mina, a rich casserole or pie layered with either meat or cheese and vegetables. And Moroccan Jews, like Ruth Stulman's family (see page 270), mark the end of the holiday with a feast called Mimouna, where the first leavened foods after Passover are served.

There is an inherent tension in the Seder. While foods like charoset recall a time of slavery, the meal is also a celebration of freedom. During Seder, we read, "Once we were slaves—now, we are free." For Sasha Shor, who was born in the former Soviet Union, that sentiment holds a deeply personal meaning. "Every year, I think about my own family's journey and I'm reminded never to take freedom for granted," she says.

The rules and customs for keeping kosher for Passover vary by community. For some, it's customary to avoid not only hametz or leavened foods during the holiday but also kitniyot, a term that encompasses rice, legumes, corn, and some other foods. The recipes in this chapter reflect how these families cook their holiday meals, so some contain kitniyot and/or ingredients that may be hard to find with a kosher for Passover certification. You can save any of these recipes for a wonderful meal after the holiday.

A Soviet Seder Led by a Seven-Year-Old

SHARED BY

Sasha Shor

When I was little, I didn't know what our religion was, because we never talked about it at home. We were Soviets. We spoke Russian and we ate Soviet dishes. I was five when we received permission to emigrate, and everything changed. Friends dropped by our apartment to say goodbye, and I can still picture my grandfather making stencils so we could put our last name on our luggage—just two bags each. In the chaos, I asked my parents why we were leaving our home. They sat me down and let me in on the family secret: we were Jewish and it was no longer safe for us to stay in the Soviet Union.

When we arrived in Nashville, it felt like we had been dropped onto another planet. Even trips to the grocery store were bewildering—what were all of these boxed foods meant to be zapped in a microwave? School was also puzzling. I was enrolled in a yeshiva where girls wore dresses that covered their knees and all the boys wore kippahs. Every class was a barrage of newness: I learned both Hebrew and English at the same time as I was taking in what it meant to be Jewish and American.

During our second spring in Nashville, my family hosted our first Seder in two generations. Armed with my coloring-book Haggadah from school, I was happy to lead the Seder, telling the story of Passover. And

FAMILY JOURNEY

Kishinev, Moldova → Nashville, TN → New York City

Sasha and her grandfather Isay Korenblat at a family
dacha in the Russian countryside, late 1970s

when it came time for the four questions, I called them out in Hebrew,
starting with: "Why is this night different from all other nights?"

I was beaming until I noticed my always joyful grandfather Isay
crying. Everyone at the table went silent as he said, "Never in a million
years could I have imagined this." Looking back, I can see how much
he left unspoken in that moment: the years of pogroms, persecution,
secret-keeping . . . all because we were Jewish.

When I host Seder at my home, I embrace both sides of my heritage.
Every inch of the table is covered with Russian zakuski, like homemade
pickled watermelon slices and salads of roasted beets studded with
walnuts and prunes. Next to them are bowls of matzah ball soup, a dish
I've reclaimed and made my own by adding chanterelle mushrooms, and
a platter with my mother's gefilte fish, one of the few Jewish recipes that
has stayed with my family through generations, in its original Old World
preparation.

As we retell the story of the Israelites escaping from ancient Egypt
every year, I think about my own family's journey, and I'm reminded
never to take freedom for granted.

Advertising creative director and chef **SASHA SHOR** always has something
delicious with her—like homemade horseradish vodka. She spent her early years
in the USSR, until her family immigrated to the U.S. It's estimated that starting
in 1970, nearly two million Jews emigrated from the former Soviet Union.

SASHA SHOR'S PASSOVER

Old-World Gefilte Fish
208

**Chanterelle-Stuffed
Matzah Balls in Broth**
210

Kislye Ogurtsy
Sour Pickles
212

**Roasted Beet Salad with
Walnuts and Prunes**
214

Vinegret
Cooked Vegetable Salad
214

**Pomegranate and
Red Wine–Braised
Short Ribs**
216

**Horseradish-Infused
Vodka**
221

—Serve with—

kosher black caviar,
preserved fish,
assorted pickles,
potato salad, horseradish

Old-World Gefilte Fish

Growing up, Sasha called this dish by its Russian name, farshirovannaya ryba, but in Yiddish, it's known as gefilte fish—both mean "stuffed fish." She explains, "The meat of a whole boned fish such as a carp or pike was ground, mixed with tons of sautéed onions, eggs, and soaked bread (matzah meal for Passover), and then shaped back into an elongated mound inside the intact skin to resemble a whole fish."

Like many Jewish recipes, this was a clever way to stretch food for celebrations. Today in Ashkenazi homes, it's more common to see patties or quenelles of gefilte fish (see page 50), but Sasha's mom still makes the classic version. You can make it either way with this recipe.

A fishmonger in a Jewish area will know how to prepare the fish properly, but so will most others with a bit of explanation, Sasha notes. "Most importantly, make sure that they keep the skin whole." If they remove the head and tail, be sure to ask for them in a separate bag so you can freeze them and, along with the bones, use them for fish stock. *(Pictured on pages 206–207)*

MAKES 6 to 8 servings

5 tablespoons (75 ml) vegetable oil

5 tablespoons (75 ml) extra-virgin olive oil

3 medium yellow onions (about 1 pound/450 g), chopped

1 large sweet onion (12 ounces/340 g), such as Vidalia, chopped

Kosher salt and freshly ground black pepper

3 pounds (1.3 kg) pike, whitefish, carp, or other mild flaky white-fleshed fish fillets if making patties, or one whole 5-pound (2.2 kg) pike, cleaned and gutted, with 3 pounds (1.3 kg) of the flesh reserved for the filling (see headnote)

3 large eggs, lightly beaten

2 cups (230 g) matzah meal, plus more if necessary

1½ teaspoons sugar

⅓ cup (10 g) finely chopped fresh dill, plus whole sprigs for garnish

1 cup (30 g) lightly packed fresh flat-leaf parsley leaves, finely chopped, plus whole sprigs for garnish

Horseradish and/or pickled onions for serving

FOR GEFILTE FISH PATTIES: In a very large skillet, heat 3 tablespoons each of the vegetable oil and olive oil over medium heat. Add both onions and sauté, stirring often, until lightly golden, 10 to 15 minutes. Season the onions with 1½ teaspoons salt and ½ teaspoon pepper and continue cooking, stirring often, until the onions take on a deeper golden color, about 15 minutes longer. Remove from the heat and let the onions cool completely in the pan.

Cut the fish fillets into 2-inch (5 cm) chunks. Layer the fish chunks and sautéed onions evenly in a food processor (do not overfill the food processor; work in batches if necessary) and pulse the mixture until they just come together. The result should resemble a coarse mixture, not a paste.

Transfer the fish-onion mixture to a large bowl and add the eggs, matzah meal, 2½ teaspoons salt, 1 teaspoon pepper, the sugar, chopped dill, and chopped parsley. Using your hands, fold the mixture over itself to aerate and combine all the ingredients; the texture should be like thick oatmeal, and the mixture should hold its shape. If it is too wet, add a bit more matzah meal. Cover and refrigerate for 1 hour to firm up.

Preheat the oven to 350°F (175°C). Line a baking sheet with foil and lightly oil the foil or spray it with nonstick cooking spray.

MAKE THE GEFILTE FISH PATTIES: Moisten your hands with water and shape the fish mixture into oval-shaped patties about 2 by 3 inches (5 by 7.5 cm). Set the patties on another baking sheet or tray; you should have about 30 patties.

Heat the remaining 2 tablespoons each vegetable oil and olive oil in a large skillet over medium heat. Sauté the patties, turning once, working in batches if necessary, until lightly browned on both sides, just about 1 minute per side.

Place the patties on the foil-lined baking sheet, cover tightly with more foil, and bake until the patties have firmed up and are cooked through, about 20 minutes.

Arrange the patties on a serving platter and garnish with lots of dill and parsley sprigs. Serve with plenty of horseradish and/or pickled onions on the side.

FOR STUFFED WHOLE FISH: Make the fish mixture following the instructions above, using the flesh removed from the whole fish, but do not shape into patties.

Line a baking sheet with foil. Spray another large piece of foil with nonstick cooking spray and set it oiled side up on top of the lined baking sheet. Open out the fish skin, outer side down, on the oiled foil. Pile the fish mixture lengthwise onto one side of the skin. Lightly oil your hands and shape the fish mixture into a mound that resembles the shape of the fish, following the curves and shape of the skin. Fold the other side of the skin over the mounded fish mixture, pressing it into place so the filling is fully encased. Seal the whole fish with the oiled foil, wrapping tightly to keep the fish together as it bakes.

Place the fish in the oven and bake for 1 hour. Check the fish by carefully opening the foil slightly and piercing the fish mixture with a sharp knife: it should feel firm, like a fish cake. If it is still too wet or soft, reseal and bake for 10 to 12 minutes longer. Remove from the oven and turn the heat up to 400°F (205°C).

Allow the fish to cool slightly, then open the foil to expose the top of the fish; do not remove it from the foil. Return to the oven and roast until slightly browned, 5 to 7 minutes. Remove the fish from the oven and let cool slightly.

Unwrap the fish and transfer it to a platter. Using a sharp knife, cut into 1½-inch (3.75 cm) slices, with the skin still attached.

Garnish with lots of dill and parsley sprigs. Serve with plenty of horseradish and/or pickled onions on the side.

Chanterelle-Stuffed Matzah Balls in Broth

Sasha likes to stuff tender matzah balls with chanterelles, a subtly flavored mushroom that has nutty and fruity notes. If you can't find them, use whatever varieties of mushrooms you can get; even white or cremini mushrooms will taste delicious here. Sasha likes to make the filling with butter and crème fraîche, but olive oil and nondairy cream cheese work well for a kosher version.

The matzah balls take a bit of time to make, but the filling can be made up to 2 days in advance and refrigerated, and the matzah balls can be formed (though not cooked) a day ahead of time. Store them spaced apart on a baking sheet covered with plastic wrap in the fridge until you are ready to cook and serve them. Once you've cooked the matzah balls in the chicken broth, they can be kept warm in the broth for a couple of hours, until you're ready to serve this mid-Seder. For a homemade chicken broth recipe, try the broth from Mitchell Davis's Matzah Ball Soup (see page 47), or if you prefer, you can use vegetable broth.

MAKES 6 to 8 servings; 12 to 16 matzah balls

FOR THE FILLING

2 tablespoons unsalted butter or extra-virgin olive oil

2 tablespoons finely chopped shallot

4 ounces (115 g) chanterelle mushrooms (or other wild mushrooms or white or cremini mushrooms), trimmed and cut into ¼-inch (6 mm) slices

Kosher salt

1½ teaspoons finely chopped fresh flat-leaf parsley

1½ teaspoons crème fraîche or nondairy cream cheese

Freshly ground black pepper

FOR THE MATZAH BALLS

4 large eggs, beaten

¼ cup (60 ml) seltzer or water

¼ cup (60 ml) melted schmaltz or duck fat

1 cup (115 g) matzah meal

1½ teaspoons kosher salt

Freshly ground black pepper

3 quarts (3 L) homemade or canned chicken broth (not low-sodium), heated

1 pound (450 g) fresh spinach or Swiss chard, stemmed and steamed just until wilted

Good-quality truffle oil for serving (optional)

Fresh dill for serving

MAKE THE FILLING: Heat 1 tablespoon of the butter in a large skillet over medium-high heat until it shimmers. Add the shallot and sauté, stirring often, until translucent and starting to caramelize, 2 to 3 minutes. Transfer the shallot to a small bowl to cool.

Wipe out the pan with a paper towel, add the remaining 1 tablespoon butter, and heat over medium heat. Add the mushrooms and ¼ teaspoon salt and sauté, flipping and stirring the mushrooms so they cook evenly, until they are tender and starting to brown at the edges, 4 to 5 minutes. Transfer the mushrooms to a bowl and set aside to cool.

When the mushrooms are cool, chop into a very fine dice. Drain off any liquid.

recipe continues

Add the mushrooms to the bowl with the shallot, then add the parsley and crème fraîche and stir until well blended. Season generously with salt and pepper. Set aside.

MAKE THE MATZAH BALL MIXTURE: In a large bowl, combine the eggs, seltzer, and schmaltz. In a small bowl, stir together the matzah meal with the salt and several twists of black pepper.

Add the matzah meal to the egg mixture and stir until well combined. Refrigerate, uncovered, for 30 to 45 minutes.

SHAPE AND FILL THE MATZAH BALLS: Line a baking sheet with parchment or wax paper. Remove the matzah ball mixture from the fridge. Moisten your hands with water, scoop out some of the matzah ball mixture, and shape it into a 1½- to 2-inch (3.75 to 5 cm) ball. Cradle the ball in one hand and poke a hole into the center with your other thumb. Fill the hole with a teaspoon of mushroom filling, and then seal the hole by easing the mixture around the filling and reshaping it into a ball. Gently roll the ball between your palms to smooth it. Aim for 2 matzah balls per person; so if you're serving 8, make the matzah balls on the smaller side.

Put the chicken broth in a large pot and bring to an active simmer/low boil over medium-high heat. Very gently add the matzah balls to the hot broth, cover, and simmer until cooked through, about 1 hour.

To serve, put 2 hot matzah balls in each soup bowl, ladle in the hot chicken broth, and add a spoonful of the wilted greens. Garnish each bowl with a few drops of truffle oil, if using, and torn fresh dill.

Kislye Ogurtsy
Sour Pickles

Kirby cucumbers are ideal for pickling because their skins are firm and can withstand long soaking. You can use the same method to pickle small green tomatoes, green beans, firm-skinned cherry tomatoes, red or green jalapeños, cauliflower florets, or carrot slices. If you plan to serve the pickles at a Passover Seder, be sure to start at least a week before, so they have time to ferment.

The tangy and salty brine left in the jar is an added bonus—don't waste it! Use it to make dirty martinis or bloody Marys. *(Pictured on page 207)*

MAKES 20 to 25 pickles

2 or 3 large cabbage leaves, washed and torn into a few pieces each

20 to 25 small kirby cucumbers, washed

8 to 10 garlic cloves, halved lengthwise

12 to 14 whole black peppercorns

4 to 6 very fresh dill sprigs

2 bay leaves

1 jalapeño, thinly sliced (optional)

1 teaspoon red chile flakes (optional)

FOR THE BRINE

2 quarts (2 L) room-temperature water

2 tablespoons kosher salt

SPECIAL EQUIPMENT

A wide-mouth 1-gallon (4 L) jar

A small clean ramekin or other small heavy object that fits inside the mouth of the jar

A clean cloth to cover the jar (muslin, a thin kitchen towel, or doubled cheesecloth)

A rubber band or kitchen twine to secure the fabric

Layer the cabbage leaves, cucumbers, garlic, peppercorns, dill sprigs, and bay leaves in the jar, along with the jalapeños, chile flakes, or both, if using. Do not push hard on the cucumbers, or the skins may break.

MAKE THE BRINE: Pour the water into a pitcher or large jar, add the salt, and stir until it dissolves.

Pour the brine into the jar with the cucumbers, covering them completely with the liquid. Set a ramekin or small weight on top of the cucumbers to keep them submerged. Cover the jar with a cloth and secure with a rubber band or twine. Set the jar in a dark space at room temperature.

Check the pickles after a week to ensure that everything is still submerged. Taste now and see if you want "half sours." For "full sours," you'll need to wait a full week more. When the pickles are to your taste, refrigerate them to slow the fermentation. They'll keep for at least a few weeks and up to a month.

Roasted Beet Salad with Walnuts and Prunes

This is one of Sasha's favorite zakuski (salads and other cold plates served in an elaborate spread to accompany vodka or other drinks in Russian tradition). "The textures and flavors are so varied and amazing together with the sharpness of the garlic and the creamy mayonnaise dressing. Some people use less garlic or omit the prunes, but I think using both really makes this salad so great," she says. Serve it with matzah during Passover or bread during the rest of the year—and chase it with a shot of ice-cold vodka. *(Pictured on page 206)*

MAKES 6 to 8 servings

1½ pounds (675 g) red beets (5 to 6 medium), scrubbed and trimmed

2 to 3 medium garlic cloves, finely minced

½ to 1 cup (125 to 250 g) mayonnaise

1 cup (120 g) walnuts, finely chopped

8 to 10 pitted prunes, chopped into ½-inch (1.25 cm) pieces

Kosher salt and freshly ground black pepper

Chopped fresh dill for garnish

Preheat the oven to 400°F (205°C). Line a baking sheet with parchment paper or foil.

Tightly wrap the beets individually in foil. Place the beets on the lined baking sheet and roast until they are soft and easily pierced with a fork, 45 to 60 minutes (or longer if your beets are very large). Remove from the oven and let the beets cool until you can handle them.

Unwrap the beets and put them in a large bowl. Cover the bowl with plastic wrap and let the beets cool for another 30 minutes, which will allow the skins to come off more easily.

Wearing plastic gloves or using a paper towel, slip the skins off the beets. Cut away any stubborn skin with a knife or peeler. Grate the beets on the large holes of a box grater into a large bowl.

Add the garlic, ½ cup (125 g) of the mayonnaise, the walnuts, prunes, and salt and pepper to taste to the beets and stir until everything is combined. Taste and add more mayonnaise, salt, and pepper, if you like.

Refrigerate the salad until chilled and serve cold.

Vinegret
Cooked Vegetable Salad

Cold chopped vegetable salads were always a part of the zakuski spread in Sasha's home growing up, but they were often part of dinner as well. Her vinegret brings together cubes of boiled potatoes, beets, and carrots, along with peas and a pop of tang from dill pickles or sauerkraut. Follow her advice and prepare the salad a bit before serving. "Letting the salad sit for 30 minutes in the fridge after dressing it will bring all the flavors together and allow the dressing to really soak into and lightly pickle the vegetables," she says. *(Pictured on page 207)*

2 large beets (about 1 pound/450 g), scrubbed and trimmed

2 medium boiling potatoes (about 12 ounces/340 g), such as Yukon Gold or a red-skinned variety, scrubbed

Kosher salt

2 large carrots (about 7 ounces/200 g), peeled and cut into ½-inch (1.25 cm) cubes

6 tablespoons (90 ml) red wine vinegar, or more to taste

¼ teaspoon sugar, or more to taste

Pinch of freshly ground black pepper

⅓ cup (80 ml) sunflower oil or other neutral oil

3 medium dill pickles (about 6 ounces/ 170 g), cut into ½-inch (1.25 cm) cubes, or 1 cup (250 g) sauerkraut

1 cup (125 g) frozen green peas, thawed

¼ cup (7 g) chopped fresh dill (reserve some larger fronds for garnish)

Preheat the oven to 425°F (220°C). Line a baking sheet with parchment paper or foil.

Tightly wrap the beets individually in foil. Place the beets on the lined baking sheet and roast until they are soft and easily pierced with a fork, about 1 hour (or longer if your beets are very large).

Meanwhile, put the potatoes in a medium saucepan, cover with water, and salt generously. Bring to a boil, and boil until tender, about 20 minutes; drain well and set aside until cool enough to handle.

Peel the potatoes and cut into ½-inch (1.25 cm) cubes. Transfer to a large bowl and set aside.

Put the carrots in a medium saucepan, cover with generously salted water, bring to a boil, and boil until tender, about 25 minutes. Drain well and add to the potatoes.

When the beets are ready, remove them from the oven and carefully peel off the foil. Place them in a large heavy plastic bag, seal the bag, and leave the beets to cool for another 30 minutes.

Wearing plastic gloves or using a paper towel, slip the skins off the beets. Cut them into ½-inch (1.25 cm) cubes and add to the bowl with the potatoes and carrots.

In a small bowl, combine the vinegar with 1 teaspoon salt, the sugar, and pepper and whisk until the salt has dissolved. Whisking constantly, slowly pour in the oil. Continue to whisk until the dressing is blended and creamy. Taste the dressing and adjust with more vinegar, sugar, salt, and pepper as necessary to achieve an even balance of tangy, sweet, salty, and peppery.

Add the pickles, peas, and chopped dill to the bowl of vegetables. Pour in most of the dressing and toss to combine. Cover and refrigerate for at least 15 minutes and up to 30 minutes, to allow the flavors to marry.

Taste the salad again and add more dressing, if you like. Transfer to a serving bowl, garnish with dill fronds, and serve cold.

Pomegranate and Red Wine–Braised Short Ribs

Sweet-and-sour braised meat dishes are staples in Sasha's family—everyone from her grandmother to her mom and aunt has their own version. "These dishes were often made at the start of the week and eaten for a few days into the week, getting better by the day," Sasha says. These short ribs braised with tangy pomegranate juice and red wine and fragrant with the Moroccan spice mix ras el hanout are her take on the braises she grew up with.

You can make this recipe using a slow cooker instead of braising the short ribs in the oven. For the slow cooker, brown the short ribs on the stovetop first as directed in the recipe, then transfer them to the slow cooker, along with the sautéed onions and garlic and the braising liquid, and cook on low for 8 hours. You can also make the dish a day ahead and reheat gently on the stovetop before serving.

Sasha recommends serving the ribs with fried potatoes, or with something creamy like polenta, parsnip puree, or mashed potatoes, along with fresh parsley, fresh dill, and freshly chopped garlic.

MAKES 6 to 8 servings

7 to 8 pounds (2.7 to 3.6 kg) bone-in short ribs

Kosher salt and freshly ground black pepper

1 tablespoon ras el hanout

2 tablespoons vegetable oil

4 medium yellow onions (about 1½ pounds/ 675 g), cut into ¾-inch (2 cm) pieces

6 to 8 garlic cloves, halved lengthwise

2½ cups (600 ml) homemade or canned low-sodium beef broth

¼ cup (85 g) honey

3 tablespoons tomato paste

2 cups (480 ml) good-quality dry red wine

3 cups (720 ml) unsweetened pomegranate juice

3 tablespoons pomegranate molasses (optional)

Juice of 1 large orange

2 teaspoons brown sugar

Strips of orange peel from 1 large orange (removed with a peeler)

4 or 5 thyme sprigs, wrapped in a square of cheesecloth and tied into a small bundle with kitchen string

Take the short ribs out of the fridge and let them sit at room temperature for 30 to 45 minutes. Preheat the oven to 300°F (150°C).

Generously season the short ribs all over with salt and pepper and the ras el hanout. Heat the vegetable oil in a very large Dutch oven or other ovenproof heavy-bottomed pot (at least 10 quarts/10 L) over medium-high heat. Working in batches to avoid crowding the pot, sear the short ribs, turning occasionally, until well browned on all sides. Transfer the ribs to a bowl and set aside.

If there's more than about 2 tablespoons of fat left in the pot, spoon off the excess fat. Add the onions to the pot and sauté over medium heat until soft and light gold, about 20 minutes. Add the garlic and stir.

Add ½ cup (120 ml) of the broth and scrape the bottom of the pot with a spatula to dissolve the pan juices, then add the honey and tomato paste and stir to blend. Add the remaining 2 cups (480 ml) broth, the wine, pomegranate juice, pomegranate molasses, if using, orange juice, and brown sugar and stir well.

Return the short ribs to the Dutch oven, along with any juices that have accumulated in the bowl. Tuck the orange peel and thyme bundle in among the ribs and cover with the lid. Bring the liquid to a lively simmer over medium-high heat, then transfer the Dutch oven to the oven. Cook the short ribs until the meat is falling off the bones, 2½ to 3 hours; start checking for doneness after 2 hours. Remove from the oven and let the short ribs rest, covered, for at least 30 minutes.

Remove the lid from the pot and spoon off the excess fat from the surface, then taste the braising liquid and adjust the seasoning with more salt and pepper if needed. If the braising liquid seems thin, remove the short ribs and simmer the liquid until thickened and more concentrated in flavor; return the meat to the liquid and simmer to reheat.

Serve the short ribs with the braising liquid, spooned over your choice of accompaniment (see headnote).

Horseradish-Infused Vodka

In Sasha's home when she was growing up, vodka and Cognac were served at every celebration, and, she says, there was always something to celebrate. Shots were taken, then chased with something savory like pickles. Today she likes to make various infused vodkas, but lemon-horseradish is her go-to flavoring.

MAKES 1 liter

1 large lemon

One 5-inch (12.5 cm) piece fresh horseradish root, cleaned, rinsed, outer layers removed, and cut into thin ribbons (discard the inner core)

1 liter good-quality vodka

Using a vegetable peeler or a sharp paring knife, remove the zest of the lemon in wide strips, leaving the white pith behind. If some strips still have a lot of pith left on them, which will be bitter, slice off as much of it as possible with a sharp knife.

Push the lemon zest and horseradish ribbons into a clean 1-liter bottle (use one that you can seal tightly). Using a funnel, pour the vodka into the bottle until it is full. Seal the bottle and put it in a dark spot at room temperature, such as a cupboard or liquor cabinet. After 1 or 2 days, gently shake the bottle to redistribute the peel and horseradish.

Let the vodka infuse for another 2 or 3 days and taste it. If you like the flavor, transfer the bottle to the freezer and keep it there for storage. If you prefer a bolder flavor, reseal the bottle and allow it to infuse for 2 more days, then transfer to the freezer.

Serve the vodka very cold, preferably after freezing it for at least 6 hours or overnight.

A Mexico–Meets–New York Kind of Seder

SHARED BY

Fany Gerson

The first real Seder I hosted was a year after I graduated from culinary school. I was about twenty and living in a tiny New York apartment, far from my family in Mexico City. When I realized I didn't have anywhere to go for Seder, I decided that I was going to make my home the place that people—whether Jewish or not—could come to. I was keeping the tradition I grew up with but making it my own.

I was homesick and wanted to make the dishes that we ate at my grandmother Ana's house. My great-grandmother, Babi Lena, who emigrated from Ukraine to Mexico in 1926, was the one who cooked these dishes originally. Babi's menu was pretty traditional Ashkenazi, but she gave it a few Mexican updates. She served her matzah ball soup with lime and made a "red" gefilte fish served warm in a tomato sauce that was spicy from lots of white pepper.

At the time, I'd never made Babi's recipes, so I called relatives as well as a cook who worked at Ana's house and had been making the gefilte fish for years—I ended up with five different versions of the recipe. I looked at them, relied on my memory, and started cooking, imagining Babi by my side guiding me and giving me permission to make it my own as a new immigrant.

FAMILY JOURNEY

Annapol, Ukraine (present-day Hannopil', Ukraine) → *Mexico City* → *New York City*

Fany in Mexico City, 1984

Every time I've cooked for the holiday since, I've felt her presence. One of the years when I made matzah ball soup with bone marrow, I felt like she was there, saying, "That's how we used to do it." I'm not sure she ever made it that way, but I imagined her hands guiding me. Much as she created dishes bridging her two worlds, I created my own, which are rooted in nostalgia for Mexico and for a relationship with her that has lived on in my imagination.

We've had up to thirty people at our Seder. One year I didn't even have a dining table, so we sat on the floor around a coffee table, ate from mismatched plates and Tupperware, and drank from plastic cups or empty containers. I told my best friend in New York, Ian, who has since passed away, that I hoped one day to be like my aunt Sari and host the way she did. She has a beautiful home and an incredible collection of silverware. He told me, "You know what? Maybe you will and maybe you won't, but this is what's beautiful about it, this is what you have, it's all heart."

He was right. Twenty years later, I still don't have a complete set of anything or enough space for everyone—we often sit on the floor—but it doesn't matter. I love, love, love hosting in our small apartment and I wouldn't have it any other way. I now get to share these traditions with our son, Gael, as my babi continues to be by my side.

It's customary on Passover to open one's home and welcome family and friends to the table. For more than twenty years, Mexico City–raised pastry chef and cookbook author **FANY GERSON** has done just that.

Gefilte Fish in Spicy Tomato Sauce

After emigrating from Ukraine to Mexico City, Fany's great-grandmother Lena added a few Mexican touches to her Ashkenazi Passover menu, such as a "red gefilte fish" served in a smoky, chile-spiked tomato sauce.

You can find dried chipotle and guajillo chiles in many well-stocked grocery stores and at Mexican markets. The chipotles are deliciously smoky, but quite hard, so be sure to soak them until they're fully tender to ensure that your sauce will have the best texture. Guajillos are fruity with a medium heat level; their flexible flesh will soften easily. Toasting both types of chiles in a skillet before soaking brings out all their flavor nuances.

You can make this dish a day in advance. Store the gefilte fish patties and the sauce separately in the refrigerator and rejoin them to gently reheat.

MAKES 6 to 8 servings; 12 fish patties

FOR THE SAUCE

2 pounds (900 g) tomatoes

1 or 2 garlic cloves, not peeled

5 or 6 guajillo chiles, stemmed and seeded

1 or 2 dried chipotle chiles or canned chipotle chiles, stemmed and seeded

½ small white onion, coarsely chopped

1½ teaspoons kosher salt

2 tablespoons avocado or vegetable oil

FOR THE FISH PATTIES

1 small white onion (about 4 ounces/115 g), roughly chopped

1 small carrot (about 2½ ounces/70 g), peeled and roughly chopped

1 pound (450 g) skinless red snapper, carp, rockfish, or flounder fillets, any pin bones removed, cut into 1-inch (2.5 cm) pieces

⅓ cup (40 g) matzah meal

1½ teaspoons kosher salt

Freshly ground white pepper

1 or 2 large eggs

About ⅓ cup (80 ml) avocado or vegetable oil

MAKE THE SAUCE: Preheat the broiler. Line a baking sheet with aluminum foil and place the tomatoes and garlic on it. Broil, turning the tomatoes and garlic every few minutes, until the tomato skins are blistered and slightly charred and the garlic feels soft to the touch, 10 to 15 minutes. Remove from the broiler and set aside to cool.

In the meantime, heat a medium skillet over medium-high heat. Add the guajillo and dried chipotle chiles and toast for about a minute on each side, pressing each one down with a spatula so the entire chile comes in contact with the hot pan. (If using canned chipotles, skip the toasting and soaking steps and add them to the blender in the next step.) Transfer the chiles to a bowl and cover with very hot water; set aside to soften for 10 to 15 minutes.

When the chiles are soft, drain them in a sieve set over a bowl; reserve the liquid.

recipe continues

When the tomatoes and garlic are cool, peel the garlic and put the tomatoes and garlic in the blender, along with the onion, half of the chiles, and the salt. Puree until smooth, then add about ½ cup (120 ml) of the chile soaking liquid and blend again until smooth. Taste, and if you'd like more chile heat, add more of the soaked chiles. (Discard any you don't end up using, or reserve for another use.)

Heat the oil in a large deep skillet or wide saucepan over medium heat. Pour the tomato-chile sauce into the pan and bring it to a boil. Reduce the heat to low and simmer for 10 minutes, adding a few spoonfuls of water if the sauce seems too thick. Taste the sauce and adjust with more salt if needed; cover and set aside while you prepare the fish patties.

MAKE THE FISH PATTIES: Put the onion and carrot in a food processor and pulse until finely chopped. Add the fish and pulse until it is finely chopped but not mushy.

Transfer the fish mixture to a large bowl and add the matzah meal, salt, a pinch of white pepper, and 1 egg. Mix gently but thoroughly with your hands; if the mixture seems dry, beat the second egg with a fork and add a bit more. The mixture should be moist but hold together when you shape it.

Dampen your hands with cold water and scoop out about ⅓ cup (50 g) of the fish mixture. Shape into a 2-by-3-inch (5 by 7.5 cm) oval patty and gently place on a clean platter. Repeat with the remaining fish mixture, moistening your hands in water as needed; you should have 12 patties.

Heat the oil in a large skillet over medium heat. Working in batches if necessary to avoid crowding the pan, add the fish patties and fry gently, turning once, until lightly browned, about 1 minute on each side.

Bring the tomato-chile sauce to a simmer and carefully slide the browned fish patties into the sauce. Simmer until they are cooked through, about 20 minutes. Remove from the heat.

Lift the patties from the sauce and arrange on a platter. Spoon the sauce on top and serve hot.

Matzah Ball Soup a la Mexicana with Chiles and Cilantro

Fany combined memories of her family's matzah ball soup (with lime) and her love of Mexican chicken soup to create this recipe. The result is a wonderful hybrid of traditions: classic matzah balls in a broth flavored with chiles, cilantro stems, and sprigs of epazote, a member of the mint family used in Mexican cooking. The final presentation features a classic Mexican garnish of chopped white onion, fresh chiles, avocado, and cilantro, with a squeeze of lime juice for a bright contrast. *(Pictured on page 231)*

MAKES 6 to 8 servings; about 24 matzah balls

FOR THE BROTH

1 large whole chicken (5 to 6 pounds/ 2.2 to 2.7 kg) or 1 smaller chicken plus 8 chicken wings

1½ white onions (about 8 ounces/225 g), halved

4 medium carrots (about 8 ounces/225 g), peeled and sliced into ¼-inch (6 mm) rounds

3 celery stalks (about 6 ounces/170 g), cut into large chunks

1 leek, split lengthwise, rinsed well, and thinly sliced

1 or 2 serrano or other hot fresh chiles, halved lengthwise

1 large garlic clove

2 bay leaves

8 cilantro stems

8 flat-leaf parsley sprigs

2 epazote sprigs (optional)

1 tablespoon kosher salt

5 or 6 whole black peppercorns

About 4 quarts (4 L) water

FOR THE MATZAH BALLS

5 large eggs

1¼ cups (145 g) matzah meal

2½ teaspoons kosher salt

¼ teaspoon freshly ground black pepper

½ teaspoon baking powder

½ teaspoon baking soda

¼ cup (60 ml) melted schmaltz, duck fat, or bone marrow, or vegetable oil

¼ cup (30 g) finely grated white onion

3 tablespoons finely chopped fresh herbs, such as dill, flat-leaf parsley, and chives

FOR THE GARNISH

1 small white onion (about 3 ounces/85 g), finely chopped

2 serrano chiles or 1 jalapeño, cored, seeded, and finely chopped

1 cup (30 g) chopped fresh cilantro

1 or 2 avocados, halved, pitted, peeled, and diced

3 or 4 limes, cut into wedges

MAKE THE BROTH: Put the chicken in a large stockpot (at least 10-quart/10 L capacity) and add the onions, carrots, celery, leek, chile, garlic, bay leaves, cilantro, parsley, epazote, if using, the salt, peppercorns, and water. If the water doesn't cover the ingredients, add more to cover. Bring the water to a boil over medium-high heat and then quickly adjust the heat so the broth will simmer when partially covered. Partially cover the pot and simmer until the chicken is fully cooked, 50 to 60 minutes, skimming off the foam as needed. Remove from the heat.

recipe continues

Carefully remove the chicken (and wings, if using) from the broth and transfer to a bowl to cool. When the chicken is cool enough to handle, pull off the meat, shred it, and set aside in a bowl. Discard the skin.

Return the chicken bones to the pot and continue cooking the broth at a simmer for another 1 to 2 hours, adding more water if needed to keep the ingredients covered. Remove the pot from the heat and let the broth cool slightly, then strain it into a clean pot and set aside; discard the chicken carcass and the vegetables.

MAKE THE MATZAH BALLS: Separate 3 of the eggs, putting the whites into a large grease-free bowl and making sure no yolks get into the whites; reserve the yolks in a small bowl.

In another large bowl, combine the matzah meal, salt, pepper, baking powder, and baking soda and whisk to blend.

In a medium bowl, whisk the 2 whole eggs with the 3 yolks, the schmaltz, grated onion, and herbs. Beat the egg whites by hand or with a handheld electric mixer until firm peaks form. Stir the schmaltz mixture into the matzah meal mixture, then fold one-third of the beaten egg whites into the mixture until incorporated; the mixture will seem stiff at first but will loosen as you add more whites. Gently fold in the remaining whites until no streaks remain.

Press a sheet of plastic wrap directly against the surface of the batter and refrigerate for about 30 minutes, until firm.

Fill a small bowl with water and set near your work surface. Scoop up rounded tablespoons (20 g) of the matzah batter and arrange them on a baking sheet. Moisten your hands with water and roll each scoop of batter into a ball, handling them as gently as possible.

Taste the broth and adjust with more salt if needed, then bring to a simmer over medium-high heat. Add the matzah balls as gently as possible and cook in the simmering broth, turning them a few times, until they are plump and cooked through, about 30 minutes.

Stir the shredded chicken into the soup and simmer just until it is warmed through.

Put a few matzah balls in each soup bowl and ladle in the broth and chicken. Offer the garnishes at the table so diners can serve themselves.

Fennel and Cucumber Salad

A brief marination in the fridge brings all the flavors of this bright and crunchy salad together. *(Pictured on page 225)*

MAKES 6 to 8 servings

2 large fennel bulbs (about 2 pounds/ 900 g), stalks and fronds cut off

3 Persian cucumbers or 1 English (seedless) cucumber (about 12 ounces/340 g), thinly sliced

¼ cup (7 g) chopped fresh dill

¼ cup (7 g) chopped fresh flat-leaf parsley

¼ cup (50 g) thinly sliced red onion (optional)

⅓ cup (80 ml) extra-virgin olive oil

1 tablespoon finely grated lemon zest

⅓ cup (80 ml) fresh lemon juice

1 teaspoon kosher salt

Freshly ground black pepper

Slice the fennel bulbs lengthwise in half and cut out the cores. Using a mandoline, thinly shave the fennel crosswise. If you don't have a mandoline, use a sharp knife to slice the fennel as thin as possible.

Put the fennel, cucumbers, dill, parsley, red onion, if using, olive oil, lemon zest, and about ¼ cup (60 ml) of the lemon juice in a bowl. Season with the salt and several twists of pepper and toss thoroughly. Taste and adjust with more lemon juice, salt, and pepper if needed.

Cover the bowl with plastic wrap and refrigerate for at least 30 minutes and up to 2 hours before serving. Serve cold.

Brisket Tamales

"The brisket tamales are a newer addition to our Seder; it was something my husband came up with and it really solidified during the pandemic," Fany explains. The idea came from wanting to bring together traditions from both sides of their family—Fany's Ashkenazi and Mexican heritage and Daniel's New York and Mexican—all in a kitchen with a rather small oven.

Making tamales is a project that's best done with friends or family. You can make and steam these several days ahead and keep them stored in the refrigerator, well wrapped. They can also be frozen for months. In either case, reheat in a steamer or microwave. Finished tamales will stay warm for about 2 hours in the steamer.

Brisket can be leaner or fattier, depending on which part of the cut you buy. The "flat" is leaner and the "point" is fattier (but of course that means it's full of flavor). Two pounds (900 g) of raw meat will yield about 1 pound (450 g) of cooked meat, but buy a bit more to allow for excess shrinkage in case your piece is quite fatty. *(Pictured on page 234)*

MAKES 28 tamales

FOR THE FILLING

2 tablespoons kosher salt

¼ teaspoon freshly ground black pepper

2 tablespoons sweet paprika, or more to taste

1½ teaspoons hot paprika or ground chile piquín, or more to taste

2½ to 3 pounds (1.1 to 1.4 kg) beef brisket, trimmed of excess fat

2 to 3 tablespoons vegetable oil

1 small white onion (about 4 ounces/115 g), cut into quarters

2 medium carrots (about 5 ounces/140 g), peeled and cut in half

3 large garlic cloves, chopped

One 14-ounce (397 g) can whole peeled tomatoes, with their juices

2 bay leaves

FOR THE TAMALES

1 cup (200 g) vegetable shortening

1 teaspoon kosher salt

1½ cups (360 ml) homemade (from Matzah Ball Soup a la Mexicana, page 229) or store-bought low-sodium chicken broth, plus more if needed

1½ teaspoons baking powder

2 pounds (900 g) fresh masa, or 3¼ cups (400 g) instant corn masa flour mixed with 2½ cups (600 ml) water

28 dried corn husks, 6 to 7 inches (15 to 17.5 cm) at the wide end, plus more for tying and for lining the pot, softened in hot water

Roasted Tomatillo Salsa (recipe follows) for serving

MAKE THE FILLING: Preheat the oven to 375°F (190°C).

Mix 1 tablespoon of the salt, the pepper, sweet paprika, and hot paprika in a small bowl. Coat the brisket generously with this mixture.

In a large Dutch oven or other heavy-bottomed ovenproof pot, heat the vegetable oil over medium-high heat. Add the brisket and cook, turning once, until nicely browned on both sides, about 10 minutes. Remove the brisket and set it aside on a platter.

Reduce the heat to low, add the onion, carrots, and garlic, and cook until the garlic is golden and the vegetables are slightly softened, about 8 minutes.

Add the tomatoes and their juices to the pot, breaking the tomatoes into smaller pieces with a spatula; stir, scraping up any bits that have stuck to the bottom of the pot. Bring the mixture to a simmer and add the brisket. If necessary, add

enough water to fully cover the meat, then add the bay leaves and the remaining 1 tablespoon salt. Taste the liquid and add more salt if needed.

Cover the pot with the lid or foil, transfer to the oven, and braise until the meat is fork-tender, 1½ to 2½ hours. Check the meat every half hour, basting it with braising liquid if needed to keep it moist. Remove from the oven and let cool.

Remove the brisket from the pot and strain the cooking liquid into a container; discard the vegetables and bay leaves. Shred the meat with your fingers and a fork; you'll need about 1 pound (450 g) of the shredded meat.

In a bowl, mix the shredded brisket with ¼ to ½ cup (60 to 120 ml) of the cooking liquid, or more if needed, to make a moist, flavorful filling. Taste and adjust the seasoning with more salt, pepper, and sweet or hot paprika. Set aside.

MAKE THE MASA: Put the vegetable shortening in the bowl of a stand mixer fitted with the whisk attachment and beat at medium speed until very light, about 1 minute. Add the salt and about 1 tablespoon of the chicken broth and beat until the shortening is white and slightly fluffy, about 2 minutes. Add the baking powder and beat it in, then take turns adding the masa and the remaining broth in 3 or 4 additions each.

Continue beating at medium speed for about 10 minutes, until the dough is homogenous and very fluffy and aerated. The consistency should be similar to a soft cake batter; add a bit more broth if needed. To see if the masa is ready, drop ½ teaspoon of it into a cup of cold water: It should float. If it does not, beat for an additional 4 to 5 minutes and test again.

ASSEMBLE THE TAMALES: Drain the corn husks and blot the excess water with paper towels. Tear a few corn husks into at least 56 very thin strips, which you will use to tie the tamales.

recipe continues

1. Lay out a corn husk with the narrow end toward you. Using a spoon or spatula, spread a heaping 3 tablespoons of masa into a 2- to 3-inch (5 to 7.5 cm) square on the upper part of the corn husk, leaving at least a ½-inch (1.25 cm) uncoated border at the top of the husk and a bit more on the sides. 2. Place 1 tablespoon of the brisket filling in a line down the middle of the masa, leaving a border of plain masa on the sides that's at least ½ inch (1.25 cm) wide.

3. Pick up the sides of the corn husk and bring them together, which should cause the sides of the masa square to join and enclose the filling. Fold the corn husk to one side and wrap it around the tamale. 4. Using 2 of the corn husk strips, tie the top and bottom of the tamale to secure the filling and keep the tamale from unwrapping. Continue until you have used all the masa and filling. As you fill and fold the tamales, stand them as vertically as possible in a bowl or other container.

COOK THE TAMALES: Pour some water into a tall pot fitted with a steamer rack. Use as much water as possible while keeping the level below the rack; you don't want the steamer to boil dry during cooking. Line the steamer with one or two layers of the remaining soaked corn husks. Stand the tamales up in the steamer rack. They will probably fit tightly, but if there is any empty space left in the steamer, tuck in some corn husks to prevent the tamales from slipping down.

Arrange a few more corn husks on top of the tamales, cover, and bring the water to a boil. Adjust the heat so that you have a nice steady amount of steam, and cook the tamales until they feel firm to the touch and you can see that the masa is pulling away from the corn husks, 50 to 60 minutes (keep an eye on the water level and add more if needed). The tamales will still be moist but will firm up slightly as they cool. Remove from the heat.

Serve the tamales in the corn husks and let your guests open them like a present on their own plates and dollop some tomatillo salsa on top.

Roasted Tomatillo Salsa

You can make the tart and spicy base of this salsa up to 2 days in advance, but wait until just before serving to add the onions and avocado. Serve it with Fany's brisket tamales (page 232). *(Pictured on page 225)*

MAKES about 2 cups (350 g)

1 pound (450 g) tomatillos (about 8 large), husks removed, rinsed, and dried

1 garlic clove, not peeled (or more, if you like garlic)

2 serrano or jalapeño chiles

½ cup (15 g) coarsely chopped fresh cilantro leaves and tender stems

Kosher salt

1 small avocado, halved, pitted, peeled, and diced

½ cup (75 g) finely chopped white onion (optional)

Adjust an oven rack to about 4 inches (10 cm) below the broiler element and preheat the broiler. Line a small rimmed baking sheet or baking dish with foil (the tomatillos will release a lot of juice).

Arrange the tomatillos, garlic, and chiles on the baking sheet and broil until they are charred and very soft, flipping them once or twice so they get evenly browned; this should take between 10 and 20 minutes, depending on your broiler. (Keep an eye on the garlic and remove it early if it's starting to burn.) Remove from the broiler and let the ingredients rest until cool enough to handle.

Peel the garlic. Remove the stems from the chiles (if you want a milder salsa, remove the seeds as well). Put the tomatillos and all their juices, the garlic, one of the chiles, the cilantro, and about ½ teaspoon salt in a blender and blend until the salsa has the texture you like— chunky or smooth. Taste and add more salt if needed. If you'd like the salsa hotter, add the second chile and pulse to blend. (Otherwise, reserve the second chile for another use.)

If using the onion, put it in a strainer, rinse under cold water, and drain well.

Just before serving, stir the avocado and onion into the salsa.

Roast Chicken with Apricots

This apricot chicken recipe is Fany's creation, but it was inspired by an apricot chicken her family made. The flavorful pan juices are blended with an apricot butter, making a savory-sweet sauce to pass at the table. This project recipe is best saved for a holiday or a weekend when you want to enjoy spending time in the kitchen.

MAKES 6 to 8 servings

½ cup (115 g) dried apricots

4 tablespoons (60 g) unsalted butter or nondairy butter

5 garlic cloves

Kosher salt and freshly ground black pepper

3 tablespoons fresh lemon juice

3 tablespoons extra-virgin olive oil, plus 1 teaspoon

One 4- to 5-pound (1.8 to 2.2 kg) chicken

8 thyme sprigs

2½ cups (600 ml) homemade or canned low-sodium chicken broth

1 small onion, cut into 1-inch-thick (2.5 cm) wedges

½ cup (60 g) finely chopped shallots

¼ cup (60 ml) red wine vinegar

2 tablespoons apricot preserves

½ cup (15 g) chopped fresh herbs, such as chives, flat-leaf parsley, and mint (optional)

Put the apricots in a small saucepan, cover with water by about 1 inch (2.5 cm), and bring to a boil. Adjust the heat to a simmer and cook until the apricots are very tender, about 30 minutes (the darker Turkish apricots may take longer to soften). Drain and let the apricots cool.

Put the softened apricots, the butter, and 1 garlic clove in a food processor and process to a smooth, thick puree. Scrape the mixture into a small bowl and season with 1 teaspoon salt and ¼ teaspoon pepper; stir to blend.

Transfer 2 heaping tablespoons of the apricot butter to a small container and refrigerate for later. Put the remaining apricot butter in a small bowl and whisk in the lemon juice and the 3 tablespoons olive oil to make a glaze. Set aside.

Arrange a rack in the center of the oven and preheat the oven to 450°F (230°C).

Place the chicken on a cutting board and pat it dry with paper towels. Season the cavity with 1 teaspoon salt and a large pinch of pepper and stuff with half of the thyme sprigs. Tie the legs together loosely with kitchen twine.

Season the outside of the chicken generously with salt and pepper and set it breast side up in a small roasting pan. Try to choose a pan that's not too much larger than the chicken; a 9-by-13-inch (23 by 33 cm) baking dish is fine, slightly larger is better. Carefully pour the broth into the roasting pan and arrange the onion wedges, the remaining 4 garlic cloves, and the remaining thyme sprigs around the chicken.

Roast the chicken for 15 minutes, then reduce the oven temperature to 375°F (190°C) and roast for another 20 minutes.

Remove the chicken from the oven and brush or spread it with the apricot glaze (the glaze will be thick), making sure to get the lower parts of the legs and the wings. Return the chicken to the oven and roast for another 25 minutes, then coat with apricot glaze again.

Return the chicken to the oven and roast until it is fully cooked, another 15 to 30 minutes; a thermometer inserted in the thickest part of

a thigh should read at least 175°F (80°C). To test the chicken without a thermometer, wiggle a drumstick, which should feel loose, and tilt the bird in the pan to let some juices run out—they should be clear, not pink. When the chicken is done, remove it from the oven.

Tilt the chicken and pour all the juices into the roasting pan, then transfer the chicken to a platter, cover loosely with foil, and let rest for 15 minutes. Strain the pan drippings into a small bowl, pressing on the onion and garlic, and set aside.

While the chicken is resting, heat the remaining 1 teaspoon oil in a small saucepan over medium heat. Add the shallots and cook until they soften a bit, about 3 minutes. Pour the vinegar into the saucepan, bring to a lively simmer, and cook until the liquid has mostly reduced, about 5 minutes.

Add the apricot preserves and the reserved pan drippings to the saucepan, whisk together, and bring to a simmer. Taste the sauce; if it is very liquidy, simmer for a few more minutes to concentrate the flavors and slightly thicken it. Whisk in the reserved apricot butter (directly from the refrigerator), adding it a little at a time while whisking to make a creamy, emulsified sauce. Remove the sauce from the heat, taste, and season with salt and pepper as needed. Keep in a warm spot, then transfer to a sauceboat right before serving.

Carve the chicken and arrange on a platter, garnished with the chopped fresh herbs, if using. Serve with the apricot sauce on the side for passing at the table.

Olive Oil Smashed Potatoes

These chunky "smashed" potatoes get their richness from olive oil, which is balanced with plenty of fresh herbs, lemon zest, and garlic. *(Pictured on page 224)*

MAKES 6 to 8 servings

2½ pounds (1.3 kg) red potatoes, scrubbed and quartered

Kosher salt

5 to 6 tablespoons (75 to 90 ml) extra-virgin olive oil, plus more (optional) for drizzling

½ cup (15 g) chopped fresh flat-leaf parsley

3 garlic cloves, finely chopped

Freshly ground black pepper

Finely grated zest of ½ lemon or lime

2 tablespoons finely chopped fresh chives

Put the potatoes in a large pot, add 2 tablespoons salt, and cover with cold water. Bring to a boil over medium-high heat, then reduce the heat to a simmer and cook, uncovered, until the potatoes are fork-tender, about 20 minutes.

Meanwhile, put ¼ cup (60 ml) of the olive oil in a small saucepan and gently heat over medium heat. Add the parsley and garlic and cook until the garlic is fragrant and slightly golden, 2 to 3 minutes, taking care not to brown it. Pour the oil into a small bowl and set aside to cool.

When the potatoes are tender, scoop out about 1 cup (240 ml) of the cooking water and set aside. Drain the potatoes and return them to the pot over low heat. Stir the potatoes to evaporate the surface moisture, then turn off the heat and smash the potatoes with a potato masher or large fork until chunky.

Add the parsley-garlic oil and another tablespoon or two of olive oil to the potatoes and fold to mix. Season generously with salt and pepper and fold in the lemon zest. Taste the potatoes and season with more salt and pepper and a bit of the reserved potato cooking water if needed to make them moist.

Transfer the potatoes to a platter, drizzle on a bit more olive oil, if you like, and garnish with the chives. Serve warm.

Green Beans with Almonds

Fany's take on the classic green beans amandine adds a welcome crunch to her Passover menu. *(Pictured on page 224)*

MAKES 6 to 8 servings

Kosher salt

1½ pounds (675 g) green beans, trimmed

¼ cup (60 ml) extra-virgin olive oil

½ cup (60 g) sliced or slivered almonds

2 tablespoons finely chopped shallots

1 garlic clove, very finely chopped

1 tablespoon fresh lemon juice

Freshly ground black pepper

Bring a large pot of water to a boil and add 1 tablespoon salt. Meanwhile, fill a large bowl with cold water and some ice cubes and set aside. Add the beans to the boiling water and cook until bright green and barely crisp-tender, about 2 minutes. Drain in a colander and transfer to the ice water.

Once the beans are cool, drain them well and spread them on a clean kitchen towel or paper towels to dry completely.

Heat the oil in a large skillet over medium-low heat. Add the almonds and cook, stirring occasionally, until golden brown all over, 3 to 5 minutes.

Using a slotted spoon, transfer the almonds to a plate. Reduce the heat to low and add the shallots and garlic to the skillet. Cook, stirring constantly, until fragrant, about 30 seconds. Increase the heat to medium and add the beans. Cook, tossing occasionally, until the beans are tender and lightly browned in some places, 5 to 8 minutes.

Remove the skillet from the heat, add the lemon juice and salt and pepper to taste, and toss to distribute the seasonings.

Arrange the beans on a serving platter, sprinkle with the almonds, and serve.

Boca Negra with Tomatillo Sauce
Flourless Chocolate Cake

Flourless chocolate cake is a Passover staple in many Jewish homes. Fany's is a take on the Mexican dessert boca negra, which means "black mouth," because your mouth turns black from all the chocolate in this very fudgy cake. Since chocolate is the main ingredient, use the best you can find. Fany also adds chipotle chiles for a surprising smoky-spicy kick.

While Fany uses a regular cake pan, it may be easier to remove the cake from the pan if you use a springform. Because the cake is baked in a water bath, you'll need to wrap the springform tightly with foil (see below).

The cake is served with a sauce made from tangy tomatillos, which are balanced by the toffee-like sweetness of piloncillo. If you can't find piloncillo, use 1 cup packed (215 g) dark brown sugar and add 1 tablespoon molasses. You can make the tomatillo sauce up to a week in advance and keep refrigerated; if necessary, add a bit of water if it seems too thick when you serve it—it should be thick but pourable. The cake needs to chill for at least 2 hours and up to overnight.

MAKES one 8-inch (20 cm) round cake

FOR THE CAKE

12 tablespoons (1½ sticks/170 g) unsalted butter or nondairy butter, cut into small pieces, plus 1 teaspoon for the pan

1 cup (200 g) plus 1 tablespoon sugar

6 medium dried chipotle chiles

10 ounces (280 g) high-quality semisweet chocolate, finely chopped

6 tablespoons (90 ml) fresh orange juice

4 large eggs

1½ tablespoons cornstarch or almond flour

Pinch of kosher salt

FOR THE TOMATILLO SAUCE

1 pound (450 g) tomatillos, husks removed, rinsed and coarsely chopped

1 vanilla bean, split lengthwise

8 ounces (225 g) piloncillo (see headnote)

¼ cup (50 g) sugar

⅓ cup (80 ml) water

1 small cinnamon stick

MAKE THE CAKE: Preheat the oven to 325°F (160°C). Cut a round of parchment paper to fit the inside of an 8-inch (20 cm) round cake pan (you don't need the parchment if using a springform pan). Grease the bottom and sides of the cake pan or an 8-inch (20 cm) springform with the 1 teaspoon butter, line the bottom with the parchment, if using, and grease the parchment with a bit more butter. Dust the interior of the pan with the 1 tablespoon sugar, shaking and turning the pan to distribute it all around, and tap the pan to remove the excess. If using a springform pan, wrap the bottom and sides securely in foil, making sure to tightly seal any seams so water can't seep into the pan.

Remove and discard the stems, seeds, and veins from the chipotles. Heat a medium skillet over medium-high heat, then lay the chiles in the skillet and toast them for a couple of minutes, until fragrant, pressing them flat with a spatula and flipping them frequently so they don't burn.

recipe continues

Transfer the chiles to a bowl and cover with very hot water. Soak until softened, 20 to 30 minutes, or longer if the chiles still have hard spots. Drain the chiles, reserving the liquid.

Put the chiles in a blender or food processor and process until you have a smooth paste, adding a bit of the soaking water as needed. Press the paste through a sieve into a bowl to make it completely smooth. Measure out 1½ tablespoons of the paste; if you have more than that, you can freeze the extra for another use.

Put the chocolate in a large heatproof bowl. Combine the remaining 1 cup (200 g) sugar and the orange juice in a small pot and heat over medium heat, stirring, until the sugar is dissolved. Bring the liquid just to a simmer, then remove from the heat and immediately pour over the chocolate. Let stand for about 1 minute, then stir until all the chocolate is melted (you can use a whisk, but don't beat the mixture, simply stir, as you don't want to incorporate air).

Stir the 12 tablespoons butter little by little into the still-warm chocolate mixture until melted. Add the eggs one by one, stirring until each egg is incorporated before adding the next one. Add the chipotle paste, cornstarch, and salt and stir until the batter is smooth.

Pour the batter into the prepared cake pan. Set up a water bath: Put a large deep baking dish in the oven (large enough to hold the cake pan). Place the filled cake pan in the center of the dish and carefully pour enough hot water into the baking dish (around the cake pan) to reach about halfway up the sides of the cake pan.

Bake the cake until a thin, crusty layer forms on top and the cake feels firm when gently pressed with your finger, 55 to 75 minutes.

MAKE THE TOMATILLO SAUCE: While the cake is baking, put the tomatillos in a medium saucepan. With the tip of a paring knife, scrape the sticky seeds from the split vanilla bean and add the seeds and bean to the tomatillos, then add the piloncillo, granulated sugar, water, and cinnamon stick (the piloncillo will soften and dissolve as the sauce cooks). Bring the sauce to a simmer over medium heat and cook, stirring frequently to dissolve the piloncillo, until the tomatillos are very tender, 15 to 20 minutes. Remove from the heat.

Remove and discard the vanilla bean and cinnamon stick and, with a food processor, puree the mixture into a slightly chunky but uniform sauce. Transfer to a bowl, cover, and chill the sauce completely.

When the cake is ready, remove the water bath from the oven, remove the cake pan from the water bath, and cool the cake for about 10 minutes. If using a springform pan, remove the foil after cooling. Transfer the cake to the refrigerator and chill, covered, for at least 2 hours and up to overnight.

When ready to unmold the cake from a regular cake pan, dip a small sharp knife in hot water, dry it quickly, and run it around the edges of the cake to release it from the pan. Dip the bottom of the cake pan in very hot water for about 3 minutes and then unmold onto a cake plate; peel off the parchment. Or, if you used a springform pan, unclip and remove the sides, slide a spatula under the cake to loosen it from the base of the springform, and transfer to a serving plate.

Serve the cake at room temperature. To slice the cake, use a sharp knife dipped into hot water and dried between each slice to ensure that the sides of each piece are smooth. Serve each slice with a spoonful of tomatillo sauce.

Mexican Chocolate–Covered Caramelized Matzah

Fany tops sheets of matzah with both bittersweet and Mexican chocolate, cinnamon, and flaky salt. Mexican chocolate is made from cacao, sugar, cinnamon, and sometimes other flavorings. It is usually sold in disc form and is readily available.

Be sure to bake the matzah long enough for the caramel topping to become deeply golden brown, which will create a toffee-like flavor and crunch; if the caramel doesn't bake enough, the flavor will simply be sweet. You can make the toffee a few days in advance and store it at room temperature in an airtight container or make it further in advance and keep it in the freezer. *(Pictured on page 240)*

MAKES at least 8 servings

4 to 6 sheets unsalted matzah

8 ounces (2 sticks/225 g) unsalted butter or nondairy butter, cut into pieces

1 cup (215 g) firmly packed light brown sugar

½ teaspoon kosher salt

¼ teaspoon vanilla extract

¼ teaspoon ground cinnamon, preferably Mexican

1½ cups (240 g) bittersweet or semisweet chocolate chips

About 3 ounces (90 g) Mexican chocolate, finely chopped (½ cup)

¼ to ½ teaspoon flaky salt (optional)

Preheat the oven to 350°F (175°C). Line a rimmed baking sheet with foil, making sure it comes up and over all four sides. Line the pan with parchment paper.

Arrange the matzahs neatly on the baking sheet, breaking them into smaller pieces as needed to make an even layer with no gaps.

In a medium saucepan, melt the butter with the brown sugar over medium-high heat, stirring to dissolve the sugar. Bring the mixture to a boil and cook for 3 minutes, stirring constantly with a whisk.

Remove the mixture from the heat and whisk in the kosher salt, vanilla, and cinnamon. Immediately pour the hot caramel over the matzah, spreading it evenly with a heatproof spatula and taking care to keep the matzah in an even layer.

Bake the matzah until the caramel bubbles and becomes deep golden, 12 to 15 minutes.

Remove the pan from the oven and distribute the chocolate chips evenly over the caramel topping. Let sit until the chocolate is mostly melted, 4 to 5 minutes, then spread it into an even layer.

Distribute the chopped Mexican chocolate over the melted chocolate and sprinkle with the flaky salt, if using. The Mexican chocolate won't melt, but it will stick to the melted chocolate layer. Let stand until the matzah is completely cool and the chocolate has firmed up.

Break the matzah into a few large pieces and store in an airtight container in a cool, dry spot for up to 3 days. Break into smaller pieces to serve.

A Spring Table Inspired by My Greatest Teachers

SHARED BY

Rinat Tzadok

I've spent countless hours in kitchens from Tel Aviv to New York, baking and cooking, learning from everyone I've worked with along the way. But the most enduring marks on my cooking were left by my earliest teachers—my family—and the flavors and customs they brought with them to Israel.

My father is now in his seventies, and he's never known his exact birthday—he was born on his family's journey from Yemen to Israel in 1949. His father and stepmom lived just down the street from us in Hadera, next to my grandfather's synagogue. On Saturdays, I would follow him to services and wait for the black coffee with cardamom and kubaneh my grandmother made. But it was my great-grandmother Sa'adah who influenced me the most. I went to live with her after my army service. She had a homestead where she raised chickens in her backyard and often cooked over a small propane stove outside. For Passover, she made her own matzah in a taboon and dried her own spices for her hawaij blend for Yemenite soup. Her cooking was intuitive and resourceful and her table simple but thoughtful.

FAMILY JOURNEY

Ouazzane, Morocco → *Givat Ada, Israel* →
Hadera, Israel → *Tel Aviv*

Yemen → *Azur, Israel* → *Tel Aviv*

Rinat in Givat Olga, Israel, 1984

On my mother's side of the family, my Moroccan aunt Mesodi was my culinary guide. She lived with my grandfather Moshe, and we visited them every weekend. Partially paralyzed by polio, she couldn't cook herself, but starting when I was ten or eleven, she taught me the fundamentals of Moroccan cooking, both the flavors and the techniques. In their home, dishes like fish patties with artichokes and chicken meatballs in a turmeric-tinted broth with celery were made fresh daily; leftovers were never served. And the vegetables always reflected what was in season. They knew the magic of how to make an abundant table from little.

It's only recently that I've seen all of these culinary principles from my family really surface in my own cooking. When I host friends and family, whether for Shabbat or Passover Seder, my menus are rooted in tradition, but even more so in those early kitchen lessons. Like my grandfather Moshe, I shop for ingredients just before cooking them, and like Sa'adah, I make the most of whatever I have on hand. Their resourcefulness is at the root of my creativity as a cook.

RINAT TZADOK is a gifted chef , recipe developer, and content creator. She leads research and development for Lehamim, an acclaimed bakery in Israel.

—*Serve with*—

matzah, Seder plate,
pickled vegetables and olives,
parsley and scallions,
green and red schug,
hilbeh

Charoset Balls

During the Passover Seder, foods like bitter herbs, matzah, and charoset—a sweet paste made from fruits and nuts—help tell the story of the Exodus from Egypt. There are different interpretations of the symbolism of charoset, but it's most often seen as representing the mortar the Jews used for constructing buildings when they were slaves in ancient Egypt. The custom of eating charoset is ancient. As the late culinary scholar Gil Marks explained in his *Encyclopedia of Jewish Food*, it was widespread as early as 200 C.E.

There are countless ways to make charoset. Jewish cooks across the Diaspora have prepared it with the various ingredients available to them— apples and walnuts in Eastern Europe, dates in parts of North Africa and the Middle East. Rinat's charoset draws inspiration from both sides of her heritage. The cardamom and sesame seeds, she notes, are from her Yemenite family, while the dates, almonds, and hazelnuts come from the Moroccan side. Like her mom, Rinat forms the charoset into snack-sized balls, which can be enjoyed at Seder or anytime as an energy snack.

MAKES about 3 dozen 1-inch (2.5 cm) balls

½ cup (55 g) raw walnuts

½ cup (55 g) blanched raw almonds

⅓ cup (40 g) blanched raw hazelnuts

¼ cup (30 g) raw sesame seeds

1 cup (200 g) Medjool dates, pitted

½ teaspoon ground cinnamon

¼ teaspoon ground cardamom

¼ cup (60 ml) sweet red wine

1 tablespoon honey

Preheat the oven to 300°F (150°C). Line a baking sheet with parchment paper.

Spread the walnuts, almonds, hazelnuts, and sesame seeds on the baking sheet and toast in the oven, stirring once or twice for even toasting, until aromatic and golden, about 10 minutes. Remove from the oven and set the nuts aside to cool.

Meanwhile, put the dates in a small heatproof bowl, cover with boiling water, and soak for 5 minutes to soften. Drain the dates thoroughly.

Put the dates, walnuts, almonds, hazelnuts, sesame seeds, cinnamon, cardamom, wine, and honey in a food processor and process the mixture until it forms a paste that's uniform but not completely smooth. If the mixture seems too dry, add up to 1 tablespoon hot water and process a bit more (but you want the mixture to be stiff enough to roll into balls). Transfer the charoset to a bowl, cover tightly, and refrigerate for at least 20 minutes, and up to overnight.

To shape the balls, coat your hands with a bit of neutral oil, scoop up a heaping teaspoon of the mixture, and roll the charoset into 1-inch (2.5 cm) balls. The charoset balls can be stored in an airtight container in the fridge for up to 2 weeks.

Arrange the charoset balls on a serving plate and serve at room temperature.

Eggplant Salad

Rinat describes this eggplant dish from her mom as a vegetarian take on chopped liver. She often serves it in lettuce cups topped with horseradish for a kick. *(Pictured on page 246)*

MAKES 6 to 8 servings

2 large eggplants (about 2 pounds/900 g), peeled and cut into 1-inch (2.5 cm) cubes

About 6 tablespoons (90 ml) extra-virgin olive oil

1½ teaspoons kosher salt

3 large eggs

2 medium yellow onions (about 12 ounces/ 340 g), finely chopped

¼ teaspoon freshly ground black pepper

Lettuce leaves for serving

Grated fresh or prepared horseradish for garnish

Preheat the oven to 400°F (205°C). Line a baking sheet with parchment paper.

Put the eggplant in a large bowl and drizzle on about ¼ cup (60 ml) of the olive oil, tossing the eggplant cubes as you add the oil so it gets distributed evenly. Season with 1 teaspoon of the salt and toss again.

Spread the eggplant cubes in an even layer on the prepared baking sheet and roast until they are deeply golden brown and very tender, 45 to 60 minutes. Set the eggplant aside, lightly covered with parchment paper or foil so the steam can continue to soften the eggplant.

Meanwhile, put the eggs in a small saucepan and cover with water by at least 1 inch (2.5 cm). Bring to a boil, adjust the heat to a vigorous simmer, and cook the eggs for 9 minutes. Drain the eggs, run cold water over them for a minute or two, and set aside to cool completely.

recipe continues

Heat the remaining 2 tablespoons olive oil in a large skillet (large enough to hold all the eggplant) over medium heat. Add the onions and sauté until soft and golden, 12 to 15 minutes.

Add the eggplant and stir to mix with the onions. Remove from the heat and set aside to cool.

Peel and finely chop the hard-boiled eggs. Pile the eggplant and onion mixture on a large cutting board or in a large wide bowl and scatter the chopped eggs over the top, then sprinkle with the remaining ½ teaspoon salt and the pepper. Using a fork or wooden spoon, mash the eggplant with the eggs until blended but still slightly chunky and well mixed with the salt and pepper. Taste and adjust the seasoning with more salt and pepper if needed.

Transfer the salad to a serving bowl and serve with a side of grated horseradish alongside lettuce leaves so that guests can create their own lettuce cups, or preassemble for your guests.

Swiss Chard Salad

This spicy, garlicky, and lemony Swiss chard salad comes from Rinat's mother. The dish is delicious when warm, right from the skillet, but it's even better when it's chilled before it's served—the time in the refrigerator allows the lemon juice to marinate the chard leaves a bit. *(Pictured on page 247)*

MAKES 6 to 8 servings

3 bunches Swiss chard, rinsed and dried
¼ cup (60 ml) extra-virgin olive oil
5 garlic cloves, finely chopped
¾ teaspoon ground cumin
¾ teaspoon sweet paprika
½ teaspoon red chile flakes
1½ teaspoons kosher salt
½ teaspoon freshly ground black pepper
1½ tablespoons fresh lemon juice

Trim the bottoms of the chard stems and cut the stems from the leaves. Chop the stems into ½-inch (1.25 cm) pieces and set aside. Stack a few chard leaves at a time, roll up into a loose cylinder, and cut across into ½-inch (1.25 cm) slices. Cut the slices crosswise into ½-inch (1.25 cm) pieces and set aside.

Heat the olive oil in a large skillet over medium heat. Add the garlic, cumin, paprika, and chile flakes and warm the spices for 30 seconds, then add the chopped chard stems. Sauté until they start to soften, about 5 minutes.

Add the chopped chard leaves, salt, and pepper, toss everything together, and continue cooking over medium heat until the leaves and stems are tender, about 15 minutes. Remove from the heat and fold in the lemon juice.

Transfer the chard to a bowl and let cool to room temperature, then refrigerate the salad for at least 20 minutes before serving.

Herb and Almond Salad

This festive chopped salad with bright notes of soft herbs, preserved lemon, and crunchy nuts has a surprising addition of tiny marzipan "pearls." Rinat likes to soak whole unblanched almonds for 6 hours before peeling them, which gives them a tender bite, but you can use blanched raw almonds if you want to skip the soaking. *(Pictured on page 247)*

MAKES 6 to 8 servings

FOR THE DRESSING

2 tablespoons fresh orange juice, or more to taste

1 tablespoon fresh lemon juice, or more to taste

1 teaspoon honey or maple syrup

½ garlic clove, grated or finely chopped

½ teaspoon kosher salt

2 tablespoons extra-virgin olive oil

FOR THE SALAD

2 cups (60 g) arugula

½ cup (15 g) fresh flat-leaf parsley leaves

Leaves from 3 sprigs za'atar, thyme, or oregano

3 Persian cucumbers, not peeled, finely diced

2 scallions, white and light green parts, finely chopped

1 jalapeño, cored, seeded, and finely chopped

¾ cup (90 g) unblanched raw whole almonds, soaked in cool water for 6 hours, drained, peeled, and roughly chopped

½ cup (60 g) sesame seeds

⅓ cup (40 g) slivered almonds, lightly toasted

3 tablespoons marzipan, rolled into small pearls (optional)

2 tablespoons finely chopped preserved lemon (optional)

MAKE THE DRESSING: Put the orange juice, lemon juice, honey, garlic, and salt in a small bowl and whisk to combine. Whisk in the olive oil and continue whisking until the dressing is emulsified. Taste and add more lemon juice, orange juice, and salt as needed. Set aside.

MAKE THE SALAD: Finely chop about half of the arugula, half of the parsley leaves, and half of the herb leaves and put in a large mixing bowl.

Add the remaining arugula, parsley, and herb leaves to the bowl, then add the cucumbers, scallions, jalapeño, chopped almonds, sesame seeds, slivered almonds, marzipan pearls, if using, and preserved lemon, if using. Gently toss all the ingredients to mix well.

Drizzle the dressing over the salad and toss to coat. Serve right away.

Marak Temani

Yemenite Soup with Spring Greens

In Israel, Yemenite soup, or marak temani in
Hebrew, is a richly spiced broth with beef
or chicken and potatoes. Rinat's vegetarian
version is lighter, but it shares some of the same
signature flavors, including hawaij, a spice blend
from Yemen—often made with turmeric, cumin,
black pepper, and cardamom—that you can find
at some well-stocked grocery stores, at Middle
Eastern markets, or online.

Be sure to use regular Swiss chard, with
white ribs, in this recipe, as the rainbow, red, and
yellow varieties will make the soup look muddy.
Rinat serves the soup with hilbeh, a fenugreek
condiment, and with the Yemeni hot sauce
schug, which is always on her Passover table.
You can use Erez Pinchas's schug from the Yom
Kippur chapter.

MAKES 6 to 8 servings

FOR THE BROTH

1½ tablespoons extra-virgin olive oil

3 medium celery stalks (about 6 ounces/ 170 g), chopped into large pieces

3 medium carrots (about 6 ounces/170 g), peeled and chopped into large pieces

2 medium leeks (about 8 ounces/225 g), halved lengthwise, rinsed, and chopped into large pieces

1 medium yellow onion (about 5 ounces/140 g), halved

1 medium celery root (about 6 ounces/170 g), peeled and chopped into large pieces

2½ quarts (2.5 L) water

1 bay leaf

2 whole allspice berries

Two ¼-inch (6 mm) slices peeled fresh ginger

Three or four ¼-inch (6 mm) slices peeled fresh turmeric

1 tablespoon kosher salt

FOR THE SOUP

2 bunches Swiss chard, rinsed and dried

¼ cup (60 ml) extra-virgin olive oil

1 medium yellow onion (about 5 ounces/140 g), chopped

1 heaping tablespoon hawaij spice mix (see headnote)

1 teaspoon kosher salt

½ teaspoon freshly ground black pepper

1½ to 2 pounds (675 to 900 g) fresh fava bean pods (to yield 1½ cups/225 g beans)

3 tablespoons fresh lemon juice, or more to taste

FOR SERVING

Schug (page 93) or hilbeh

Roughly chopped fresh cilantro and/or flat-leaf parsley

MAKE THE BROTH: Heat the olive oil in a large stockpot over medium heat. Add the celery,

carrots, leeks, onion, and celery root and cook, stirring occasionally, until the vegetables are slightly softened, about 10 minutes.

Add the water, which should cover the vegetables; if not, add a bit more. Add the bay leaf, allspice, ginger, turmeric, and salt and bring to a boil over high heat. Reduce the heat to an active simmer, cover the pot, and cook for 1 hour.

Remove the broth from the heat and let cool for at least an hour.

MAKE THE SOUP: Cut the chard ribs from the leaves and finely chop the ribs. Set aside. Chop the leaves, or stack them a few at a time, roll up into a loose cylinder, and cut across into thin ribbons. Set aside.

Heat the olive oil in a large stockpot over medium-high heat. Add the chopped onion and cook until golden, 8 to 10 minutes. Add the chopped chard ribs and cook for 8 minutes, stirring occasionally. Stir in the hawaij spice mix and cook for another 2 to 3 minutes, stirring constantly.

Strain the broth and discard the vegetables. Add the broth, chard leaves, and salt and pepper to the pot and bring the soup to a boil, then immediately reduce the heat so it just simmers. Cook until the chard is tender, about 20 minutes.

Meanwhile, bring a medium pot of water to a boil. Split open the fava pods and remove the beans. Blanch the beans in the boiling water for about 30 seconds, then drain. When cool enough to handle, split the white membranes surrounding the beans, using a paring knife or your thumbnail, and pop out the bright green beans inside.

Add the peeled fava beans to the soup and simmer for 5 minutes, then turn off the heat and add the lemon juice. Taste and adjust the flavors with more lemon, salt, and pepper if needed.

Serve the soup on its own or garnish each serving with schug, cilantro, and/or parsley.

Spiced Fish Patties with Artichokes

In this dish from Rinat's Moroccan family, delicate fish patties are bathed in an aromatic sauce of spicy chiles, bright tomato, and fragrant cilantro, with artichoke hearts for a touch of spring. Rinat uses a mix of grouper and cod; both are sweet, mild varieties of ocean fish, but any fish that's not too oily will work. Chopping the fillets by hand creates an appealing loose texture, but it makes the patties slightly fragile. Pay attention as you shape them—if the mixture doesn't hold together, add a bit more matzah meal.

MAKES 6 to 8 servings

FOR THE FISH PATTIES

12 ounces (340 g) grouper fillet, finely chopped

12 ounces (340 g) cod fillet, finely chopped

Leaves from 1 bunch cilantro, finely chopped

1 medium yellow onion (about 5 ounces/ 140 g), grated

1 large egg, lightly beaten

4 garlic cloves, finely chopped

1 teaspoon finely grated lemon zest

1½ teaspoons kosher salt

¼ teaspoon freshly ground black pepper

½ teaspoon ground coriander

½ cup (60 g) matzah meal

Extra-virgin olive oil for cooking

FOR THE SAUCE

2 dried Thai chiles or other small dried hot chiles, stemmed and seeded

2 dried guajillo chiles, stemmed and seeded

¼ cup (60 ml) extra-virgin olive oil

2 fresh green chiles, such as jalapeños, cored, seeded, and roughly chopped

3 tomatoes, finely chopped, juices reserved

8 garlic cloves, thinly sliced

1 tablespoon finely chopped preserved lemon

1 teaspoon sweet paprika

1½ teaspoons kosher salt

1¾ cups (420 ml) water

Finely chopped leaves from 1 bunch cilantro

6 artichoke hearts, halved (frozen or canned is fine), or peeled cardoon stalks, thickly sliced

MAKE THE PATTIES: Put the grouper, cod, cilantro, onion, egg, garlic, lemon zest, salt, pepper, coriander, and matzah meal in a large bowl. Mix thoroughly, using a wooden spoon or your hands. Cover and refrigerate the mixture for 20 minutes.

Scoop up 3 to 4 tablespoons of the fish mixture and shape it into a 2½-inch (6.25 cm) patty. Place it on a tray and repeat with the rest of the mixture; you should have 12 to 14 patties. Cover and refrigerate for 5 minutes.

Heat 3 to 4 tablespoons olive oil in a large skillet (nonstick is okay) over medium-high heat. Gently place several patties in the pan and cook, turning once, until nicely browned, about 2 minutes on each side; don't crowd the pan. To prevent the patties from sticking to the pan, don't try to move them for the first minute, allowing a crust to form, and then use a thin spatula to flip them. Set the patties on a clean tray or plate and continue with the rest of the patties, adding more oil as needed. Set the patties aside.

MAKE THE SAUCE: Put the Thai and guajillo chiles in a small bowl and cover with boiling water. Soak for 5 minutes, then drain and pat the peppers dry. Tear or chop the chiles into ½-inch (1.25 cm) pieces.

Heat the olive oil in a wide shallow saucepan or large deep skillet over medium heat. Add the fresh chiles and torn dried chiles and fry for about 3 minutes, until the fresh chiles have softened and everything is nicely fragrant.

Add the tomatoes and their juices, the garlic, preserved lemon, paprika, and salt to the pan and cook for 2 to 4 minutes.

Add the water, increase the heat to medium-high, and bring the mixture to a boil. Add half of the cilantro and all of the artichoke hearts and stir to mix, then simmer for a few minutes to heat the artichokes through.

Gently place the fish patties in the sauce, reduce the heat to a simmer, cover the pan, and cook for 10 minutes. Carefully flip the fish patties and continue cooking, covered, for another 5 minutes, until they are slightly firm and cooked through. Don't let the sauce boil, or the patties may fall apart.

Put the patties on a large platter, spoon the sauce over, and shower with the rest of the cilantro, or arrange the patties in individual shallow bowls, ladle the sauce over, and sprinkle with the cilantro. Serve immediately.

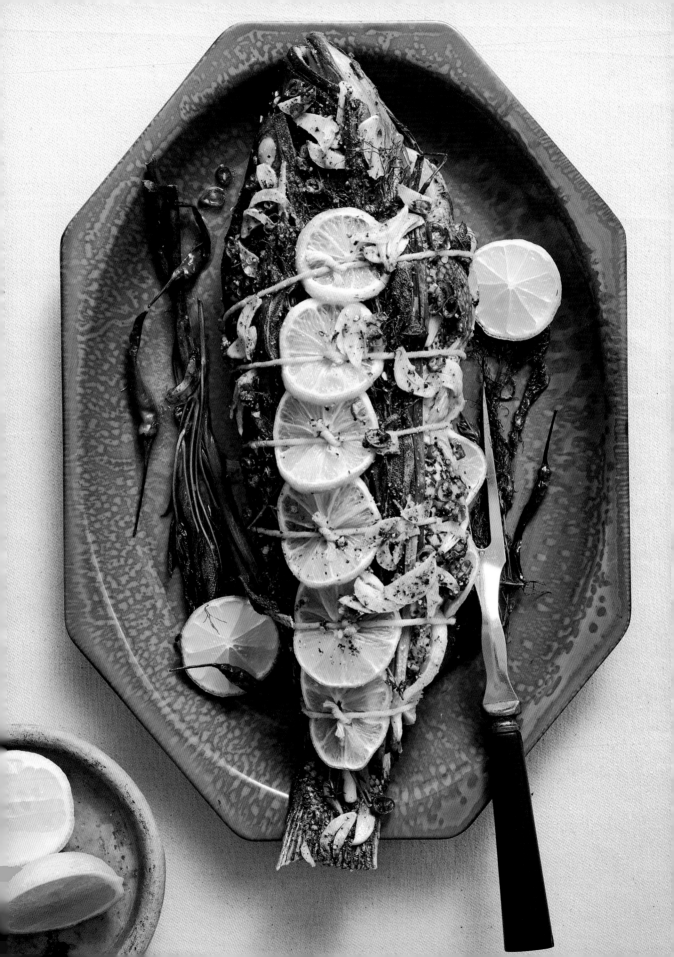

Whole Roasted Fish with Lemon and Herbs

This whole fish, adorned with lemons and fresh herbs, makes quite a statement on a holiday table. Filleting it tableside is easy, once you've watched someone else do it. If you're new to it, start by sliding the knife along the spine of the fish, then make a cut that separates the head from the top fillet and another that separates that fillet from the tail. Remove the top fillet (using a tablespoon can help). Lift the tail, which will release all of the bones and the head from the bottom fillet. It can help to check out short videos of this technique online.

Ground dried lime, sometimes called Persian lime, can be found at Middle Eastern stores and is worth seeking out for its subtle but distinctive tangy-smokiness.

MAKES 6 to 8 servings

One 4½-pound (2 kg) whole black sea bass or red snapper, scaled and cleaned

1 lemon, thinly sliced

Kosher salt

3 tablespoons extra-virgin olive oil

1 teaspoon ground dried lime (see headnote)

3 garlic cloves, thinly sliced

1 fresh hot green chile, such as jalapeño, cored, seeded, and sliced

½ teaspoon freshly ground black pepper

4 scallions, trimmed

4 fresh sage leaves

4 thyme sprigs

4 fennel fronds (optional)

Preheat the oven to 375°F (190°C). Line a rimmed baking sheet with parchment paper.

Set the fish on the baking sheet and arrange a few of the lemon slices in the belly cavity; season the cavity lightly with salt.

In a small bowl, mix the olive oil, dried lime, garlic, chile, 2 teaspoons salt, and the pepper. Rub both sides of the fish with the olive oil mixture and lay the remaining lemon slices on top of the fish.

Place the scallions, sage, thyme, and fennel fronds, if using, on top of the lemons. Wrap the fish with kitchen twine in a few places to secure the seasonings.

Cover the fish tightly with aluminum foil and roast for 15 minutes. Remove the foil and continue roasting until the fish is cooked through, another 10 minutes or so, depending on the thickness of the fish (it should register 135°F/57°C on an instant-read thermometer).

Carefully remove the twine, keeping the seasonings in place. Transfer the fish to a serving platter and carve at the table.

Roast Chicken with Spring Vegetables

A true celebration of spring, this roast chicken is surrounded by an array of vegetables that are first roasted and then braised, bathed in the chicken juices so they become soft and sweet. Take care that the vegetables aren't getting too brown as they roast; giving them a big stir at least once during roasting will help with even cooking.

Green garlic, which looks like overgrown scallions, has a mild, sweet flavor. It's an iconic springtime treat at farmers' markets, but you can substitute a couple of scallions and a garlic clove if you can't get it.

MAKES 6 to 8 servings

2 to 3 stalks green garlic or 2 scallions plus 1 garlic clove

Kosher salt

Extra-virgin olive oil

1 to 1½ pounds (450 to 675 g) fresh fava bean pods (to yield 1 cup/150 g beans)

One 5-pound (2.2 kg) chicken

3 or 4 medium celery stalks (about 8 ounces/ 225 g), cut into ½-inch (1.25 cm) slices

5 or 6 drained canned or thawed frozen artichoke hearts, halved

1 cup (140 g) fresh or frozen green peas

1 large or 2 small fennel bulbs (about 8 ounces/ 225 g), stalks and fronds removed, cut into wedges, and core removed

1 large leek (about 4 ounces/115 g), white and light green parts, sliced into ½-inch (1.25 cm) rounds, rinsed, and drained

1 head garlic, cut horizontally in half (skin on)

1 lemon, thinly sliced

1 jalapeño or other fresh hot chile, cored, seeded, and finely chopped

4 thyme sprigs

4 to 6 fresh sage leaves

1 teaspoon freshly ground black pepper

1 cup (240 ml) homemade or canned low-sodium chicken broth

Preheat the oven to 425°F (220°C).

Trim the dark green tops from the green garlic and roughly chop the lighter sections. Put into a food processor with 1 teaspoon salt and process to a rough puree. With the motor running, pour in just enough olive oil to make a smooth paste, about 1 tablespoon; it shouldn't be runny. Alternatively, put the green garlic and salt on a cutting board and chop the garlic as fine as possible, mashing it and the salt together to form a paste; then mix with about 1 tablespoon olive oil. (If using scallions and garlic, use the same method, chopping only the white and light green parts of the scallions.) Set aside.

Bring a medium pot of water to a boil. Split open the fava pods and remove the beans. Blanch the beans in the boiling water for about 30 seconds, then drain. When cool enough to handle, split the white membranes surrounding the beans, using a paring knife or your thumbnail, and pop out the bright green bean inside; set aside.

Set the chicken on a plate or small tray and coat with about ½ cup (100 g) salt, making sure all parts are evenly coated. Set aside for 30 minutes.

Meanwhile, put the celery, artichoke hearts, peas, fennel, fava beans, leek, and garlic head in a roasting pan that has fairly high sides and is large enough for the chicken and all the vegetables. Drizzle ¼ cup (60 ml) olive oil over

the vegetables and season with 1 teaspoon salt. Toss gently to distribute the oil and salt evenly.

Roast the vegetables for 30 minutes.

Meanwhile, after the chicken has sat for 30 minutes, wipe off all the salt with a damp paper towel. Be sure to get the salt out of the folds around the legs and wings, or the chicken will be too salty.

Gently slide your finger under the breast skin to separate the skin from the meat, and smear some of the green garlic paste over the meat, working your way as far back as you can, creating an even layer. Spread any remaining green garlic paste over the chicken skin. Stuff about half the lemon slices into the chicken's cavity.

Remove the roasting pan from the oven and stir the vegetables. Distribute the remaining lemon slices among the vegetables. Set the chicken in the center of the pan, moving aside some vegetables as necessary to make space. Scatter the jalapeño, thyme sprigs, and sage leaves evenly over the chicken and vegetables, then sprinkle with the pepper. Pour the chicken broth into the pan, avoiding the chicken. Drizzle the chicken breasts with a bit of olive oil.

Return the roasting pan to the oven and continue roasting until the chicken is cooked through, 1 hour and 15 minutes to 1 hour and 30 minutes; about halfway through roasting, stir the vegetables around so they are evenly cooked. When the chicken is done, the juices from the inside of the cavity should be clear, not pink, and an instant-read thermometer inserted in the thickest part of a thigh should read at least 175°F (80°C).

Tilt the chicken in the pan to pour any juices in the cavity into the roasting pan, then transfer the chicken to a platter or cutting board with a rim to catch the juices and let it rest for about 10 minutes before serving.

Carve the chicken into portions and place on a platter, with the vegetables and pan juices arranged around the chicken or served on a separate platter.

Festive Rice with Nuts, Herbs, and Onions

This rice brings together crunchy toasted seeds and almonds with onions cooked two ways. In some Jewish homes, it's customary to avoid rice, legumes, and other foods that are referred to as *kitniyot* on Passover. If this is your custom, save this delicious recipe for another occasion or holiday.

A small amount of the Middle Eastern spice blend baharat adds complexity to the dish. Baharat usually includes allspice, cumin, coriander, cardamom, cloves, and black pepper. You can find it in some well-stocked grocery stores or in Middle Eastern markets. Use it in other rice dishes, as well as for dry rubs and marinades.

MAKES 6 to 8 servings

½ cup (55 g) sliced almonds

¼ cup (35 g) shelled sunflower seeds

¼ cup (35 g) shelled pumpkin seeds

⅓ teaspoon saffron threads

2¼ cups (540 ml) plus 2 tablespoons boiling water

6 tablespoons (80 ml) extra-virgin olive oil

2 cups (300 g) finely chopped yellow onions, plus 1 medium yellow onion (about 7 ounces/ 200 g), halved and thinly sliced

1½ cups (300 g) basmati rice, rinsed under cool water until the water runs clear

1 teaspoon kosher salt

¼ teaspoon freshly ground black pepper

¼ teaspoon baharat spice mix

Finely chopped fresh flat-leaf parsley for garnish

Preheat the oven to 325°F (160°C). Line a baking sheet with parchment paper.

Spread the almonds, sunflower seeds, and pumpkin seeds on the baking sheet and toast in the oven until lightly browned, 5 to 8 minutes. Remove from the heat.

Put the saffron threads in a small bowl and cover with the 2 tablespoons boiling water; set aside.

Heat 3 tablespoons of the olive oil in a large saucepan over medium-low heat. Add the chopped onions and sauté, stirring occasionally, until soft and translucent, about 10 minutes.

Add the rice to the chopped onions and cook, stirring, to coat the rice in oil and lightly toast it, 2 to 4 minutes. Add the salt, pepper, and baharat spice mix, pour in the remaining 2¼ cups (540 ml) boiling water and the saffron water, and stir to mix well. Increase the heat to high, bring the mixture to a boil, and cover with a lid. Reduce the heat to low and cook for 18 to 20 minutes, until all the liquid has been absorbed and the rice is tender. Remove the pan from the heat and set aside, covered, for 10 minutes, then fluff the rice with a fork.

While the rice is cooking, heat the remaining 3 tablespoons olive oil in a large skillet over medium-high heat. Add the sliced onions and fry until browned and crisp, 5 to 6 minutes, taking care to not let them get too brown, or they will be bitter. Remove from the heat.

Fold about half of the nut mixture into the rice and put the rice in a large serving bowl. Top with the fried onion, the remaining nut mixture, and parsley. Serve hot.

Chocolate Mousse with Nut "Granola" and Olive Oil

Rinat often makes this ethereally light yet deeply chocolatey mousse on Friday nights because it uses olive oil instead of cream or other dairy, meaning it can be served at a kosher meat meal. It would be excellent on its own, but Rinat's crunchy spiced nut topping, baked like a granola and lightly sweetened with maple syrup, takes

the dessert to a new level. The mousse needs at least 10 hours to set up properly, so it's best to make it the day before serving.

MAKES 6 to 8 servings

FOR THE NUT MIXTURE

⅓ cup (40 g) raw pistachios, roughly chopped

¼ cup (30 g) almonds, roughly chopped

3 tablespoons grated unsweetened coconut

½ teaspoon kosher salt

½ teaspoon crushed coriander seeds

¼ teaspoon ground cardamom

¼ teaspoon freshly ground black pepper

2 tablespoons maple syrup

FOR THE MOUSSE

4 large eggs, at room temperature

9 ounces (250 g) 70% bittersweet chocolate, finely chopped (1¾ cups)

⅔ cup (160 ml) boiling water

3 tablespoons plus 1 teaspoon (50 ml) extra-virgin olive oil, plus more for garnish

1 teaspoon rosewater (optional)

3 tablespoons plus 1 teaspoon (40 g) sugar

⅛ teaspoon flaky sea salt

MAKE THE NUT MIXTURE: Heat the oven to 325°F (160°C). Line a baking sheet with parchment paper.

Put the pistachios, almonds, coconut, kosher salt, coriander, cardamom, pepper, and maple syrup in a small bowl and toss to mix thoroughly. Spread the mixture on the prepared baking sheet and bake until the nuts and coconut turn light brown and the mixture is fragrant, about 10 minutes, stirring the mixture a few times to

make sure it toasts evenly. Don't let any of the ingredients get too dark; the mixture will crisp up as it cools. Remove from the oven and set aside.

MAKE THE MOUSSE: Separate the eggs, putting the whites into the bowl of a stand mixer fitted with the whisk attachment (or in a large bowl) and the yolks in a small bowl.

Fill a medium saucepan with about 1 inch (2.5 cm) water and set a stainless steel bowl on top; the bottom of the bowl should not touch the water. Put the chopped chocolate, boiling water, and olive oil in the bowl and heat over medium heat, stirring constantly, until the chocolate has melted and becomes smooth. Add the rosewater, if using, and mix well, then remove from the heat.

One at a time, whisk the egg yolks into the chocolate mixture, fully incorporating each yolk before adding the next. Set aside to cool completely.

Whip the egg whites in the stand mixer on medium speed (or use a handheld electric mixer) until the whites are foamy and no longer translucent. Gradually add the sugar as you continue to whip the whites, and then whip until soft, stable peaks form.

Using a rubber spatula, fold the egg whites a few scoops at a time into the cooled chocolate mixture, taking care to preserve as much volume as possible. Gently fold in the flaky salt.

Transfer the mixture to a pretty glass or ceramic serving bowl, cover with plastic wrap, and chill in the refrigerator for at least 10 hours before serving.

Serve the mousse with a drizzle of olive oil and a small spoonful of the pistachio mixture atop each portion.

A Mina Recipe from Izmir That's Six Generations Strong

SHARED BY

Alexandra Zohn

I never met my great-great-grandmother Rosa, but my grandmother Rita adored her. Every time we ate one of Rosa's recipes, Rita would tell us about her—how Rosa wore her hair in a bun with a rose even while she cooked, how she moved to Mexico City from Turkey around 1920, and how when she was elderly, she preferred the company of young people, so she would go to a café and make friends with everyone there.

The story my grandmother told the most was the one about how when Rosa was little, it wasn't customary for girls to learn to read in her community in Izmir. So, at sixty, Rosa taught herself to read using newspapers and was so delighted that she could finally join in conversations with informed opinions.

Rosa's recipes were often a part of the weekly Monday lunches and holiday meals my grandmother hosted for our entire family—aunts, uncles, cousins. We weren't religious, but the traditional dishes were key to the holidays, connecting us to our ancestors, even the ones we didn't

FAMILY JOURNEY

Izmir, Turkey → *Mexico City* → *New York City*

Alexandra's grandmother Rita in the late 1960s

know much about. For Passover, that meant charoset, matzah fritters called buñuelos, and minas, pies layered with sheets of matzah stacked high with either meat or spinach, cheese, and potatoes.

Before I moved to the U.S., I went to my grandmother's home and tried to write down her recipes in a notebook—for her, "one cup" means a glass from her cabinet. I packed that notebook along with a tortilla press and a pan from Rosa. They were heavy, but it felt like carrying part of my identity and family's traditions with me.

I wish I had met Rosa, but I know she's part of my DNA. Her recipes are the best way I have to communicate with her.

Born and raised in Mexico City's diverse Jewish community, **ALEXANDRA ZOHN** now lives in New York City, where she is a holistic health coach.

Mina de Espinaca
Matzah and Spinach Pie
268

—*Serve with*—

green salad with radish,
braised mixed vegetables

Mina de Espinaca
Matzah and Spinach Pie

A staple of Sephardi Passover tables, mina de matza (sometimes simply called mina) is a type of savory pie stacked with sheets of matzah and fillings like seasoned meat, eggplant, or spinach and cheese. With layers of mashed potatoes and spinach both laced with Parmesan, this one from Alexandra's family makes a wonderful main for a vegetarian Seder or Passover lunch.

MAKES 6 to 8 servings

2 russet or 3 Yukon Gold potatoes (about 1½ pounds/675 g), scrubbed, halved if large

Kosher salt

1½ cups (about 6 ounces/170 g) shredded Parmesan cheese

8 ounces (225 g) cream cheese, at room temperature

2 large eggs, lightly beaten

1 pound (450 g) baby spinach, finely chopped

2 tablespoons extra-virgin olive oil

4 or 5 sheets matzah (7-inch/17.5 cm squares)

MAKE THE POTATOES: Put the potatoes in a medium saucepan, cover with water, add 1 tablespoon salt, and bring to a boil over high heat. Reduce the heat to medium-low and cook until the potatoes can be easily pierced with a knife, 20 to 25 minutes. Drain and let cool until the potatoes are cool enough to handle but still warm.

Peel the potatoes and put them in a large bowl. Mash them with a potato ricer or fork until smooth, with no chunks. Add 1½ teaspoons salt, ¾ cup (85 g) of the Parmesan cheese, the cream cheese, and the eggs and mix well with

a rubber spatula or wooden spoon until the mixture is smooth and uniform. Taste and adjust the seasoning with more salt, if you like. Set aside.

MAKE THE SPINACH MIXTURE: Put the chopped spinach in a medium bowl and add ½ cup (55 g) of the Parmesan and 1 teaspoon salt. Mix until the cheese and salt are evenly distributed. Set aside.

Preheat the oven to 350°F (175°C). Grease a 10-inch (25 cm) springform pan with 1 teaspoon of the olive oil.

Fill a container that's large enough to hold a matzah sheet with about an inch (2.5 cm) of water and stir in ¼ teaspoon salt. Line a plate or tray with paper towels.

Soak the matzahs one at a time in the water until the sheets are flexible yet still firm enough to hold their shape; this could take anywhere from 30 seconds to a minute or two. Gently place each soaked matzah on the paper towels to absorb excess moisture.

ASSEMBLE THE MINA: Line the bottom of the springform pan with a matzah, then fill in the gaps around the edges with pieces of matzah that you tear to fit. Spread half of the spinach-Parmesan mixture over the matzah in an even layer. Add another layer of moistened matzah on top, gently pressing the matzah into the spinach layer to make space for the remaining layers.

Spread the rest of the spinach mixture over the matzah layer. Place another layer of matzah over the spinach, gently pressing the matzah into the spinach to make room for the remaining layer.

Spread the potato mixture evenly over the matzah layer. Use the back of a spoon or an offset spatula to make swirls in the surface of the potatoes so they brown attractively in the oven. Sprinkle the remaining ¼ cup (25 g) Parmesan on top of the potato layer and drizzle the remaining olive oil on top.

Bake the mina until deep golden brown, 40 to 50 minutes. Remove from the oven and allow the mina to cool for about 5 minutes, then run the tip of a sharp knife around the edges of the mina to release it from the pan.

Remove the sides of the springform, transfer the mina to a serving platter, and cut into wedges. Serve hot.

Sharing Mimouna with Neighbors—in Morocco and Virginia

Ruth Stulman

When Passover ended in Rabat, Mimouna started. We would wear our most beautiful jewelry, caftans, and djellabas, and everyone in our community would open their doors. I would run from one home to the next greeting our neighbors with the word *terb'ah*, wishing them good luck and success by saying, "You win."

Sweets like pistachio cookies made with rosewater and dates stuffed with marzipan were laid out on tables in everyone's homes. Each household had its specialty, and you absolutely had to eat something when you visited. The signature sweet of the holiday was always mufleta, freshly made crepes that we would spread with butter and honey, fold into quarters or roll up into a cigar, and devour. The party would go until two or three o'clock in the morning; there was so much joy on those evenings as we ran into friends in the streets, laughed, and celebrated.

When we moved to Virginia in the early 1970s, we no longer had our Moroccan community around us, but we kept celebrating Mimouna. My mother, Perla, would invite our neighbors and members of our

---

FAMILY JOURNEY

Rabat, Morocco → *Alexandria, VA* → *Fairfax, VA* → *New York City*

Ruth's mother, Perla Amar, in Fairfax, Virginia, 1998

synagogue to the party at our house. By the time my son Gabriel was twelve, I had taken over the hosting responsibilities, proudly introducing our own friends to a custom I love. Mimouna is a beautiful moment of joy and freedom and shows people how you can celebrate anything—in our case, being Jewish.

When we hosted Mimouna at Gabriel's restaurant in 2019, we wanted to share that moment with New Yorkers. Our whole family wore caftans and djellabas; there was live Moroccan music and I taught the chefs to make our mufleta. Gabriel tells me that for him, honoring Mimouna is about being part of what he calls an unbreakable chain that links him to his heritage and culture, which he's now sharing with his own children. Sometimes my grandkids call me and say, "Terb'ah."

In Moroccan Jewish homes, the end of Passover is traditionally marked with a celebration called Mimouna, where the first leavened food is eaten. The custom has also become popular in other communities. In 2019, the Jewish Food Society hosted a Mimouna party with restaurateur Gabriel Stulman and his mother, **RUTH STULMAN**, at his restaurant Fairfax in Manhattan's West Village. Ruth grew up in the Moroccan coastal city Rabat in the late 1950s and early 1960s but today calls Virginia home.

RUTH STULMAN'S MIMOUNA

Mufleta
Moroccan Crepes
274

**Sweet Couscous with
Nuts and Dried Fruit**
275

**Marzipan-Stuffed
Dates and Walnuts**
276

Walnut Cookies
278

Pistachio Cookies
278

—Serve with—

Jordan almonds,
assorted candies,
fresh and dried fruit,
honey

Mufleta
Moroccan Crepes

When Passover ended in Ruth's childhood community in Rabat, everyone opened their doors for a joyous and sweets-filled Mimouna party. The signature treat of the celebration is mufleta, yeasted crepes that are often the first hametz, or leavened food, eaten after Passover. Ruth remembers devouring them with the traditional butter and honey, but you can also serve them with jam.

The technique for shaping and rolling the well-oiled dough so it's paper-thin and then frying the rounds stacked in multiple layers may seem challenging at first, but the dough is very forgiving. Once you've rolled and stacked a few layers, you'll get the hang of it and feel quite accomplished when you see your tall stack of tender crepes, ready to enjoy. *(Pictured on page 272)*

MAKES one 12- to 14-inch (30 to 35 cm) mufleta stack (about 24 layers)

4 cups (520 g) all-purpose flour

1 teaspoon sugar

2 teaspoons kosher salt

1 packet (2¼ teaspoons/7 g) active dry yeast

1½ cups (360 ml) lukewarm water

About ½ cup (120 ml) neutral oil, such as canola, plus more for the bowl and work surface

Melted butter for drizzling

Honey for drizzling

Put the flour, sugar, salt, and yeast in the bowl of a stand mixer fitted with the dough hook and mix on low speed until combined. With the mixer running, slowly stream in the water. If the dough seems dry at this point, add a bit more water, a teaspoon at a time, until the dough just comes together. Increase the mixer speed to medium and mix the dough for 10 to 12 minutes, until uniform and smooth.

Transfer the dough to a lightly oiled bowl, cover with plastic wrap, and let rise until doubled in size, about 40 minutes.

Pour the oil onto a rimmed baking sheet and spread it evenly. Turn the dough out onto the oiled pan and use a knife to cut it into 24 equal pieces about the size of a golf ball (40 g).

To shape the dough, stretch one-quarter of one piece of dough out, over, and into the center of the dough ball. Do this three more times, working your way around the dough—think of creating a little parachute with the dough where the four quarters meet at the middle. Make a ring by connecting the thumb and forefinger of one hand. Take the dough ball and, smooth top side first, push it through the ring, which will slightly stretch the surface of the dough, tightening the ball. Pinch the bottom of the ball closed. Coat both sides of the ball with a bit more oil from the baking sheet and place it seam side down on the sheet. Continue to shape the rest of the dough balls.

Heat a large nonstick skillet over medium-high heat. Lightly oil a clean work surface.

Set a dough ball on the oiled work surface and, using your hands and a rolling pin, stretch and flatten it into a 12- to 14-inch (30 to 35 cm) paper-thin round (try not to make any holes, but if it happens, it's okay). Carefully lift the dough and lay it in the hot pan. You'll have a few seconds to reposition any folds or creases, but don't worry if it's not perfectly flat. Immediately start stretching your next layer. Once the dough in the skillet starts to brown lightly on the bottom, use a spatula to carefully flip it over. Lay the second stretched dough round directly on top of the first and immediately start stretching your next piece of dough.

When the bottom of the dough in the pan is lightly golden, 2 to 3 minutes, flip the two layers over. Lay the third round of stretched dough on top of the stack.

Repeat this process of stretching, flipping, and adding to the dough stack until all of the layers are stacked in the skillet, like a giant crepe cake. If after you've stacked a dozen or so layers the stack becomes too difficult to flip as one, set that stack aside and start fresh with the rest of your dough. Adjust the heat as necessary while you work so that the layers don't take on too much color. Remove the stack from the skillet and place on a large plate or serving dish.

Serve the mufleta immediately. To eat, each person should peel away a layer of mufleta from the stack, drizzle it with butter and honey, and roll it into a cylinder or fold into quarters.

Sweet Couscous with Nuts and Dried Fruit

While couscous paired with vegetables, meat, or fish is best known, there are also sweet versions. This one is made with cinnamon, dried fruit, and nuts and finished with almond milk. It's easiest to use instant couscous for this recipe, but homemade (page 77) is excellent if you have the time. *(Pictured on page 273)*

MAKES 6 to 8 servings

1 pound (450 g) instant couscous

½ cup (100 g) sugar

1 teaspoon ground cinnamon

4 tablespoons (½ stick/60 g) unsalted butter or margarine, melted

¾ cup (115 g) raisins

¾ cup (150 g) pitted dates, chopped

¾ cup (100 g) dried apricots, chopped

¾ cup (90 g) blanched almonds, chopped

¾ cup (90 g) walnuts, chopped

½ to 1 cup (120 to 240 ml) almond milk

Prepare the couscous according to the package instructions, using water rather than broth. Transfer the couscous to a large serving bowl.

In a small bowl, stir the sugar and cinnamon into the melted butter. Pour over the couscous, tossing to coat. Stir in the raisins, dates, apricots, almonds, and walnuts.

Gradually add the almond milk, a little bit at a time, until the couscous is moistened to your liking; you may not need all of the almond milk. Tidy up the edge of the serving bowl and serve right away, while the couscous is still warm.

Marzipan-Stuffed Dates and Walnuts

Like Ruth's walnut and pistachio cookies (page 278), these marzipan-filled treats don't use any flour, meaning they can be made toward the end of Passover and stored for Mimouna. Much of what makes these special is their decorative look, so take your time finishing them. The exact amount of the filling you will need depends on the sizes of your dates and walnuts, but you should have plenty to make 2 dozen of each type.

Finding whole, unbroken walnut halves can be tricky, so inspect the bag or bulk bin in the store and buy a bit more than you think you will need.

MAKES about 24 pieces of each candy

2 cups (240 g) raw unblanched almonds or blanched almonds

1 cup (115 g) confectioners' sugar

4 teaspoons orange blossom water

Red food coloring

Green food coloring

24 Medjool dates

48 whole walnut halves

½ cup (100 g) granulated sugar for dusting

If using skin-on almonds, put the almonds in a large heatproof bowl and cover with boiling water. Let stand for exactly 1 minute (any longer, and they will soften too much), then drain and cover again with cold water. Gently squeeze each almond between your fingers to remove the skin. Spread on a baking sheet and allow to dry for about 30 minutes.

Put the almonds in the bowl of a food processor and pulse until finely ground. Add the confectioners' sugar and pulse to combine evenly. Add the orange blossom water and pulse until a paste forms, adding a few drops of water if needed.

Divide the marzipan paste in half. Set one half aside; you will not color it. Divide the other half into 3 equal portions. Color one portion with 4 to 6 drops of red food coloring (or more or less, depending on what color you're going for), kneading the marzipan to

distribute the food coloring evenly. Color a second portion with 4 to 6 drops (or more or less) of green food coloring. Leave the third portion uncolored.

MAKE THE DATES: Slit open one side of a date with a paring knife and remove the pit. Fill with a generous ½ teaspoon (about 4 g) each of two of the three colors of marzipan. Mold the marzipan so it fills the date nicely, then use the back of a knife to make a design in the paste by pressing indentations into it. Repeat with the remaining dates.

MAKE THE WALNUTS: Roll a rounded teaspoon (about 6 g) of the uncolored marzipan into a ball and place it in between 2 walnut halves, like a sandwich. Repeat with the remaining walnuts.

Spread the granulated sugar on a plate and roll each walnut candy lightly in sugar.

Store the candies in an airtight container in the refrigerator. Bring to room temperature before serving.

Walnut Cookies

The baking method for these walnut confections—starting them in a cold oven—is unconventional, but it produces a lovely balance of textures: crisp on the outside, tender on the inside. The cookies hold well for up to a week, so you can easily bake them a few days before a Mimouna party or another celebration. *(Pictured on page 274)*

MAKES about 40 cookies

4 cups (480 g) walnuts

1 cup (200 g) sugar

Grated zest of 1 large orange

1½ teaspoons ground cinnamon

⅛ teaspoon ground cloves

½ teaspoon kosher salt

1 large egg white

Place the racks in the upper and lower thirds of the oven. Line a rimmed baking sheet with parchment paper and grease with nonstick cooking spray or vegetable oil.

Put the walnuts, sugar, orange zest, cinnamon, cloves, salt, and egg white in the bowl of a food processor. Pulse until the walnuts are coarsely ground and the mixture is evenly combined. Transfer to a bowl.

Lightly oil your hands, scoop up a rounded tablespoon (20 g) of the mixture, and roll it into a ball about the size of a walnut; set on the prepared baking sheet. Continue with the rest of the mixture, spacing the balls about 1 inch (2.5 cm) apart.

Put the baking sheet on the top rack of the oven and turn the oven on to 350°F (175°C). Bake for 12 minutes, then move the pan from the top to the bottom rack and continue baking for another 13 minutes, until the cookies are lightly browned all over.

Transfer the cookies to a wire rack and let cool. The cookies will feel soft to the touch but will crisp up as they cool.

Store the cookies in an airtight container for up to a week.

Pistachio Cookies

These delicate cookies are flourless, which makes them light and crunchy. That also means they are gluten free and kosher for Passover.

MAKES about 40 cookies

2½ cups (350 g) raw pistachios

1 cup (200 g) sugar

½ teaspoon kosher salt

1 large egg

1 large egg yolk

1 tablespoon rosewater

Put the pistachios in the bowl of a food processor and pulse until coarsely ground. Transfer the nuts to a large bowl, add the sugar and salt, and stir to mix.

Whisk together the egg, egg yolk, and rosewater, pour into the nut mixture, and stir to blend. Chill the cookie dough for about 30 minutes.

Place the racks in the upper and lower thirds of the oven and preheat the oven to 350°F (175°C). Line two baking sheets with parchment paper.

To shape the cookies, scoop up 2 heaping teaspoons of dough for each one and drop in a

single mound onto the prepared baking sheets, leaving 2 inches (5 cm) of space between the cookies.

Bake until lightly golden and slightly browned around the edges, 18 to 22 minutes, rotating the pans top to bottom and front to back about halfway through the cooking time. Let cool on a wire rack.

The cookies keep nicely in an airtight container for up to three days.

Shavuot

THE LAND FEELS ALIVE and everything is in bloom at this time of the year. The markets are flooded with fresh produce. It's a reminder of a time when families grew their own food and brought offerings from their harvests to the Temple in ancient Jerusalem during the three pilgrimage festivals: Sukkot (see page 102) at the start of fall, Passover (see page 202) in the early spring, and Shavuot, on the cusp of summer. To measure the seven weeks (*shavuot* in Hebrew) between the Passover and Shavuot pilgrimages, and the barley and wheat harvests, it's traditional to "count the Omer," a blessing that's said each night.

Historically, there was a deep connection between the success of the harvest and daily life. During the first part of the Omer, when the crops could be destroyed by extreme weather, farmers held their breath and there were no weddings or other joyful gatherings. Once confident in a good harvest, on the minor holiday Lag B'Omer (the thirty-third day of the Omer), Jews could once again rejoice.

On kibbutzim like the one I grew up on and Ma'ale HaHamisha, where Hila Alpert (see page 288) was raised, Shavuot is the most important celebration. There, it is still primarily an agricultural holiday. It's seen as a time to rejoice in our connection to the land. We wear flower crowns and white clothing on the holiday. First fruits, newborn animals, and babies are marched in parades, tractors are decorated, and friends gather on the grass for performances by community members.

Elsewhere, Shavuot is best known as a celebration of God giving the Torah to Moses at Mount Sinai and counting the Omer as a way to prepare spiritually for the holiday. Religious communities read the Book of Ruth on Shavuot and spend the evening studying. It's customary to serve dairy dishes for a host of reasons. For example, some attribute the tradition to the idea of Israel as the land of milk and honey, while others say that it stems from the time of year when animals produced extra milk from grazing on green pastures. There's also an argument that after the Israelites received the Torah and learned of kosher laws, the first meal they were able to prepare was a dairy one.

Cheesecake has become a signature food of the holiday, but there are many others. When he was little, Alon Hadar would join his Kurdish grandmother while she made kadeh, a pastry stuffed with cheese (see page 282). Recipes like the cheese-stuffed peppers (page 300) from Ron Levy-Arie's Bulgarian grandmother Hilda are also perfect for a Shavuot meal.

I like to borrow from both holiday traditions—the connection to the land and cooking with dairy—and make the most of the fleeting season. I invite friends to a picnic, bring fruit that has just arrived at the farmers' market, and bake a cheesecake. Summer is almost here.

The Queen of Our Shavuot Table

Alon Hadar

Cooking for Shavuot with my grandmother Rachel in Jerusalem when
I was growing up is something I'll never forget. When Kurdish Jews
like our family came to Israel, they tried to rebuild our community and
keep our culture alive. Every year, on the day before the spring holiday,
my grandmother would join other Kurdish women in a friend's garden
in her Jerusalem neighborhood. Together they would build a fire and
take part of an old water heater, beating it with hammers to shape it
into a saj, an upside-down dome they placed over the fire and used as
a griddle. They always did this without any help from the men, but as a
boy, I was allowed to tag along.

Each of the "grandmothers," as I like to think of them, brought two
bowls to the gathering, one with her homemade dough and one with a
mix of soft white cheeses for kadeh, a filled flatbread they knew from
home. They worked in tandem: one grandmother would split open the
dough and another would stuff it with cheese and put it on the saj. Still,
each grandmother's kadeh was different from those of her friends. They
all had their signature touches: one mixed eggs into her cheese, another

---

FAMILY JOURNEY

Iraq or Turkey → *Jerusalem* → *New York City*

Alon with his grandmother Rachel and
grandfather Nissim in Jerusalem, mid-1990s

added butter so it would be sweeter. My grandmother used cheese from
the small Galilean city Tzfat and some Bulgarian feta to give it a salty
punch. When the kadeh were ready, the grandmothers would put out the
fire and pack up their warm flatbreads in baskets to take home.

My grandmother served hers at our holiday lunch the next day
alongside jajic, a sauce made with yogurt and fresh herbs or purslane my
father foraged in the hills near Jerusalem. The table was always set with
a salad of fresh green almonds and another made with fakus, a local
heirloom vegetable similar to a cucumber that was just coming into
season. But the kadeh was always the queen of her table. In New York
City, it's still the queen of mine.

Chef and journalist **ALON HADAR**'s grandmother was born into a Kurdish family,
but no one knows exactly where—either in northern Iraq or in southwestern Turkey.
That information was lost to time, but the cooking traditions and a strong connection to
seasonal ingredients remained. Alon continues to draw inspiration from them for
his New York City–based catering company, Hamara by Alon Hadar.

283

Kadeh

Kurdish Cheese-and-Spinach-Stuffed Bread

As a child, Alon used to help his grandmother make the stuffed flatbreads called kadeh over a fire in Jerusalem. He's adapted the recipe, making the flatbreads a bit thicker and adding spinach to the cheese filling. His kadeh are substantial enough to be the centerpiece of a Shavuot meal, but they also pack up well for a picnic.

The cheese filling uses a combination of feta, chewy halloumi, and Armenian (sometimes called Syrian) string cheese. Typically sold in skeins studded with nigella seeds, the latter cheese can easily be pulled apart into tender strings, which are then chopped into small pieces for the filling.

Alon suggests baking the kadeh a few at a time on a preheated baking stone or baking sheet. This helps preserve the high heat of the oven, allowing the breads to puff and develop a light texture. *(Pictured on page 284)*

MAKES about 20 stuffed flatbreads

FOR THE DOUGH

6½ cups plus 2 tablespoons (860 g) white bread flour

¾ cup (95 g) whole wheat flour

2½ cups (600 ml) cold water

¼ cup (60 ml) extra-virgin olive oil, plus more for greasing

3½ tablespoons sugar

2½ tablespoons kosher salt

1 tablespoon (8 g) active dry yeast

FOR THE FILLING AND ASSEMBLY

1½ pounds (675 g) baby spinach

1½ tablespoons kosher salt

2 cups (9 ounces/260 g) crumbled feta cheese

¾ cup (90 g) small pieces Armenian or Syrian string cheese

¾ cup (115 g) chopped halloumi cheese

White bread flour for rolling and dusting

3 tablespoons extra-virgin olive oil

2 tablespoons nigella seeds

MAKE THE DOUGH: Put the bread flour, whole wheat flour, water, olive oil, sugar, salt, and yeast in the bowl of a stand mixer fitted with a dough hook. Blend the ingredients for a minute or so on low speed and then knead for 15 minutes, or until a smooth dough forms.

Grease a large bowl with olive oil and transfer the dough to the bowl, turning it to coat it with oil. Cover the bowl with plastic wrap and let the dough rest in a warm place until doubled in size, about 1½ hours. (Alternatively, let the dough rise in the refrigerator until doubled, about 24 hours.)

WHILE THE DOUGH RISES, MAKE THE FILLING: Put the spinach in a large bowl and sprinkle with the salt. Massage the spinach with your hands for 1 to 2 minutes, until it wilts and releases some liquid, then set aside for 20 minutes.

Squeeze out the excess liquid from the spinach, transfer it to a cutting board, and chop it roughly. Return the spinach to the bowl and add the feta, string cheese, and halloumi. Stir until the mixture is well combined and set aside.

When the dough is ready, transfer it to a lightly oiled surface and divide it into about 20 equal pieces, about 3 ounces (80 grams) each.

Arrange the pieces of dough 1 inch (2.5 cm) apart on an oiled baking sheet, cover with plastic wrap, and let rest for 20 minutes.

Preheat the oven to 475°F (245°C) and place a pizza stone on the middle rack of the oven, if you have one. Alternatively, cover the underside of a baking sheet with aluminum foil and place it on the middle rack of the oven, upside down.

ASSEMBLE THE KADEH: Lightly flour the work surface. Roll 1 piece of dough into a 6- to 7-inch (15 to 17.5 cm) round. Put 2 heaping tablespoons of the spinach filling onto the lower half of the dough, leaving a ½-inch (1.25 cm) border around the edges. Brush a bit of water along the edges of the dough. Fold the dough over the filling, creating a half-moon shape, and seal the edges, pressing down firmly with your fingers. Crimp the edges decoratively by pressing dimples into them with your index finger, then prick the dough all over with a fork. Repeat with another 2 or 3 pieces of dough.

Put the first few kadeh on the preheated pizza stone or baking pan and continue making more kadeh a few at a time, rolling and stuffing them as the first batches bake. Bake the kadeh until golden and baked through, 8 to 10 minutes (you may need to test the baking time by cutting into one of the breads). Take the kadeh out of the oven and place on a wire rack, then immediately brush the tops of the kadeh with olive oil and sprinkle with nigella seeds. Cover the baked kadeh loosely with a cloth to keep warm as you bake the rest. Repeat until you've assembled and baked all the kadeh.

Serve warm.

Jajic
Yogurt and Purslane Dip

Alon's grandfather used to make this creamy dip on Saturday mornings to enjoy with pita and olive oil. His family also serves it on Shavuot with kadeh (opposite).

Similar to Greek tzatziki, jajic is made with a yogurt base and features cucumbers or other vegetables, or herbs. Alon's recipe mixes in purslane, which his family used to forage. The succulent herb grows wild, often in ordinary backyards, and can be found at farmers' markets. The small rounded leaves, which are fleshy with a tart, almost salty flavor, are excellent chopped for a seasoning or used whole in salads. *(Pictured on page 285)*

MAKES 6 to 8 servings

1 cup (250 g) plain whole-milk yogurt

¼ cup (60 g) sour cream

3 scallions, white and light green parts, finely chopped

¼ cup (40 g) finely chopped purslane or watercress

1 teaspoon kosher salt

¼ teaspoon freshly ground black pepper

Stir all the ingredients together in a bowl until well combined. Let sit for about 20 minutes for the flavors to marry before serving.

A Holiday Parade of Tractors, Babies, and First Fruits

SHARED BY
Hila Alpert

I was born in 1965 and grew up only seeing my parents in the early evenings and on weekends. I never slept in their home; instead, I shared a bedroom with three other kids in our kibbutz's communal children's home. Everything on the kibbutz was shared. The only thing I had of my own was a little bedside table I could put a few secrets in, like little mushroom-shaped containers of Israeli Sweet'N Low that I stole when I was five years old. When it was time for a new shirt, we could choose between brown or blue. Once, as I waited my turn, they ran out of blue shirts, so it became a choice between a brown shirt with or without tears. That was as much personal taste and individual choice as kibbutz life allowed for.

We ate breakfast and lunch in the children's house and we had to finish whatever they put on our plates—most of the people on our kibbutz had survived the Holocaust. We were taught to never waste food: you ate to get stronger, to build the country. What made me a cook was my Moroccan grandmother, who lived nearby. She used to tell me, "Sweetheart, if you don't like it, don't eat it. Your body is not a garbage can." This was the opposite of the thinking on the kibbutz.

FAMILY JOURNEY

Kibbutz Ma'ale HaHamisha, Israel → *Tel Aviv*

Members of Kibbutz Ma'ale HaHamisha, including Hila,
her father, and her brother, celebrating Shavuot, 1970s

They didn't encourage us to have our own tastes, but creativity was highly valued, as was a do-it-yourself attitude. You really saw this on Shavuot. This was the holiday that everyone took part in—it was our way to celebrate ourselves and our agricultural community. I remember, even as a little girl, the pride and excitement we all felt leading up to the holiday, women and men, young and old, all of us.

We would decorate our tractors with colorful paper cutouts and flowers for a parade. It was amazing to see how much creativity and effort we all put into it—you wanted your tractor to be the most beautiful one. Kibbutz members who tended to the cows brought the new calves to the parade, and those who worked in chicken coops brought the chicks. Farmers harvested the first fruits of the season, and babies born during the past year would be dressed in white clothes and given flower crowns. There was always music, and my friends and I joined in the folk dancing.

We thought we were the gods of the land. It was an amazing and beautiful thing to see. I remember the excitement—it's still alive in me.

HILA ALPERT is a celebrated Israeli food writer and TV presenter who grew up celebrating Shavuot in the kibbutz movement, where the holiday is deeply tied to its agricultural roots as a harvest festival.

HILA ALPERT'S SHAVUOT

Lali Salad
*Cherry, Chile, and
Cilantro Salad*
292

Phyllo Bundles with Feta,
Honey, and Black Pepper
292

Calsones
*Fresh Pasta Filled
with Cheese*
293

—Serve with—

fresh seasonal fruit

Lali Salad

Cherry, Chile, and Cilantro Salad

In Israel, this salad is a culinary icon, made popular by Habasta, a restaurant tucked into Tel Aviv's Carmel Market. The recipe originated with Hila and is called the "Lali" salad after her nickname. She grew up on a kibbutz that was one of the first in Israel to grow sweet cherries. She remembers hiding behind the leaves while harvesting them so that no one would see her as she devoured the cherries straight from the branch.

Jalapeños provide a spicy contrast to the sweetness of the cherries; taste yours before you add them to the salad to check their heat level, and then use however much of a kick you want. *(Pictured on page 291)*

MAKES 6 to 8 servings

1½ pounds (675 g) fresh sweet cherries, pitted

2 cups (60 g) chopped fresh cilantro

3 to 4 jalapeños, cored, seeded, and thinly sliced

3 or 4 garlic cloves, finely chopped

1 tablespoon kosher salt

¼ cup (60 ml) extra-virgin olive oil

Put the cherries, cilantro, jalapeños, garlic, salt, and olive oil in a large bowl and stir well until all the ingredients are evenly distributed. Chill until refreshingly cold.

Serve the salad chilled.

Phyllo Bundles with Feta, Honey, and Black Pepper

It's customary on Shavuot to eat dairy-rich foods like cheesecake, cheese-filled calsones (opposite), and blintzes. These bundles are perfect for the holiday or a weekend brunch: salty feta, crispy phyllo, and a good amount of black pepper play off the sweetness of honey.

Working with phyllo dough requires a bit of planning. To defrost it properly, transfer it to the refrigerator the night before. The next day, leave it at room temperature for an hour or two before you start preparing the recipe. Because packages of feta come in various shapes and weights, a precise measurement isn't possible here, but the end goal for these pastries is to have a "tile" of feta that's about 1¾ inches (4.5 cm) square and about ½ inch (1.25 cm) thick. You can join more than one piece of feta together as necessary, since the cheese won't be visible inside the pastry. You'll have plenty of phyllo sheets from one package, so increase the recipe if you like, to make as many bundles as you have feta for . . . and guests. *(Pictured on page 290)*

MAKES 8 bundles

6 sheets fresh or frozen phyllo (defrost the package of dough overnight in the refrigerator; see headnote)

6 tablespoons (90 g) salted butter, melted

1 pound (450 g) full-fat feta cheese, cut into 1¾-inch (4.5 cm) squares or into pieces that will make squares of this size (see headnote)

6 tablespoons (125 g) honey

1 teaspoon freshly ground black pepper

Preheat the oven to 375°F (190°C).

Cut each phyllo sheet crosswise into 3 equal strips, to make 18 wide strips. Keep the phyllo covered with a clean cloth or sheet of plastic as you work to prevent it from drying out, which it will do quickly.

Lay one phyllo strip horizontally in front of you on the work surface and brush it with melted butter. Place a second strip of phyllo vertically across the center of the first strip, forming a cross. Brush the second strip with melted butter.

Place a square of feta approximately 1¾ inches (4.5 cm) across and ½ inch (1.25 cm) thick on the center of the two layered phyllo strips, fitting two or more smaller pieces of cheese together if necessary to form the square.

Fold the right side of the bottom phyllo strip over, covering the cheese. Brush it lightly with butter. Fold the bottom of the second strip of phyllo up over the cheese and brush it lightly with butter. Fold the left side of the bottom phyllo strip over the center and brush it lightly with butter, then fold the top of the second strip of phyllo over onto the center of the phyllo bundle. Repeat until there is no remaining unfolded phyllo and you have a neat bundle.

Brush any unbuttered spots with butter and place the bundle seam side down on a baking sheet. Repeat with the remaining phyllo strips and feta (you'll have 2 phyllo strips left over; you can discard these, or reserve them for another use).

Bake until the phyllo bundles are golden brown, 15 to 20 minutes. Remove from the oven.

Arrange the phyllo bundles on a serving platter and drizzle the honey over them, then sprinkle with the pepper. Serve immediately, while the cheese is warm and the pastry is crisp.

Calsones
Fresh Pasta Filled with Cheese

A popular dish in the Syrian Jewish community, these cheese-filled calsones originated in the Kingdom of Naples and moved east in the sixteenth century when Jews were expelled from there. It later came with Syrian Jews to Jerusalem and the northern Israeli cities Tzfat and Tiberias. Here, calsones are mainly eaten on Shavuot. Each city and cook has their own subtle differences in the way they make them, explains Hila. Some add baking powder or more eggs, "but everyone is careful about the filling, which must include the hard Tzfatit cheese," she adds.

Hila cuts the Tzfatit cheese (named for the city Tzfat) with a creamier local cheese. A mix of feta and farmer's cheese works wonderfully as a substitute. *(Pictured on pages 294–295)*

MAKES 8 servings (about 200 small dumplings, fewer if rolling the dough by hand)

FOR THE DOUGH

1 teaspoon kosher salt

1 cup (240 ml) boiling water

3½ cups (455 g) all-purpose flour, plus more for dusting

1 large egg yolk

FOR THE FILLING

2 cups (280 g) sheep's-milk feta, crumbled, or Tzfatit cheese, finely grated or crumbled

2 cups farmer's cheese (300 g) or Tuv Taam cheese, crumbled

2 large egg yolks

5 tablespoons (75 g) unsalted butter, cut in small pieces

½ cup (50 g) grated Parmesan or Tzfatit cheese

recipe continues

MAKE THE DOUGH: Stir the salt into the boiling water until dissolved and then pour the water into a medium bowl.

Add 1 cup (130 g) of the flour and the egg yolk and stir until blended, then add another 1 cup (130 g) flour and stir to make a very wet, shaggy dough.

Transfer the dough to a lightly floured work surface, sprinkle on a bit more flour, and start kneading, continuing to add flour and knead until you have a soft, smooth, flexible dough. You should use all or almost all of the 3½ cups

(455 g) flour. Wrap the dough in plastic and let it rest in the refrigerator for at least 2 hours and up to overnight.

MAKE THE FILLING: Meanwhile, stir together the feta, farmer's cheese, and egg yolks and set aside in the refrigerator.

After the dough has rested, cut it into 8 pieces. Lightly sprinkle flour on one piece of dough, keeping the others covered, and roll it out with a pasta machine until just barely translucent (on many pasta machines, this will be the second-thinnest setting). You can also use a rolling pin,

rolling as thin as you can, aiming for the dough to be translucent and very thin; you will end up with fewer calsones.

1. Using a 2½-inch (6 cm) cookie cutter or small glass, stamp out rounds; you should have about 12 rounds. Gather the scraps, reroll them, and stamp out another 12 or so rounds.

2–3. Place a heaping ½ teaspoon of the filling in the center of each round. **4.** Fold the round in half to make a half-moon, and press the edges firmly to seal.

Lightly dust a baking sheet with flour and set the calsones on the sheet, keeping them as separate as possible so they don't stick to each other.

Continue with the rest of the dough, keeping the dough and the rounds covered so they don't dry out as you work.

Bring a large pot of salted water to a boil and add the calsones. Boil until the calsones are tender (they should float to the top, but be sure to test by tasting), 1 to 3 minutes depending on the thickness of your dough, and then scoop out with a slotted spoon, and transfer to a large baking dish. You may want to boil the calsones in batches and use two baking dishes.

Heat the broiler. Dot the tops of the calsones with the butter and sprinkle with the Parmesan. Broil until the surface is lightly browned and a few dumpling edges are crisp, about 5 minutes. Serve right away.

The Bulgarian Grandmother with the Golden Touch

SHARED BY
Ron Levy-Arie

Friday lunch was my grandmother Hilda's meal. We would drive to her home on Yosef Eliyahu Street in Tel Aviv for a multicourse feast served on her best plates with fancy silverware. I always tried to sit up straight in my chair out of respect for the occasion. Every week, her elegant table was dotted with Bulgarian and Sephardi delicacies like a rich cheese and egg pie, lots of salads, and sometimes bowls of cold yogurt soup, but she had a few aces she liked to draw occasionally, like chushki burek, little red peppers stuffed with cheese that she coated in flour and fried until golden.

She grew up in the well-off Arie family in the Bulgarian city of Plovdiv and fled to Tel Aviv in the early 1940s to escape the war. Some of the recipes from her community are more than five hundred years old, predating the Spanish Inquisition and the Sephardi migration to the Ottoman Empire, and others were adopted from the Ottomans. But when she married my grandfather, Hilda couldn't even fry an egg. After she remarried in the late 1960s to Sam Dormont, Hilda became a painter and an archaeological restorer and seemed to have magical hands.

FAMILY JOURNEY

Plovdiv, Bulgaria and Izmir, Turkey → Tel Aviv

Ron's grandmother Hilda in Tel Aviv,
late 1940s

Everything she touched turned to gold, including food, once she started cooking. By the time I was growing up, she was making her own pickles, jams, and pastries.

I went to an arts high school near her home and spent almost every afternoon with her. I would stop by to have lunch, talk, and watch her cook, absorbing what I could—I've always loved the kitchen. When I started cooking as a young adult, I would call her constantly to ask questions about the ingredients or check that I was using the right kind of oil. After years of practice, I finally invited her for a meal—and waited for her reaction. She fully endorsed it.

When I make her recipes today, I listen to Ottoman songs and women's choirs from Bulgaria, think of her, and hope that I inherited her golden touch.

RON LEVY-ARIE's life is steeped in music: he is a DJ and a producer of reggae festivals and concerts in Israel, and, along with his wife, he designs record covers and music posters. He is also a gifted cook who hosts pop-up dinners at cafés and restaurants in Tel Aviv. His grandmother's cheese- and butter-filled recipes are a wonderful fit for Shavuot, when it's customary to eat dairy.

RON LEVY-ARIE'S SHAVUOT

Chushki Burek
*Roasted Peppers
Stuffed with Cheese*
300

Handrajo
*Eggplant, Onion,
and Tomato Pastries*
301

"Dunce Pie"
Cheese Soufflé
303

—Serve with—

fresh fruit, chopped salad,
pickles

Chushki Burek

Roasted Peppers Stuffed with Cheese

Ron likes to use chuska peppers, a long, sweet Bulgarian variety, for this recipe from his grandmother Hilda. If you can't find them, use another small sweet pepper, such as mini bell peppers, pimentos, red Cubanelles, or Lipsticks.

Depending on the size and shape of your peppers, you may have a bit of cheese filling left over. It will last in the refrigerator for a couple of days; use it as the filling for an omelet or in a frittata. *(Pictured on page 299)*

MAKES 6 to 8 servings; 12 to 16 stuffed peppers, depending on variety

12 to 16 small sweet red peppers

1 cup (about 4 ounces/120 g) crumbled sheep's-milk cheese packed in brine, such as Bulgarian cheese or feta (Valbreso is a good choice)

⅓ cup (85 g) farmer's cheese or cream cheese

½ cup (60 g) grated kashkaval or kasseri cheese (use the small holes of a box grater)

2 tablespoons ricotta cheese

¼ cup (25 g) grated Parmesan cheese (optional)

2 large eggs

Pinch each of kosher salt and freshly ground black pepper

About 1 cup (130 g) all-purpose flour for coating

Canola oil for shallow-frying

1 tablespoon unsalted butter

1 garlic clove

ROAST THE PEPPERS: Preheat the broiler. Place the peppers on a baking sheet and broil 2 to 3 inches (5 to 7.5 cm) from the heating element, turning them occasionally, until wrinkled and charred, 10 to 15 minutes. Remove the peppers from the broiler, transfer to a bowl, cover with foil or plastic wrap, and let cool.

When the peppers are completely cool, peel away the skins as delicately as possible. Cut a vertical slit in each pepper and remove the core and seeds, keeping the peppers intact, ideally with the stems. (Don't be tempted to rinse the peppers as you peel them, which would wash away flavorful juices.)

Put the sheep's-milk cheese, farmer's cheese, kashkaval, ricotta, and Parmesan, if using, in a medium bowl and stir to blend thoroughly.

Beat the eggs with the salt and pepper in a shallow bowl. Put a mound of flour on a plate. Line another plate or small tray with paper towels.

Gently coat one pepper on all sides with flour, shaking off any excess. Place a heaping teaspoon (or two, depending on the size of your pepper) of filling into the pepper and very gently wrap the pepper around it to close. Generously flour the pepper again and place on a plate or wire rack. Repeat with the remaining peppers.

Fill a large deep skillet or wide saucepan with ¼ inch (6 mm) of oil and heat over medium-high heat. Add the butter and garlic clove. When the garlic begins to sizzle, dip one of the stuffed peppers in the beaten eggs, gently turning to coat on all sides, and carefully place it in the hot oil. Repeat with a few more stuffed peppers, being careful not to overcrowd the pan; you'll probably need to cook the peppers in two or more batches. Reduce the heat to medium; the peppers should sizzle and the oil should form small bubbles around them. Turn the peppers gently after 2 minutes, and then again after 2 more minutes. After another 2 minutes, so the peppers have fried on three sides, for a total of 6 minutes, carefully remove them from the pan and place on the plate lined with paper towels.

Serve the peppers immediately, while the coating is still crisp.

Handrajo
Eggplant, Onion, and Tomato Pastries

In Ladino, *handrajo* means "rag," but it's also the name of a vegetable ragu filling (gomo de handrajo) for savory pastries. In Ron's family, they call these log-shaped flaky pastries by the same name. Don't let it scare you off from trying the recipe from his aunt Ketty, which pairs perfectly with his grandmother Hilda's dishes from the other side of the family.

Be sure to allow enough time for the frozen puff pastry to defrost in the refrigerator—at least 6 to 8 hours or overnight. The filling is also best when made a few hours or a day ahead so it has plenty of time to cool. Once the filling is made and the dough has defrosted, shaping the pastries is simple. *(Pictured on page 302)*

MAKES 4 long pastries; 16 slices

⅓ cup (80 ml) extra-virgin olive oil

1¼ pounds (560 g) eggplant (about 2 medium), peeled and cut into ½-inch (1.25 cm) cubes

2 teaspoons kosher salt

12 ounces (340 g) onions (about 2 medium), finely chopped

2 large garlic cloves, finely chopped

1 pound (450 g) tomatoes (about 3 large), halved and grated on a box grater, skin discarded

2 teaspoons sweet paprika, or more to taste

1½ teaspoons sugar

½ teaspoon freshly ground black pepper

2 sheets puff pastry (18 ounces/500 g), preferably butter-based, thawed in the fridge for 6 to 8 hours or overnight

1 large egg, whisked

Sour cream for serving (optional)

Heat the olive oil in a large sauté pan (with a lid) over high heat. Add the eggplant cubes, spreading them into an even layer, season with the salt, and cook undisturbed for 5 minutes, or until the eggplant starts to brown.

Add the onions and garlic and stir to combine. Cover the pan, reduce the heat to medium, and cook until the eggplant, onions, and garlic are soft (taking care not to burn the garlic), about 10 minutes.

Remove the lid and cook to reduce and thicken the vegetable juices a bit, about 5 minutes.

Stir in the tomatoes, paprika, sugar, and pepper and cook until the mixture is thick and nicely blended, 5 to 10 minutes, depending on how juicy your tomatoes are, stirring and scraping the bottom of the pan occasionally to prevent sticking. Taste and add more salt, pepper, and paprika if needed. Remove the pan from the heat and cool the mixture completely.

When you're ready to assemble and bake the pastries, preheat the oven to 425°F (220°C). Line two baking sheets with parchment paper.

Place one sheet of the puff pastry on a lightly dusted work surface and roll it to a 10-by-14-inch (25 by 35 cm) rectangle, with a short side closest to you. Trim any uneven edges. Cut the sheet lengthwise in half, so you have two

5-by-14-inch (12.5 by 35 cm) rectangles. Arrange the pastry strips on one of the prepared baking sheets. Repeat with the second sheet of puff pastry and arrange on the second baking sheet. Set a small bowl of cool water nearby.

Divide half the filling evenly between the 2 pastry strips on the first baking sheet, spreading it from top to bottom along half of the width of each rectangle, leaving just less than an inch (2.5 cm) of empty border around it. Dip your finger in the water and moisten the borders to help seal the pastry. Gently fold the other half of the dough over the filling on each strip, bringing the edges of the pastry together neatly, to make a 2½-by-14-inch (6.25 by 35 cm) rectangle. Using a fork, press the edges of the rectangles to seal the pastry. With a sharp knife, cut slits in the pastry every few inches to create steam vents. If necessary, reposition the pastries so they are evenly spaced on the baking sheet, and repeat with the remaining pastry strips and filling.

Brush the pastries with the whisked egg and bake until well browned and crisped, 25 to 30 minutes. Transfer to a wire rack and cool for about 10 minutes.

Cut each strip into portions on the diagonal and serve slightly warm or at room temperature, with sour cream on the side, if desired.

"Dunce Pie"
Cheese Soufflé

Ron's grandmother used to call this soufflé-like cheese pie a dunce or fool's pie, because it's so simple anyone can make it. Rubbing the inside of the baking dish with a halved garlic clove adds a subtle hint of it to the otherwise all-cheese flavor. Kashkaval, a semi-hard cheese made from cow's and/or sheep's milk, is popular in Eastern European and Mediterranean cooking, but it may not be easy to find here. Greek kasseri, Italian caciocavallo, and even provolone are all good substitutes for this recipe.

MAKES 8 servings

1 garlic clove, unpeeled, halved lengthwise

1 tablespoon unsalted butter, at room temperature

2 tablespoons all-purpose flour

4 large eggs

¾ cup (200 g) sour cream

1 cup (240 ml) heavy cream

3 cups (10½ ounces/300 g) grated kashkaval cheese (see headnote; use the large holes of a box grater)

Position a rack in the middle of the oven with plenty of space above it so the pie can rise, and preheat the oven to 425°F (220°C). Rub the inside of a 2-quart (2 L) baking dish with the halved garlic clove, going over the entire surface of the dish a few times to release the garlic flavor. Grease the dish with the butter, sprinkle in the flour, and turn and shake the dish to coat the interior with the flour, tapping out any excess.

Put the eggs, sour cream, and heavy cream in a large bowl and whisk vigorously to blend until uniform. Gently fold in the cheese until evenly combined.

Pour the mixture into the baking dish and smooth the top. Bake until the pie is puffed and golden and the center is set and just barely firm to the touch, 30 to 40 minutes.

Remove from the oven and serve immediately. The pie will puff up in the oven but collapse shortly after you take it out.

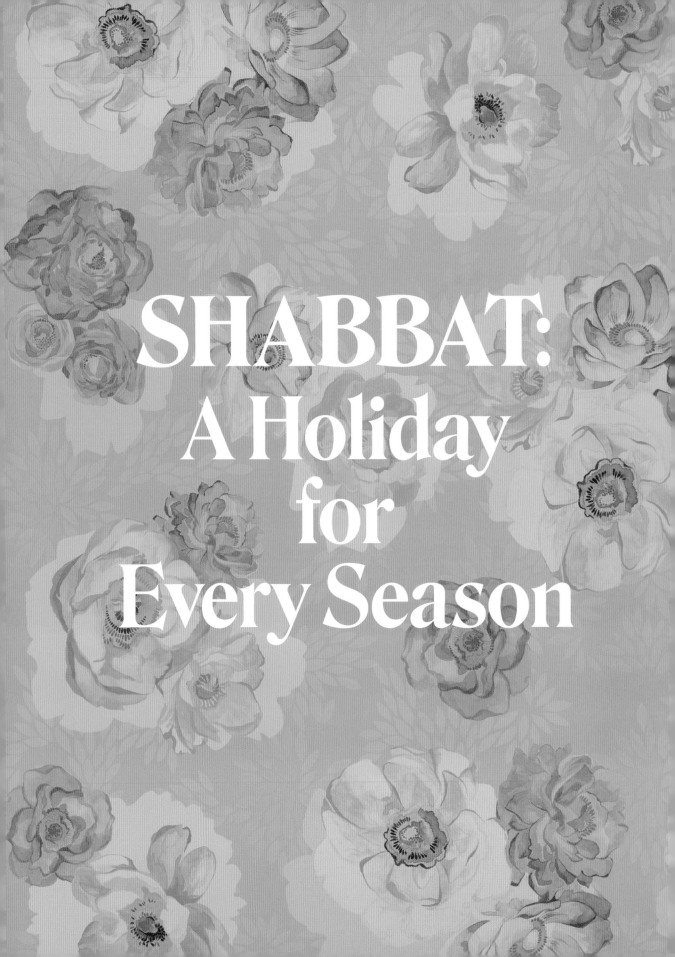

SHABBAT:
A Holiday
for
Every Season

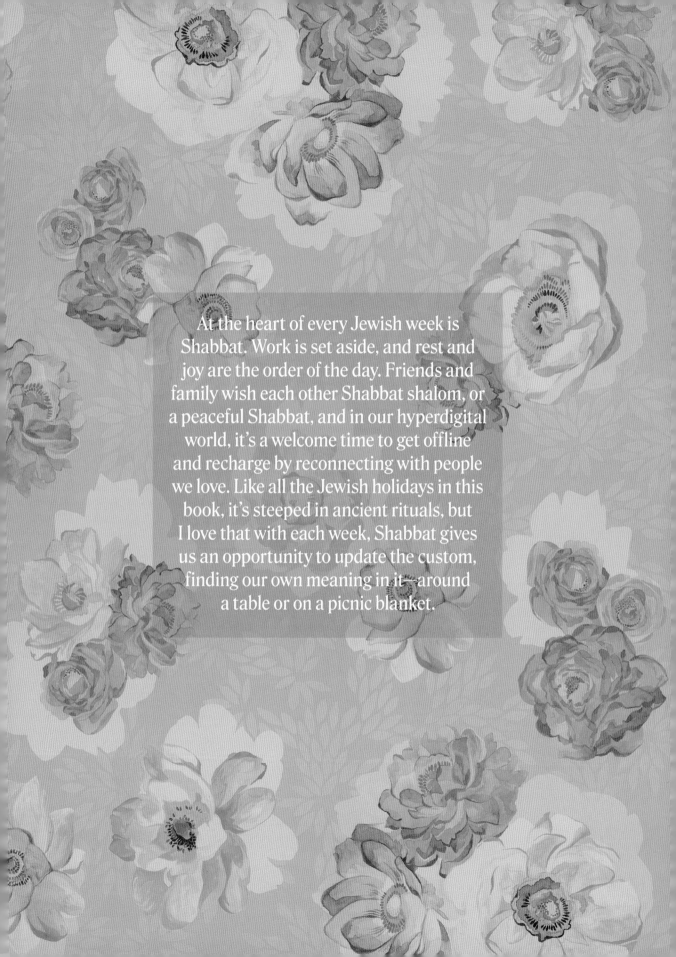

At the heart of every Jewish week is Shabbat. Work is set aside, and rest and joy are the order of the day. Friends and family wish each other Shabbat shalom, or a peaceful Shabbat, and in our hyperdigital world, it's a welcome time to get offline and recharge by reconnecting with people we love. Like all the Jewish holidays in this book, it's steeped in ancient rituals, but I love that with each week, Shabbat gives us an opportunity to update the custom, finding our own meaning in it—around a table or on a picnic blanket.

IN JEWISH LIFE, everything pauses for Shabbat, from sunset on Friday until there are three stars in the sky on Saturday night. It's a time when work is set aside, prayers are recited in observant communities, families and friends gather, and people recharge before the next week starts. Its roots can be traced to Genesis, when God worked for six days to create the heavens and the Earth and rested on the seventh day.

Preparations often start well before the holiday, with some cooks serving simple dishes on Thursdays so they can turn their attention to cooking for Shabbat. When my friend Idan Cohen was growing up in Israel, Friday afternoons were a time for his family to get together for cakes and coffee, a tradition that his great-grandparents brought with them when they left Berlin in 1933 (see page 330).

By Friday evening, or *erev Shabbat* in Hebrew, a calm and special atmosphere sets in at the homes of Jewish families who celebrate around the world. During World War II, Anna Polonsky's grandparents fought in the Resistance and lost relatives in Auschwitz. Those who survived had no interest in religion, but when Anna wanted to explore her roots as a teenager in Paris, her family started hosting Friday night dinners (see page 350).

In religious homes, thirty-nine categories of labor called melachot in Hebrew are forbidden during Shabbat, including plowing, writing, and cooking—a considerable challenge when the holiday is meant to be celebrated with lavish meals. From this came a hallmark of Jewish food: an entire category of recipes where time is the key ingredient.

The most famous of these are hearty dishes like cholent, t'bit, and adafina (also spelled *dafina*, and several other ways, depending on the community) that gently simmer or are kept warm overnight. In some parts of the world, pots of these Shabbat dishes were traditionally dropped off on Fridays at communal ovens still hot from baking loaves for the holiday, and picked up on Saturday after morning prayers.

Each of these is far more than the sum of its parts and a reflection of where the cook's family is from and the ingredients they had to work with. Sometime after Esther Serruya Weyl's community emigrated from Morocco to northern Brazil in the late nineteenth century, they replaced chickpeas with flour dumplings called café de massa in their dafina (see page 380).

While Shabbat meals traditionally were the most luxurious ones a family would eat all week, there's a resourcefulness to this cooking, too. In Iraqi homes, whole eggs are often tucked into pots of t'bit, spiced rice and chicken that's served at Shabbat lunch. In the morning, the eggs are fished out and enjoyed as part of a breakfast spread along with fried eggplant, tahini, and amba. Today, when those ingredients are stuffed into a pita, they are known as sabich. For Tami Shem-Tov, whose father shared a name with the dish, sabich is a reminder to be proud of your roots (see page 364).

On Shabbat, there's always bread on the table. Traditionally two loaves are served, referencing the double portion of manna the Israelites miraculously received for Shabbat as they wandered the desert for forty years. While challah (page 313) is the best known, there are others, like dabo, which Beejhy Barhany's community made for Shabbat as they walked for months from Ethiopia to Sudan on their journey to Israel (see page 342). There are also Yemenite breads like jachnun and kubaneh that are kept in the oven for hours and served for Saturday lunch.

There's such an incredible diversity in Shabbat tables around the world and so many ways to celebrate. Each week, it offers us an opportunity to interpret tradition and make it our own.

Shabbat Picnics and Living Jewishly

SHARED BY
Naama Shefi

I grew up celebrating Shabbat with hundreds of people every week on Kibbutz Givat HaShlosha. Everyone dressed up in their best clothes and walked with their families to the communal dining hall for a special meal on Friday evening at 7 p.m. There was no religious ceremony, but the gathering was sacred. We lingered over fruit compote for dessert and wandered outside after the meal to sit on the grass with our friends.

In Israel, no matter how religiously observant or secular you are, the atmospheric shift on Fridays is inescapable. A tranquil festivity reverberates throughout the country as everyone gets ready to host or head off to a Shabbat dinner—often with many generations sitting around the table, catching up on their weeks and sharing their lives.

In New York City, where I live now with my husband, Ilan, and our daughter, Ella, life rarely slows down, but I always make space for Shabbat and try to re-create the sense of community in my own way. I feel lucky to have friends who make New York a home, and we often spend Shabbat together—taking our time over the meal and drinking wine while the kids run around high on sugar.

FAMILY JOURNEY

Kibbutz Givat HaShlosha → *Tel Aviv* → *New York City*

Enjoying gefilte fish since 1985

My menu is inspired by my Friday morning walks through the farmers' market and by the Jewish Food Society archive, with dishes like seasonal salads, spinach fritters, cured fish, and challah I bake with Ella. Sometimes I add my mom's two signature recipes: a zucchini casserole and a frozen chocolate dessert. The menu is always changing, and while I love to cook, sometimes Shabbat dinner is as simple as chicken schnitzel and roasted potatoes. There's really only one rule: a meal made from scratch.

Shabbat meals don't need to be formal to feel special. When the weather is nice, I turn dinner into a picnic and lay a blanket down on the grass next to my apartment building on the Lower East Side or in one of the city's many parks.

The food is delicious, but it's the acts of gathering and connecting that are most precious to me. Every week, Shabbat reminds me that celebrations are always in season.

The author of this book, **NAAMA SHEFI** is the founder and executive director of the Jewish Food Society and the founder of Asif: Culinary Institute of Israel.

NAAMA SHEFI'S SHABBAT

Challah
313

**Eggplant Salad with
Garlic and Parsley**
314

Quick Matbucha
Moroccan Tomato Salad
317

Spinach Rissoles
Spinach Fritters
320

Preserved Fish
323

Zucchini Pashtida
Zucchini Casserole
324

Herby Potato Salad
326

Naknik Shokolad
Chocolate "Salami"
329

—Serve with—
fresh fruit,
cheese plate,
olives and pickles,
anchovies

Challah

I learned to make this challah from my good friend Uri Scheft, who is a genius baker and the owner of Lehamim bakery in Tel Aviv. Our families often travel together, so I've seen Uri bake challahs in Tuscany, on the Greek island of Andros, in Mexico City, and, of course, in New York City and Tel Aviv. It's amazing to see him at work—he has such a way with dough.

I often make this recipe, adapted from his book *Breaking Breads*, with my daughter, Ella, on Fridays for our Shabbat dinner. I like that it makes three loaves (or two loaves and some rolls), so I can give one to a neighbor. It's also great left over, used for avocado toast or French toast, or turned into breadcrumbs for schnitzel.

I asked Uri if he had any crucial tips to share and he said less is more: knead the dough less and proof it less than you might expect, so you end up with loaves that are lighter and fluffier.

MAKES 3 loaves

FOR THE DOUGH

1⅔ cups (400 ml) cool water

1 tablespoon plus 1¾ teaspoons (15 g) active dry yeast

7¾ cups (1 kg) all-purpose flour, plus more for shaping

2 large eggs

½ cup (100 g) sugar

1 tablespoon kosher salt

5 tablespoons (75 ml) sunflower or other neutral oil, plus more for greasing the bowl

FOR THE EGG WASH AND FINISHING

1 large egg

1 tablespoon water

Pinch of kosher salt

¼ cup (35 g) sesame seeds

MAKE THE DOUGH: Put the water and yeast in the bowl of a stand mixer fitted with the dough hook and mix on low speed for a few seconds. Add the flour, eggs, sugar, salt, and oil and mix for about 3 minutes, until a dough forms.

Increase the speed to medium and mix the dough until it becomes smooth, about 5 minutes. Turn the dough out onto a lightly floured surface and knead it into a ball.

Lightly grease a large bowl with oil. Place the dough in the bowl and lightly grease the top of the dough ball. Cover loosely with a towel and set the bowl aside to proof at room temperature for about 45 minutes, or until the dough increases by about three-quarters.

SHAPE AND BRAID THE CHALLAH: Line two baking sheets with parchment paper. Turn the dough out onto a lightly floured surface and divide it into 3 equal pieces (if you have a scale, weigh each piece to be sure they're even). Divide each piece into 3 equal pieces.

Using your fingers, flatten each piece of dough into a rough rectangle about 5 by 7 inches (12.5 by 17.5 cm). Starting with a short side of the rectangle, roll the dough up tightly into a fat strand. Pinch the seams together and roll the dough under your hands into a 12-inch (30 cm) rope with tapered ends. Repeat with the remaining pieces.

Take 3 ropes of dough and place them vertically in front of you, side by side. Pinch the top ends of the ropes together and loosely braid them, bringing the left rope over the center one and then the right rope over what's now the center rope, continuing until you reach the end. Pinch the ends together to seal and tuck the ends under the loaf.

Transfer the challah to one of the parchment-lined baking sheets and repeat to make 2 more challahs; put two challahs on one baking sheet and the third one on its own sheet. Loosely cover the challahs with a towel and set aside to proof at room temperature until doubled in size, about 45 minutes.

Place the oven racks in the upper and lower thirds of the oven and preheat the oven to 425°F (220°C).

MAKE THE EGG WASH: In a small bowl, whisk the egg, water, and salt together. Gently brush the challahs with the egg wash, making sure to lightly cover all the strands and the edges. Sprinkle each challah generously with sesame seeds, making sure to get the sides again too.

Bake the challahs for 15 minutes, then rotate the pans front to back and top to bottom and continue baking until the challahs are golden and sound hollow when you tap them on the bottom, about 10 more minutes.

Remove the challahs from the oven, let cool to room temperature, and enjoy.

Eggplant Salad with Garlic and Parsley

My husband's grandmother Ketty was an extraordinary cook who helped inspire me to start the Jewish Food Society. Of all her recipes, this is the one that makes the most frequent appearance on my table, for both holidays and casual everyday meals. It's excellent served on its own as a salad or spread on top of a slice of challah.

The eggplants are roasted, but the tomatoes are left uncooked, so it's best to make this during the summer, when tomatoes are in season at the farmers' market. You want the roasted eggplant slices to fall apart as you mix the salad, so be sure they are fully cooked and tender all the way through. And while Ketty made this with simple white vinegar, I like to experiment with some of the artisanal ones I come across.

MAKES 6 to 8 servings

2 large eggplants (about 2 pounds/900 g), peeled in alternating vertical strips and cut into ½-inch (1.25 cm) rounds

Kosher salt

About ½ cup (120 ml) extra-virgin olive oil

Freshly ground black pepper

2 tablespoons white wine vinegar or Champagne vinegar

4 garlic cloves, grated or very finely chopped

2 medium tomatoes (about 8 ounces/225 g), cut into ¼-inch (6 mm) dice

¼ cup (15 g) finely chopped fresh flat-leaf parsley, plus more for garnish

Place the racks in the upper and lower thirds of the oven and preheat the oven to 350°F (175°C). Line two baking sheets with parchment paper.

Spread the eggplant slices on a tray and sprinkle them generously with salt. Set aside for at least 10 minutes, then wipe off the salt from the eggplants and pat the slices dry with a paper towel.

Pour the olive oil into a shallow bowl. Quickly dip both sides of each eggplant slice in the oil to coat (or brush on the oil with a pastry brush) and transfer to the baking sheets, arranging the slices in one layer. Season the slices on both sides with about 1 tablespoon salt and 1 teaspoon pepper.

Roast the eggplant for about 30 minutes. Flip the slices and continue roasting until they are a deep golden brown and fully tender, about 20 more minutes.

Remove from the oven and set the eggplant slices on a plate or tray to cool, stacking the slices and loosely covering them so they steam and continue to soften a bit.

When the eggplant is cool enough to handle, cut each slice into quarters and put in a large bowl.

Add the vinegar and garlic to the eggplant and stir to mix. Add the tomatoes and parsley and mix again, vigorously this time; you want the eggplant to break down into the texture of a coarse dip. Taste the salad and adjust the seasoning with more salt and pepper if needed.

Garnish the salad with parsley and serve.

Quick Matbucha
Moroccan Tomato Salad

I love matbucha, a spicy Moroccan tomato salad or dip that's a staple in Israel. It's great to have on hand and a perfect complement for challah (page 313). In classic recipes, the tomatoes simmer for hours, but as a working mom, I don't always have time for that. I learned this quicker version from my close friend Rinat Tzadok—see page 246 for her incredible Passover spread. Her version of matbucha uses cherry tomatoes, which means you can make it year-round. The amount of chile heat is up to you; for a milder matbucha, use a small Anaheim chile.

MAKES 6 to 8 servings

6 tablespoons (90 ml) neutral oil

6 to 8 garlic cloves, thinly sliced

3 cups (about 1 pound/450 g) cherry tomatoes, halved, juices reserved

1 or 2 small serrano chiles or other small hot fresh chiles, cored, seeded, and thinly sliced

1 teaspoon sweet paprika

¼ teaspoon sugar

Kosher salt and freshly ground black pepper

Heat the oil in a large skillet over medium heat. Add the garlic and cook until softened, 1 to 2 minutes; don't let the garlic brown.

Add the tomatoes and their juices, the chiles, paprika, and sugar and season generously with salt and pepper. Bring the mixture to a simmer, partially cover, and cook gently for 10 minutes.

Uncover and adjust the heat so the mixture continues to simmer nicely. Cook, stirring and scraping the bottom of the pan frequently so the tomatoes don't scorch, until the juices reduce and the matbucha becomes jammy, 15 to 20 minutes. Taste and adjust the seasoning with more salt and pepper if needed.

Remove from the heat and let cool. Serve the matbucha at room temperature.

Spinach Rissoles
Spinach Fritters

When I first launched the Jewish Food Society, my close friends Ofer and Ya'ara were incredibly supportive. They hosted a cooking session for the Society with Ofer's mom, Bracha Luft, who is a passionate cook. She was so excited to share her recipes and ones from her husband's Bulgarian family with the archive. I serve her fritters all the time: with dips and salads for a weeknight meal, at picnics, as dinner party appetizers, and for Rosh Hashanah and Hanukkah. My daughter and her friends love them too.

Bracha finishes the fritters in a quick sauce made with bouillon powder and lemon juice, but I like to spritz them with fresh lemon instead so they keep their crunch. It's best to use regular instead of baby spinach here, since it delivers more flavor and results in a better texture.

MAKES 6 to 8 servings; about 24 fritters

1 large bunch spinach (about 1 pound/450 g), stems trimmed off, leaves rinsed and dried

4 large eggs, lightly beaten

⅔ cup (85 g) all-purpose flour

⅔ cup (35 g) panko-style breadcrumbs

1 teaspoon kosher salt

¼ teaspoon freshly ground black pepper

Vegetable oil for shallow-frying

Lemon wedges for serving

Finely chop the spinach leaves; you should have about 7 lightly packed cups (340 g).

Put the spinach in a large bowl and add the eggs, flour, breadcrumbs, salt, and pepper. Stir vigorously to mix well, then let the mixture sit for about 5 minutes so the flour and crumbs can absorb the moisture.

Line a large platter with paper towels. Pour about ¼ inch (6 mm) of oil into a large skillet and heat over medium-high heat until hot. Using a large soup spoon, scoop up some of the spinach mixture and add it to the pan, patting it down with the spoon to make a small patty about 2 inches (5 cm) in diameter. Add a few more scoops, but don't crowd the pan. (If the first patty doesn't hold together in the pan, stir a few more breadcrumbs and another sprinkling of flour in the spinach mixture and try again.)

Fry the spinach fritters until lightly browned on the first side and starting to firm up a bit, 3 to 4 minutes. Carefully flip the fritters (they'll still be slightly fragile) and cook until the other side is browned in spots and the fritter feels cooked. The fritters won't become entirely browned; you'll see a few browned spots but you'll mostly see dark green spinach.

Transfer the fritters to the paper towel–lined platter and continue with the rest of the spinach mixture, scooping out any little bits that may burn from the pan and adding more oil as needed; let the new oil heat up before adding more of the fritter mixture.

Serve the fritters hot or at room temperature, with lemon wedges.

Preserved Fish

Sometimes I like to imagine that it's the turn of the twentieth century, herring is in vogue, and Jewish street peddlers are still selling pickles from barrels on the Lower East Side. To me, cured fish feels Jewish. This version from my friend Rinat (see page 244) looks fancy, but it is incredibly easy to make. I like to serve it on Shabbat, and I change the accompaniments often. Sometimes I finish the plate with sliced serrano pepper or tomato seeds, or I just serve the fish on its own with flaky salt.

The most important thing is to use the best fish you can find. I like to buy mine at the Union Square Greenmarket or at a fish market on the North Fork of Long Island. I typically use red snapper, but you can use another variety—just be sure it's incredibly fresh. You can flavor the fish by adding aromatics such as bay leaves or whole peppercorns to the oil in the jar, if you like.

MAKES 6 to 8 servings

½ cup (70 g) kosher salt

1 pound (450 g) skinless red snapper fillets

Extra-virgin olive oil

FOR SERVING

1 small serrano chile, cored, seeded, and thinly sliced

1 ripe tomato, halved

Fresh lemon juice (optional)

Flaky salt

Bread

Cover a plate generously with kosher salt. Lay the fish fillets on the salt and spread more salt over the top of the fish. Cover the plate and refrigerate for 25 minutes.

Fill a large bowl with ice water. Rinse the salted fish in the ice water and pat completely dry with paper towels.

Cut the fish into rectangular strips about ½ inch (1.25 cm) wide and 1½ to 2 inches (4 to 5 cm) long; your pieces will depend on the shape of your fish fillets.

Place the fish in a sterilized 1-pint (500 ml) mason jar or other glass container. Pour in enough olive oil to cover the fish.

To serve immediately, gently lift the fish pieces from the jar, letting the excess oil drain off, and arrange in one layer on a serving plate. Drizzle with olive oil, sprinkle with about 5 slices of serrano, and squeeze the juices and seeds of the tomato over the fish. Squeeze on a few drops of lemon juice, if using, sprinkle with flaky salt, and serve with bread.

To prepare in advance, seal the jar or container, place in the refrigerator, and let cure for up to 4 days. Let come to room temperature, then serve as above.

Zucchini Pashtida
Zucchini Casserole

Growing up on a kibbutz, I ate most of my meals in the communal dining hall, but sometimes my mom, Pnina, cooked for our family. She always tried to make something healthy, like this pashtida. Similar to a crustless quiche, pashtida is made with eggs, often mixed with vegetables and cottage cheese; in the 1980s, it was very of the moment in Israel. We've come a long way in terms of cooking since then, but this dish is still part of my family's repertoire.

I've adapted my mom's recipe a bit—and sometimes I like to swap some of the all-purpose flour for chickpea flour, which lends the dish a nutty quality. Be sure to choose slender, firm zucchini for the best texture. If your squash is a bit more mature and seedy, salt the slices for about 10 minutes and then wipe off the salt and pat them dry before using. The dish is best when the zucchini is sliced very thin, so use a mandoline if you have one.

MAKES 6 to 8 servings

Extra-virgin olive oil

2 tablespoons panko-style or regular dry breadcrumbs, plus more for the pan

1 large onion (about 10 ounces/280 g), finely chopped

1 to 1¼ pounds (450 to 560 g) zucchini (2 to 3 medium), sliced into thin rounds

Kosher salt

3 large eggs

¾ cup (190 g) plain whole-milk Greek yogurt

½ cup (50 g) plus 2 tablespoons finely grated hard cheese, such as Parmesan, kasseri, or kashkaval

¼ cup (60 ml) whole milk

¼ cup (30 g) all-purpose flour

Freshly ground black pepper

2 to 3 tablespoons chopped fresh dill or flat-leaf parsley, or a mix

Place a rack in the upper third of the oven and preheat the oven to 350°F (175°C). Grease a 9-inch (22.5 cm) pie pan with olive oil. Dust the pan with breadcrumbs and tap out any excess crumbs.

In a large skillet, heat 3 tablespoons olive oil over medium heat. Add the onion and cook, stirring occasionally, until very soft and fragrant, 8 to 10 minutes. Transfer the onion to a large plate or tray and set aside.

Increase the heat to medium-high, and if the pan seems dry, add another ½ tablespoon olive oil. Add the zucchini, sprinkle with salt, and sauté until the zucchini slices have softened a bit but are not completely cooked through, about 5 minutes. Transfer the zucchini to the plate with the onions and let cool for about 10 minutes.

In a large bowl, stir together the eggs, yogurt, the ½ cup (50 g) grated cheese, and the milk until smooth. Stir in the flour and season the mixture with 1 teaspoon salt and a few twists of black pepper. Fold in the dill, onion, and zucchini, mixing well.

Pour the mixture into the prepared pie pan, smoothing the surface so the zucchini slices lie flat. Sprinkle with the 2 tablespoons breadcrumbs and the remaining 2 tablespoons cheese.

Bake the pashtida until firm and golden brown, 55 to 65 minutes. If you like, turn on the broiler and cook for a few more minutes for a crispy golden-brown surface. Remove from the oven.

Let the pashtida cool for a few minutes before serving warm, or let cool completely and serve at room temperature.

Herby Potato Salad

My friend chef Peter Hoffman wrote a book called *What's Good? A Memoir in Fourteen Ingredients*, and I would often ask him that exact question when we ran into each other at the farmers' market. He taught me how to make this herby potato salad, which is vibrant and fresh. The trick is to lash the potatoes with a vinegary dressing while they are still warm so they absorb the flavor, and then to toss them with heaps of herbs.

Lovage is a leafy herb that has a delicate celery-like flavor. If you can't find it, you can chop some celery leaves or just use a bit more parsley, tarragon, and dill.

MAKES 6 to 8 servings

10 to 12 medium waxy potatoes (about 2 pounds/900 g), such as Nicola or Yukon Gold, peeled

Kosher salt

2 teaspoons Dijon mustard

2 tablespoons apple cider vinegar

2 tablespoons fresh lemon juice, or more to taste

3 tablespoons extra-virgin olive oil, or more to taste

1 cup (30 g) roughly chopped flat-leaf parsley

¼ cup (7 g) roughly chopped fresh lovage

¼ cup (7 g) roughly chopped fresh tarragon

1 tablespoon roughly chopped fresh dill

Herb flowers for garnish (optional)

Put the potatoes in a large saucepan, cover with water, salt the water generously, and bring to a boil. Boil the potatoes until they're easily pierced with a fork, about 20 minutes.

Drain the potatoes in a colander and run them under cold water for a few seconds. When they are cool enough to handle (but are still quite warm), cut them into 1-inch (2.5 cm) chunks and put them in a large bowl.

In a small bowl, whisk together the mustard, vinegar, lemon juice, and 1 teaspoon salt, then whisk in the olive oil until the dressing is creamy and emulsified. Pour the dressing over the still-warm potatoes and gently fold to distribute it.

Add the parsley, lovage, tarragon, and dill and gently fold again to mix. Taste and adjust with more olive oil, salt, and lemon juice if necessary.

Garnish the potato salad with herb flowers, if using, and serve at room temperature.

Naknik Shokolad
Chocolate "Salami"

On my family's kibbutz, we mostly ate together in a communal dining hall. Before the homes had full kitchens, this was a dessert that everyone could make—all you need is one burner and a freezer. In Hebrew, we call it naknik shokolad, which means "chocolate salami," because it looks like a sausage (in Italy, where it's an iconic dessert, it's salame di cioccolato). While it's incredibly simple to make, it still feels elegant. I always have a log of it in my freezer, and when I'm short on time, I serve slices for dessert along with a digestif, tea, or coffee.

Make sure to use good-quality chocolate. And when you break up the petit beurre cookies (also known as tea biscuits), aim for small pieces but not crumbs. If you like, you can also mix in pecans, almonds, and/or raisins—the recipe is very forgiving. Well wrapped, a log will keep in the freezer for up to 2 months.

MAKES two 15-inch (37.5 cm) "salamis"

½ cup (100 g) sugar

3½ ounces (100 g) bittersweet chocolate (70%), finely chopped

2 tablespoons unsweetened cocoa powder

½ cup (120 ml) whole milk

¼ cup (60 ml) red wine

1 teaspoon vanilla extract

4 tablespoons (60 g) unsalted butter

12 ounces (340 g) plain petit beurre–type cookies, plus more if necessary

¾ cup (about 90 g) pecans, sliced almonds, and/or raisins (optional)

In a small saucepan, combine the sugar, chocolate, cocoa powder, milk, wine, vanilla, and butter and cook over medium-low heat, stirring, until the sugar is dissolved, the chocolate and butter are melted, and the texture is smooth, about 5 minutes. Remove from the heat.

In a large bowl, crush and crumble the cookies into small pieces—ideally no larger than about ½ inch (1.25 cm), but the size of the pieces can vary.

Pour the warm chocolate mixture over the crushed cookies. Add the pecans, almonds, and/or raisins, if using. Stir until the ingredients are combined and the mixture has a loose dough-like consistency. Add a few more crushed cookies if the mixture is too thin to hold its shape.

Lay a large piece of parchment paper, about 12 by 18 inches (30 by 45 cm), on the counter. Transfer half of the chocolate mixture to the parchment paper and shape it into a rough log 15 inches (37.5 cm) long. Wrap the log tightly in the parchment and roll it back and forth to tighten and neaten the log, smoothing it with your hands. Twist the ends of the parchment paper to seal the mixture. Repeat with another sheet of parchment paper and the remaining mixture to create another log.

Freeze the chocolate logs for at least 3 hours.

To serve, use a sharp knife to cut the logs into ¼-inch (6 mm) slices and arrange on a plate.

Cakes for a Pre-Shabbat Kaffee und Kuchen

SHARED BY

Idan Cohen

The most religious thing about my family is having afternoon coffee with cake. Judaism is second to this German ritual.

As a kid, I'd wake up every Friday morning to the noise of clanging pans and the hum of the electric mixer, flour flying everywhere around my mother in the kitchen. If I commented on the noise, she would say, "If you're going to complain, you're not going to get any cake."

She's an excellent baker and would make two, three, sometimes even four cakes on those mornings. These often included a poppy seed babka, or, when the berries were in season, a strawberries-and-cream roulade. A "stadium cake," a dessert made with choux pastry filled with a coffee cream and topped with chocolate glaze, was the cake you got on your birthday.

Many of these recipes were from my mother's mother, Elisheva, and her mother, Marianne Schlochauer. They lived in a very small German village in the center of Israel called Ramot HaShavim, which my great-grandparents helped establish. Here, most conversations on the street

FAMILY JOURNEY

Alt-Ukta, East Prussia (present-day Ukta, Poland) → *Berlin* →
Ramot HaShavim, Mandatory Palestine (present-day Israel) →
Ra'anana, Israel → *New York City*

From left to right: Idan with his brother, Itay; mother, Anat; and
sister, Adi, on a family picnic near the Sea of Galilee, 1984

were in German and it was well known that you shouldn't knock on
someone's door during schlafstunde, afternoon rest time. Our 4 p.m.
coffee and cake ceremony came after that rest time.

In our house we drank instant coffee all week long, but on Fridays,
my dad would grind the beans and let me smell them before he made
coffee in the percolator. My aunts, uncles, and cousins would come over
after schlafstunde for a slice of cake and coffee, and if the weather was
nice, we would sit outside. These Friday gatherings were holy. They were
a way of honoring tradition with shared rituals that paced life.

Today's routine does not quite allow for nap time, but I never skip
baking a fresh cake to add to the Shabbat dinner table.

IDAN COHEN is a startup founder as well as an exceptional home cook, winemaker,
and beekeeper. He lives with his wife and their two girls in Manhattan's East Village, where
their pantry is always stocked with his homemade jams, hot sauce, and pickles.

Poppy Seed Babka

Eastern and Central European immigrants to Israel held on to many of their baking traditions, and today some of their cakes are popular with Israelis of all backgrounds. This poppy seed cake is a perfect example.

The filling is the key to this recipe, so be sure to buy poppy seeds from a good source so you get the freshest seeds. You can buy already-ground seeds or, like Idan, grind your own. He combines the sugar in the recipe with the poppy seeds and grinds them together in a spice grinder or food processor with a very sharp blade.

MAKES 2 babkas

FOR THE DOUGH

1 packet (2¼ teaspoons/7 g) active dry yeast

6 tablespoons (75 g) sugar

⅔ cup (150 ml) lukewarm whole milk

3 large eggs

3¾ cups (500 g) bread flour, plus more for dusting

10⅔ tablespoons (165 g) unsalted butter, cut into cubes, at room temperature

2 teaspoons kosher salt

FOR THE FILLING

1½ cups (360 ml) whole milk

1½ cups plus 2 tablespoons (320 g) sugar

2 cups (300 g) ground poppy seeds

¼ cup (80 g) honey

1 tablespoon fresh lemon juice

FOR THE SYRUP

½ cup (100 g) sugar

¼ cup (60 ml) water

MAKE THE DOUGH: Put the yeast, sugar, and milk in the bowl of a stand mixer fitted with the dough hook and mix briefly on low speed. Add the eggs and flour and knead for 3 minutes, then add the butter and continue mixing until it has been incorporated. Add the salt and then knead for about 7 minutes; the dough will make a slapping noise against the sides of the bowl when it's ready.

Transfer the dough to another bowl (or remove the bowl from the mixer stand and leave the dough in the bowl) and cover. Let the dough rise until doubled in size, 1 to 2 hours. Or let it rise overnight in the fridge; if you do so, allow the dough to come to room temperature before proceeding.

MEANWHILE, MAKE THE POPPY SEED FILLING: In a small saucepan, combine the milk, sugar, and poppy seeds and bring to a gentle simmer over medium heat. Cook until the bubbles become large and the mixture becomes very thick and glossy, 15 to 20 minutes.

Whisk in the honey and lemon juice, remove from the heat, and let cool completely at room temperature.

Divide the dough in half. Place one piece on a lightly floured surface, dust very lightly with flour, and cover with a large sheet of wax paper. With a rolling pin, roll the dough into a rectangular sheet about 10 by 15 inches (25 by 38 cm) and about ¼ inch (6 mm) thick. Remove the wax paper and spread half of the poppy seed paste in an even layer over the dough, leaving a border of about ½ inch (1.25 cm) all around (the filling will spread as you roll the babka). Starting with a long edge, roll the dough up gently into a log and transfer to a baking sheet or tray. Repeat with the remaining dough and filling.

Put the logs in the freezer for 15 to 20 minutes to firm up.

Grease two 9-by-5-inch (22.5 by 12.5 cm) loaf pans.

Cut the logs in half lengthwise and twist the two halves of each one together loosely two or three times to form a braid. Place the shaped babkas in the loaf pans, tucking the ends under to fit. Let the babkas rise in a warm place until the dough is puffy and almost fills out the loaf pans, 1 to 2 hours.

Preheat the oven to 350°F (175°C). Bake the babkas for 30 minutes, then increase the oven temperature to 375°F (190°C). Bake for another 15 to 20 minutes, until the babkas are golden and cooked through. Remove from the oven.

MEANWHILE, MAKE THE SYRUP: Bring the sugar and water to a boil in a small saucepan over high heat. Remove from the heat and stir until the sugar dissolves.

As soon as the babkas come out of the oven, brush or pour the syrup evenly over the tops, letting it run down the insides of the loaf pans so it can soak the bottom of the babkas as well as the sides and top. Let cool completely.

Run a knife around the inside edge of the pan to release the babkas and remove them from the pans. Slice and serve.

"Stadium Cake"
Paris-Brest-Style Pastry

When Idan's family was going to celebrate someone's birthday at the Friday afternoon coffee and cake gatherings, his mother would make this impressive pastry she calls stadium cake. It's similar to the French classic Paris-Brest, a ring of choux pastry (the same dough used to make éclairs) split and filled with pastry cream lightened with whipped cream. In her version, the cream is flavored with coffee and vanilla and the top is generously drizzled with chocolate ganache.

This recipe has a few different elements, but some of them can be prepared ahead of time. You can make the ganache up to 2 days ahead, refrigerate, and then rewarm in a double boiler just until it becomes pourable. The coffee-flavored pastry cream can be made a day ahead and refrigerated; whisk to loosen it before you fold in the whipped cream. Make sure to fully bake the pastry so it provides a crisp counterpoint to the rich cream. *(Pictured on page 333)*

MAKES 8 to 10 servings

FOR THE PASTRY CREAM

2 cups (480 ml) whole milk

1 vanilla bean, split, seeds scraped out, or 1 teaspoon vanilla extract

2 teaspoons instant coffee, or more to taste

½ cup (100 g) plus ½ teaspoon sugar

3 tablespoons cornstarch

¼ teaspoon kosher salt

4 large egg yolks

2 tablespoons unsalted butter, cut into pieces

¾ cup (180 ml) heavy cream

FOR THE PÂTE À CHOUX

1 cup (240 ml) water

8 tablespoons (1 stick/115 g) unsalted butter, cut into pieces, at room temperature

1 teaspoon sugar

½ teaspoon kosher salt

1 cup (130 g) all-purpose flour

3 large eggs

FOR THE EGG WASH

1 large egg, beaten with 2 tablespoons water

FOR THE CHOCOLATE GANACHE

4 ounces (115 g) dark chocolate (60 to 70%), finely chopped (¾ cup)

6 tablespoons (90 ml) heavy cream

1½ teaspoons corn syrup (optional)

MAKE THE PASTRY CREAM: Put the milk and vanilla bean and seeds, if using, in a medium saucepan and bring just to a simmer over medium heat. Immediately remove from the heat and stir in the instant coffee. Cover and set aside to steep for 10 minutes. (If using vanilla extract, there's no need to steep the milk, just let it cool for a few minutes and then add the vanilla.)

Taste the milk mixture and add a bit more coffee if you like, stirring to dissolve; keep in mind that the coffee flavor will be "diluted" by the whipped cream.

Put the ½ cup (100 g) sugar, the cornstarch, and salt in a medium bowl. Add the egg yolks and whisk until the mixture becomes pale and smooth, about 2 minutes.

Pour the cooled steeped milk through a strainer into the egg yolk mixture a little at a time, whisking constantly until everything is well blended; discard the vanilla bean (don't pour hot milk into the egg yolks, as it could cook the yolks).

Return the mixture to the saucepan and cook over medium heat, whisking constantly and vigorously, until it thickens and comes to a boil. Boil the pastry cream for at least 2 minutes, whisking constantly; it should develop the consistency of thick pudding. (Be careful, because the hot pastry cream will sputter.) Remove from the heat and whisk in the butter until completely incorporated.

Strain the pastry cream through a fine-mesh sieve into a medium bowl. Fill a larger bowl with water and ice and set the bowl of pastry cream in it. Cover with plastic wrap and chill in the fridge for 30 minutes.

In a large bowl, using a handheld electric mixer, whip the cream with the remaining ½ teaspoon sugar on medium-high speed until it forms stiff peaks; take care not to go beyond that, to the point where the cream starts to separate.

Take the pastry cream from the refrigerator, whisk it vigorously until smooth, and then carefully fold in the whipped cream with a rubber spatula. Cover and refrigerate for at least 1 hour to set.

Preheat the oven to 375°F (190°C).

MAKE THE PÂTE À CHOUX: Put the water, butter, sugar, and salt in a large heavy-bottomed saucepan and bring to a boil, stirring to melt the butter. (Don't let the water continue to boil, because too much evaporation will reduce the quantity.) Add the flour all at once and, using a wooden spoon, stir the flour into the water and cook, stirring constantly, for 2 to 3 minutes, until a ball of dough forms and pulls away from the sides of the pan. Transfer the dough to a large bowl and set aside to cool for about 2 minutes.

Add one egg to the dough, mixing until it is fully incorporated before adding the next and mixing it in. Add the third egg, mix until incorporated, and set the pan aside.

Using a pot lid or pan as a template, draw a 9-inch (23 cm) circle on a sheet of parchment paper to use as a guide for the pastry ring. Flip the paper over (this will keep the pastry dough from touching the ink or pencil line) and line a baking sheet with it.

Transfer the pâte à choux to a pastry bag fitted with a large plain tip, or no tip at all (if you don't have a pastry bag, you can use a heavy plastic food storage bag; snip off one of the bottom corners). Pipe a thick ring of dough following the template. Pipe a second ring of dough just inside and slightly touching the first. You'll probably still have some dough in your pastry bag, so pipe a third ring on top and in between the first two rings to build the pastry ring a bit higher. Smooth out any bubbles or bumps with your fingertip. Lightly brush the ring with the egg wash.

Bake the pastry until puffed and deep golden brown, 45 to 50 minutes. Try not to open the oven during the early part of the baking time, or the pastry may collapse. Remove from the oven and cool the pastry on a rack.

MEANWHILE, MAKE THE CHOCOLATE GANACHE: Put the chopped chocolate in a large heatproof bowl. Heat the cream in a saucepan (or the microwave) until it is very hot and just barely simmering. Immediately pour the cream over the chocolate and let sit for 1 to 2 minutes. Then pour in the corn syrup, if using, and stir the chocolate and cream until the chocolate is melted and the ganache is completely smooth and glossy.

ASSEMBLE THE PASTRY: With a serrated knife, slice the cooled pastry ring horizontally in half.

recipe continues

Carefully remove the top layer and set aside. If the interior crumb in the bottom of the pastry looks very moist, scrape out a bit with a spoon, to make more room for the pastry cream and to keep the pastry crisp.

Fill a pastry bag fitted with a large star tip with the coffee pastry cream and pipe the cream into the ring. (If you don't have a pastry bag or a star tip, you can use a heavy plastic food storage bag and snip off one of the bottom corners. The cream won't look as decorative, and but it will still taste delicious.) Place the top layer of choux pastry on top of the whipped cream and drizzle or spread the warm ganache over the top. Refrigerate for at least 1 hour.

Serve chilled, cut into portions with a serrated knife.

Strawberries-and-Cream Roulade

Idan's mother would wait until strawberries were in season to make this light cake with a whipped cream filling. While strawberries are the classic choice, you could use other berries or sliced ripe peaches.

If you haven't made a roulade before, the technique may seem tricky, but just take your time—and know that any imperfections will be covered by the dusting of confectioners' sugar. Note that the cake needs to sit in the refrigerator for at least 3 hours (and up to 1 day) before serving. *(Pictured on page 332)*

MAKES 6 to 8 servings

FOR THE CAKE

¾ cup (100 g) all-purpose flour

1 teaspoon baking powder

4 large eggs, separated

¾ cup (150 g) granulated sugar

1 teaspoon vanilla extract

Confectioners' sugar for dusting

FOR THE FILLING

2½ cups (600 ml) very cold heavy cream

2½ tablespoons plus 2 teaspoons granulated sugar

1¼ teaspoons vanilla extract

1 pound (450 g) strawberries, hulled and sliced ¼ inch (6 mm) thick

FOR DECORATION

A few strawberries, hulled and sliced ¼ inch (6 mm) thick

½ cup (120 ml) very cold heavy cream

1½ teaspoons granulated sugar

¼ teaspoon vanilla extract

MAKE THE CAKE: Preheat the oven to 375°F (190°C). Grease a large rimmed baking sheet (13 by 18 inches/33 by 45 cm) with nonstick cooking spray, line with parchment paper, and spray the paper.

Whisk the flour and baking powder together in a small bowl.

Put the egg whites in the bowl of a stand mixer fitted with the whisk attachment and whip on medium speed until soft peaks form, about 2 minutes. Continuing to whip, gradually pour in the granulated sugar and then whip until firm peaks form, another 3 to 4 minutes. Add the vanilla and then add the egg yolks one at a time, continuing to whip briefly after each addition.

Remove the bowl from the mixer stand and gently fold in the flour mixture just until incorporated, taking care to preserve as much of the egg white volume as possible.

Spread the cake batter in the parchment-lined baking sheet and use a spatula to smooth the surface. Bake until the top of the cake is lightly golden, springs back when lightly pressed, and feels set, 8 to 10 minutes. Don't overbake the cake, or it may crack when you roll it. Remove from the oven and let cool to room temperature.

recipe continues

Lightly dust a piece of parchment paper with confectioners' sugar, lay it on the counter, and flip the cake onto it. Peel off the top sheet of parchment and discard, then roll up the cake in the bottom piece of parchment. Let sit for 5 to 10 minutes.

MEANWHILE, MAKE THE FILLING: Put the 2½ cups (600 ml) heavy cream, 2½ tablespoons of the granulated sugar, and the vanilla in the bowl of a stand mixer fitted with the whisk attachment. Whip on low speed for 2 minutes, then increase the speed to medium and whip for another 4 to 6 minutes, until the cream forms stiff peaks. Keep an eye on the cream, and don't let it whip to the point of curdling.

Carefully unroll the cake. Spread the cream over the cake, all the way to the edges.

Arrange the strawberries in an even layer on the cream and sprinkle with the remaining 2 teaspoons granulated sugar. Roll the cake up again (without the parchment), wrap lightly in plastic, and refrigerate until the cream has firmed up, at least 3 hours and as long as overnight.

When ready to serve, dust the cake with confectioners' sugar. Using a stand mixer fitted with the whisk attachment or with a hand whisk, whip the ½ cup (120 ml) cream, incorporating the sugar and vanilla just as the cream begins to form soft peaks. Continue to whip until it forms stiff peaks. Fit a pastry bag with a small star tip, fill the bag with the whipped cream, and pipe a few decorative lines down the length of the roulade; decorate with more strawberries.

Blessing Dabo in the Middle of the Desert

SHARED BY
Beejhy Barhany

I come from an ancient Jewish community in Ethiopia, where welcoming Shabbat is a great honor. In my family's village in Tigray, the preparation took days. My aunties, mom, and grandmom would start sifting flour for dabo—a special bread—on Thursday and bake the loaves on Friday.

When the sun was coming down before Shabbat began, an elder would ring a bell and we would put on our best robes and carry our dabo to the synagogue to be blessed by a religious leader called a kes. We always left behind a portion for those in need and took the rest home to eat with the chicken stew called doro wat, as well as lentil and collard green stews served on injera. Ethiopian food is all about sharing and eating together—that's the culture and the mentality I come from.

One evening when I was four years old, my aunt woke me up in the middle of the night and told me we were leaving and to get dressed quickly. I sat on a horse behind my grandmother and started to cry because I didn't get to say goodbye to my favorite pet or my friends. I didn't know that for months, our entire village of more than three

FAMILY JOURNEY

Tigray, Ethiopia → *Khartoum, Sudan* → *Pardes Hana, Israel* →
Ashkelon, Israel → *Kibbutz Alumim, Israel* → *New York City*

From left to right: Beejhy's grandmother Bezabesh Worku, Beejhy,
her aunt Terefinish Ferede, and her cousin David Hailu in Sudan, 1983

hundred people had been planning to leave and start a journey to the
Promised Land, a place our community had yearned for for thousands
of years.

We weren't legally allowed to leave the country, and if we were
caught, we would have been executed immediately. So we walked
at night, stopping during the day at Jewish villages where we could
intermingle and no one would notice us. We continued from one village
to the next for months. That is how we managed to reach Sudan.

The journey was treacherous. We encountered thieves, and there
were days when we had to dig for muddy water just to wet our lips. But
even in the midst of all of that, in the middle of the desert, we stopped to
make dabo in a pot over a fire, bless it, and observe Shabbat. The dabo
has been traveling with us throughout all our journeys and our lives. It's
here on my table in Harlem.

BEEJHY BARHANY is the chef and owner of Tsion Cafe in Harlem and the founder
of BINA Cultural Foundation. Through her work, she celebrates and raises awareness of
the Ethiopian Jewish (also known as Beta Israel) community.

BEEJHY BARHANY'S SHABBAT

Dabo
Ethiopian Bread
346

Gomen
*Collard Greens
with Garlic and Ginger*
347

Messer Wot
Red Lentil Stew
348

—Serve with—

injera, chopped salad,
berbere spice mix,
hot sauce

Dabo
Ethiopian Bread

In Amharic, the word *dabo* means bread, but in the Ethiopian Jewish community, it typically refers to lightly sweet loaves like this one, which are served on Shabbat and holidays, explains Leah Koenig in *The Jewish Cookbook*. When Beejhy was little, she remembers the women in her family starting to prepare dabo on Thursdays so it would be ready for Shabbat.

The dabo is easy to make and is the perfect accompaniment to a bowl of hearty messer wot, the Ethiopian lentil stew (page 348), and gomen, collard greens with garlic and ginger (opposite).

MAKES 1 loaf

1 to 1¼ cups (240 to 300 ml) warm water

1 packet (2¼ teaspoons/7 g) active dry yeast

4 cups (520 g) all-purpose flour

¼ cup (50 g) sugar

1 tablespoon kosher salt

1½ teaspoons vegetable oil

1 large egg

Put ½ cup (120 ml) of the warm water in a small bowl, add the yeast, and stir. Set aside.

Put the flour, sugar, and salt in the bowl of a stand mixer fitted with the dough hook and mix on low speed for a few seconds to blend. Add the yeast-water mixture, 1 teaspoon of the oil, and the egg and mix on medium-low speed until blended.

Gradually add another ½ cup (120 ml) warm water to the flour mixture, and then continue mixing until the dough is well blended, smooth, and soft, about 3 minutes, adding up to ¼ cup (60 ml) more water if needed to bring the dough together. Knead on medium speed until the dough springs back after you poke it with your finger, another 6 minutes or so.

Grease your hands with the remaining ½ teaspoon oil and shape the dough into a ball. Put the dough in a large bowl and cover it with a towel. Let rise for 1 hour.

Line a baking sheet with parchment paper. Pull the dough away from the sides of the bowl to release it, gently pressing on it to push out excess air but keeping the ball intact. Transfer the dough to the parchment-lined baking sheet and cover loosely with a towel. Let it rise until doubled in size, 40 minutes or so.

Preheat the oven to 400°F (205°C).

Bake the bread until it is golden brown and sounds hollow when you tap the bottom, 25 to 30 minutes.

Remove from the oven and let cool on the baking sheet. Serve at room temperature.

Gomen
Collard Greens with Garlic and Ginger

After returning from Friday night prayers in their village, Beejhy and her family would enjoy dishes like these silky collard greens, cooked for a long time with garlic, ginger, and spices. The dish gets a hint of heat from minced fresh jalapeño added at the very end of the cooking time (although that is optional). *(Pictured on page 344)*

MAKES 6 to 8 servings

2 large yellow onions
(about 14 ounces/390 g)

4 garlic cloves

A 2-inch (5 cm) piece fresh ginger, peeled

½ cup (120 ml) vegetable oil

2 pounds (900 g) collard greens, stemmed and cut crosswise into ½-inch (1.25 cm) ribbons

2 teaspoons kosher salt

½ teaspoon freshly ground black pepper

½ teaspoon ground cumin

½ teaspoon ground nutmeg

1 jalapeño, cored, seeded, and finely chopped (optional)

Put the onions, garlic, and ginger in a food processor and process to a smooth puree.

Heat the oil in a large, deep skillet or Dutch oven over medium heat. Add the onion puree and cook, stirring occasionally, until slightly reduced and darker in color, 10 to 15 minutes.

Add the collards, salt, pepper, cumin, and nutmeg and cook until the collards are starting to soften, adding a bit of water as needed if the pan seems dry, about 20 minutes.

Cover the pan, reduce the heat, and simmer the collards, stirring occasionally, until very tender, 30 to 40 minutes longer. Taste and adjust the seasoning with more salt and pepper if needed. Stir in the chopped jalapeño, if using. Serve hot.

Messer Wot
Red Lentil Stew

The spice blend berbere is the backbone of Ethiopian cuisine, Beejhy explains. It brings complex, hot-sweet-earthy notes to stews like this simple vegetarian one. You'll have a bit more spice mix than you need for the messer wot, so store the rest in an airtight container and use it as a rub for fish, chicken, or meat; add it to other Ethiopian recipes; or sprinkle it on top of eggs.

MAKES 6 to 8 servings; 2 quarts (2 L)

FOR THE BERBERE SPICE MIX

2½ tablespoons hot paprika

½ teaspoon ground cardamom

½ teaspoon ground ginger

½ teaspoon onion powder

½ teaspoon ground coriander

½ teaspoon ground cumin

½ teaspoon kosher salt

¼ teaspoon ground cloves

¼ teaspoon ground cinnamon

¼ teaspoon ground nutmeg

¼ teaspoon ground fenugreek

¼ teaspoon freshly ground black pepper

FOR THE STEW

2 medium red onions (about 14 ounces/390 g), quartered

2 large yellow onions (about 1 pound/450 g), quartered

6 garlic cloves

A 2-inch (5 cm) piece fresh ginger, peeled and roughly chopped

1 cup (240 ml) neutral oil, such as grapeseed or vegetable

Generous ½ cup (125 g) tomato paste

5 cups (1.2 L) water

2 tablespoons berbere spice mix (above)

2 teaspoons kosher salt

2 cups (400 g) red lentils, rinsed and drained

MAKE THE SPICE MIX: Put all the spices in a bowl and mix well. Set aside.

MAKE THE STEW: Put the red and yellow onions, garlic, and ginger in a food processor and process to a fine paste. (Do this in batches if your food processor bowl isn't large.)

Heat the oil in a Dutch oven or other large heavy-bottomed pot over medium heat. Add the onion paste and sauté, stirring occasionally, until the mixture has reduced a bit and turned light brown, about 20 minutes.

Reduce the heat to medium-low and add the tomato paste, 1 cup (240 ml) of the water, the 2 tablespoons berbere spice mix, and salt and cook, stirring and scraping the bottom of the pot occasionally, until the mixture thickens slightly, about 15 minutes.

Add the lentils and the remaining 4 cups (1 L) water and stir well. Increase the heat to high and bring the stew to a boil, stirring occasionally, then cover the pot and reduce the heat to low, adjusting it as necessary so the stew simmers gently. Simmer, stirring occasionally, until the lentils are soft and cooked through, 35 to 40 minutes. Taste and adjust the seasoning with more salt if necessary. Serve hot.

A French-Ashkenazi Shabbat

SHARED BY
Anna Polonsky

After Auschwitz, no one in my family kept their faith; no one who was left wanted to hear about God or religion. My dad was born in Paris in 1946, right after the war, and I think the experience of being a French Jew was hard during that time. His relatives had come to France decades earlier to escape pogroms in Kyiv and Poland and fell in love with French music, philosophy, and culture. They did well for themselves, setting up various businesses and building new lives in Paris.

When France collaborated with the Nazis during the war, thousands of Jews, including some of my relatives, were deported to Auschwitz. Many who survived the war felt betrayed by their country. Still, my family saw France as their home. For my dad, Judaism is his culture and his history, and his family kept their recipes and the holidays as part of their calendar, but there was no religious practice. That's how he raised me.

When I was a teenager, I started to become curious about my roots. We said we were Jewish, but I didn't really know what that meant. So I started reading Jewish texts and going to temple on Yom Kippur—I

FAMILY JOURNEY

Lodz, Poland, and Kyiv, Ukraine → Paris → New York City

Anna with her father, Claude, in France, 1989

would meditate on what I'd done wrong and what I could do better, but I did that without any belief in God. We started hosting what I called secular Shabbat dinners at our home. I would pick a theme from a Jewish text and talk about it, giving a modern or personal explanation of it, and my dad would choose a recipe to prepare.

Sometimes he made family recipes he'd learned from his grandmother or his mother, like apple strudel or the meatballs my family calls yiddishe boulettes. The first time I ate cholent was at one of those dinners. Cholent is Jewish, but the word comes from the Old French and some say the dish is the origin of cassoulet—it feels fitting for my family.

I want to preserve these recipes. For me, they are a canvas for conversation, a way to get into stories about our family that I've never heard before. So much of what's survived has been through oral history, and that's always haunted me. My mom often says, "It's invaluable to know where you are from in order to know where to go in life."

Everything creative director **ANNA POLONSKY** touches is stylish. Her Shabbat dinners are inspired by the secular ones she grew up with in Paris, when her family would eat cholent and listen to klezmer music and the Rolling Stones.

Herb Salad with Shallot Vinaigrette

Soft herbs are the star of this delicate salad, so be sure to use the freshest and most pristine ones you can find. Using a variety of them is key, but otherwise, there's a fair amount of flexibility in the recipe. If you don't like one of the herbs, feel free to replace it with more of the others. In general, aim for about twice as much parsley and cilantro as any of the other herbs. *(Pictured on page 352)*

MAKES 6 to 8 servings

2 tablespoons white wine vinegar, or more to taste

2 tablespoons finely chopped shallots, or more to taste

½ teaspoon kosher salt

¼ teaspoon freshly ground black pepper

6 tablespoons (90 ml) extra-virgin olive oil

2 cups (60 g) lightly packed fresh cilantro leaves and tender stems

2 cups (60 g) lightly packed fresh flat-leaf parsley leaves and tender stems

1 cup (30 g) lightly packed fresh basil leaves, torn if large

1 cup (30 g) lightly packed fresh chervil leaves and tender stems

¾ cup (22 g) lightly packed fresh chives cut into ¾- to 1-inch (2 to 2.5 cm) pieces

½ cup (15 g) lightly packed fresh tarragon leaves

In a small bowl, whisk the vinegar, shallots, salt, and pepper together. Slowly drizzle in the olive oil, whisking to make a creamy, emulsified dressing. Taste and add more of any of the ingredients as necessary until the dressing tastes bright but not too sharp. Set aside.

Wash all the herbs well in cool water and spin in a salad spinner until completely dry. Chop or tear any large herb sprigs into smaller pieces.

Put the herbs in a large salad bowl, toss to mix, and drizzle on about half the dressing. Toss, taste, and add more dressing, if you like. Serve immediately.

Cauliflower Beignets

Anna's great-grandmother used to make cauliflower fritters like these for Anna's father, Claude, and when he saw a recipe for them from chefs and cookbook authors Yotam Ottolenghi and Sami Tamimi, he started making them. While the ingredients in this slightly modified version are humble, together they are more than the sum of their parts.

Anna serves the beignets with a dairy-based yogurt sauce, but if you're serving them at a kosher meat meal, nondairy cashew yogurt also works well.

MAKES 6 to 8 servings; about 20 beignets

FOR THE BEIGNETS

Kosher salt

1 medium cauliflower (about 1 pound/450 g), cored and cut into medium florets

1 cup (130 g) all-purpose flour

¼ cup (30 g) finely chopped shallots

3 tablespoons chopped fresh flat-leaf parsley, plus more for garnish

1 garlic clove, finely chopped

4 large eggs

1½ teaspoons ground cumin

1 teaspoon ground cinnamon

1 teaspoon freshly ground black pepper

Sunflower oil or other neutral oil for deep-frying

FOR THE YOGURT SAUCE

1 cup (225 g) Greek yogurt or nondairy cashew yogurt

Finely grated zest of 1 lime

2 tablespoons fresh lime juice

2 tablespoons chopped fresh cilantro

2 tablespoons extra-virgin olive oil

Kosher salt and freshly ground black pepper

PREPARE THE CAULIFLOWER: Bring a large pot of water with 2 tablespoons salt to a boil. Add the cauliflower florets and boil until tender, 8 to 10 minutes. Drain and transfer to a bowl.

When the cauliflower is cool enough to handle, mash it with a fork until slightly chunky; set aside.

MAKE THE YOGURT SAUCE: In a small bowl, stir together the yogurt, lime zest and juice, cilantro, and olive oil. Season to taste with salt and pepper. Cover and set aside in the refrigerator.

MAKE THE BEIGNET BATTER: Put the flour, shallots, parsley, garlic, eggs, cumin, cinnamon, 1½ teaspoons salt, and the pepper in a large bowl and whisk until you have a smooth batter. Fold in the mashed cauliflower and mash a bit more, making sure all the cauliflower is coated in batter; the mixture will be slightly thick.

FRY THE BEIGNETS: Line a large plate or tray with paper towels. Fill a large deep saucepan with about 2 inches (5 cm) of oil and heat over medium-high heat to 365°F (185°C). If you don't have a thermometer, check the oil temperature by dropping in a pinch of the batter; if it sizzles vigorously, the oil is hot enough.

With a large spoon, scoop up about a golf ball–sized portion of batter and carefully slide it into the oil; add another few beignets, but don't crowd the pan. Fry the beignets, turning once, until deep golden brown on both sides, 3 to 5 minutes per side. Monitor the oil temperature during frying, adjusting the heat as needed. Transfer the beignets to the paper towel–lined plate to drain. Repeat with the remaining batter, cooking the beignets in batches.

Arrange the beignets on a serving platter, garnish with parsley, and serve hot, with the yogurt sauce on the side.

Eggs with Schmaltzy Onions

Anna says her father's entire childhood was connected to this humble dish; his parents would make it for him as a meal or a snack. In the family, it's called tzibeles, which means "onions" in Yiddish. Here the onions are lightly caramelized in schmaltz before the eggs are added. *(Pictured on page 352)*

MAKES 6 to 8 servings

3 to 4 tablespoons melted schmaltz or duck fat, or sunflower oil

3 to 4 medium onions (1 to 1½ pounds/ 450 to 675 g), roughly chopped

Kosher salt and freshly ground black pepper

6 to 8 large eggs

Heat the schmaltz in a large skillet over medium heat. Once it is hot, add the onions, season lightly with salt and pepper, and cook, stirring and scraping the bottom of the pan so the onion juices don't burn, until the onions are very soft and lightly caramelized, 20 to 30 minutes.

Crack the eggs into a medium bowl and whisk briefly to blend. Pour the eggs into the pan and immediately mix the eggs and onions together. Let the eggs cook for 1 to 2 minutes, until they start to set, and season lightly with salt and pepper. Once the eggs are set on the bottom, stir the mixture and continue cooking until the eggs are just cooked, keeping them in large curds, another 2 to 3 minutes.

Serve right away.

Cholent

One of the hallmarks of Jewish cooking is a category of dishes where time is the key ingredient. On Shabbat, observant Jews abstain from work, including cooking. To ensure that a festive meal could be served for Saturday lunch, hearty, long-cooked dishes like classic Ashkenazi cholent and Sephardi adafina (page 380) evolved. In some communities, cooks took their pots to neighborhood bakeries or communal ovens on Fridays, where the dishes sat in the still-warm oven until after Saturday-morning prayers.

The name *cholent* likely comes from two Old French words: *chaud*, meaning "warm," and *lent*, meaning "slow," explains Joan Nathan in *Quiches, Kugels, and Couscous: My Search for Jewish Cooking in France*. Some argue the dish is the predecessor of cassoulet. As with some cassoulet recipes, the Polonsky family finishes their cholent with breadcrumbs, which are toasted under the broiler just before serving.

Beef cheeks are a perfect cut for this dish—they turn meltingly tender with long, slow cooking—though they can be hard to find. Boneless short ribs make a fine substitute. *(Pictured on page 352)*

MAKES 6 to 8 servings

¾ cup (160 g) dried beans, such as Great Northern, cannellini, or cranberry

1½ tablespoons extra-virgin olive oil

1 cup (150 g) finely chopped onion

1½ teaspoons sweet paprika

Half a small dried chile

2 cups (480 ml) homemade or store-bought low-sodium beef broth

2 beef cheeks, halved, or 1¼ pounds (565 g) boneless beef short ribs

One 14-ounce (397 g) can diced tomatoes, drained

1 large carrot (about 3 ounces/90 g), peeled and thinly sliced

1 small parsnip (about 3 ounces/90 g), peeled and thinly sliced

1 large russet potato (about 8 ounces/225 g), peeled and sliced into ¼-inch (6 mm) rounds

¼ cup (30 g) finely chopped celery

2½ tablespoons pearl or hulled barley

1 tablespoon finely minced garlic

Kosher salt

3 tablespoons Arborio rice

¼ teaspoon freshly ground black pepper

2 teaspoons dried breadcrumbs

Put the beans in a medium bowl, cover with water by 2 to 3 inches (5 to 7.5 cm), and let soak overnight.

The next day, drain the beans, put them in a medium saucepan, and cover completely with cold water. Bring to a boil and cook for 10 minutes, then remove from the heat and set aside.

Heat the oil in a medium skillet over medium heat and add the onion. Cook, stirring often, until translucent, about 5 minutes. Add the paprika and dried chile and cook for another minute, then remove from the heat and set aside.

Meanwhile, heat the beef broth in a small saucepan over medium heat until it just begins to simmer. Remove from the heat.

Drain the beans and transfer to a Dutch oven or other large heavy-bottomed pot. Add the spiced onion, beef, tomatoes, carrot, parsnip, potato,

celery, barley, and garlic, pour in the hot beef broth, and add 1 tablespoon salt.

Cover the pot and bring the mixture to a boil, then reduce to a simmer, cover the pot, and simmer gently for 5 to 6 hours, checking after the first few hours to see if the ingredients look dry; if so, add a bit more broth or water.

Add the rice and pepper, taste the cooking liquid, and add more salt if needed. Mix gently to distribute the rice.

Cover the pot again and continue to simmer until the beef is fork-tender, the beans and rice are tender, all the vegetables are fully cooked, and the liquid is rich and concentrated, another 45 to 60 minutes. Taste and adjust the seasoning with more salt and pepper if needed.

Meanwhile, heat the broiler. Remove the pot lid, sprinkle the breadcrumbs over the surface of the cholent, and broil until the crumbs are browned and the cholent is bubbling, 5 to 10 minutes. Serve hot.

Klops
Meatloaf

Anna grew up eating a meatball version of this recipe her family called yiddishe boulettes, or Jewish meatballs. When the ground meat mixture is shaped instead into a meatloaf with hard-boiled eggs in the center, the dish is sometimes called klops (which, ironically, means "meatballs" in Yiddish). If you're not a fan of hard-boiled eggs, just omit them.

Anna's family uses a mix of ground beef brisket and ground veal flank, both of which are very flavorful. Veal flank can be hard to find, though, so use whatever ground cut is available. If you can't find veal at all, use all beef—ground brisket, if you can get it, or ground chuck. *(Pictured on page 353)*

MAKES 6 to 8 servings

FOR THE KLOPS

1 pound (450 g) ground veal, ideally veal flank

1 pound (450 g) ground beef brisket or chuck

5 cups (750 g) finely chopped onions

½ cup (40 g) fresh breadcrumbs or ⅓ cup (40 g) matzah meal

4 garlic cloves, minced

1½ teaspoons kosher salt

2 large eggs

3 hard-boiled eggs (optional)

FOR THE GARNISH

3 tablespoons vegetable oil

4 large yellow onions (about 2 pounds/ 900 g), thinly sliced

Kosher salt and freshly ground black pepper

Preheat the oven to 350°F (175°C). Line a loaf pan (5-by-9-inch/12.5 by 22.5 cm if you're using the hard-boiled eggs, 4½-by-8½-inch/11 by 21 cm if you are not) with parchment paper to cover the bottom and the two long sides, leaving about a 2-inch (5 cm) overhang (the parchment will help you lift the meatloaf out of the pan).

In a large bowl, combine the veal, beef, onions, breadcrumbs, garlic, salt, and uncooked eggs. Mix well with your hands or a wooden spoon until all the ingredients are evenly distributed.

If you are not using the hard-boiled eggs, pile the mixture into the loaf pan and flatten the top evenly. If you are using the hard-boiled eggs, put about one-third of the meat mixture in the pan, arrange the eggs lengthwise in a row down the middle, and pack the rest of the meat mixture around and over the eggs, making sure the eggs are fully covered by the meat and smoothing the top.

Put the loaf pan on a baking sheet and bake the klops until it is deep golden brown on top and the internal temperature is at least 160°F (70°C), about 1 hour.

MEANWHILE, MAKE THE GARNISH: Heat the oil in a large skillet over medium heat. Add the onions to the pan, season lightly with salt and pepper, and cook, stirring and scraping the pan occasionally, until the onions are nicely caramelized, 25 to 35 minutes. Remove from the heat and keep warm.

To serve, grasp the two sides of the parchment paper and lift the klops out of the loaf pan and onto a serving plate. Slide the parchment out from under the klops and discard. Spread the caramelized onions on top of the klops and slice and serve while still warm.

Strudel aux Pommes

Deep-Dish Apple Pie with Citrus-Raisin Filling

Anna's family calls this dessert strudel aux pommes ("apple strudel" in French), but it might remind you more of a deep-dish apple pie with a buttery crust. Her grandmother used to make it for her dad, Claude, and, Anna explains, with each generation, the recipe has evolved. Claude changed the pastry dough and started caramelizing the apples in butter, which gives the filling a deep flavor (you can achieve the same with nondairy butter if you're serving this at a kosher meat meal).

You can make the dough and citrus filling (which uses an entire orange and lemon—peel included) a day in advance, to streamline your baking. *(Pictured on page 362)*

MAKES 8 servings

FOR THE DOUGH

4 cups (520 g) all-purpose flour, plus more for dusting

3½ tablespoons sugar

1 teaspoon kosher salt

10⅔ ounces (1⅓ sticks/290 g) cold unsalted butter or nondairy butter, cut into cubes, plus more for the pan

1 cup (240 ml) cold water

½ teaspoon vanilla extract

FOR THE FILLING

5 tablespoons (75 g) unsalted butter or nondairy butter, plus more for the pan

6 to 7 Golden Delicious apples, peeled, halved lengthwise, and cored

1 orange, halved crosswise and seeded

1 lemon, halved crosswise and seeded

2 cups (400 g) sugar

3 tablespoons golden raisins

1 tablespoon ground cinnamon

3 tablespoons dried breadcrumbs

FOR THE EGG WASH AND FINISHING

1 large egg, beaten

1 tablespoon sugar

MAKE THE DOUGH: Put the flour, sugar, and salt in a food processor and pulse a few times to blend. Add the cold butter and pulse until the pieces are the size of green peas. With the processor running, pour in half the water and blend for 15 to 30 seconds. Add the vanilla and enough of the remaining water so the dough starts to hold together in a ball; you may not need the full amount of water.

Transfer the dough to a floured surface and gently knead a few times to bring it together into a smooth ball. Divide the dough in half and shape each piece into a 6-inch (15 cm) square. Tightly cover with plastic wrap and refrigerate for at least 1 hour.

MEANWHILE, CARAMELIZE THE APPLES: Heat a large skillet over medium heat, add the butter, and place the apple pieces in the pan, flat side down. Cook, turning the apples occasionally, until lightly caramelized and golden brown all over, adjusting the heat so the butter doesn't burn. Take your time with this step so that the apples are nicely caramelized; it should take about 15 minutes. Remove the pan from the heat and set aside to cool.

recipe continues

Preheat the oven to 350°F (175°C). Grease a 9-by-13-inch (23 by 33 cm) baking dish with butter.

MAKE THE CITRUS FILLING: Put the orange and lemon in a food processor and process to a fairly smooth puree. Transfer to a medium bowl and stir in the sugar, raisins, and cinnamon. Set aside.

SHAPE THE DOUGH: Lightly flour a work surface. Roll out one piece of dough to a 13-by-17-inch (33 by 43 cm) rectangle, about ⅛ inch (3 mm) thick.

Transfer the dough to the prepared baking dish and gently press it over the bottom and up the sides, leaving a bit of an overhang on all sides. Roll out the second piece of dough to a rectangle the same size as the first and set aside.

Sprinkle the breadcrumbs evenly over the dough in the baking dish. Arrange the caramelized apples over the breadcrumbs in one layer. Pour the citrus mix evenly over the apples.

Lay the second piece of dough over the filling, taking care to drape it rather than stretch it. Pinch the dough edges together to seal on all sides, trim off all but about 1½ inches (3.75 cm), and then crimp the dough to make the edges look neat and pretty. Brush the surface of the pie with the beaten egg. With a sharp knife, cut about three 4-inch (10 cm) diagonal slits in the top of the dough. Sprinkle the sugar evenly on top.

Bake the pie until the crust is a deep golden brown and the filling is cooked through, poking an apple through one of the slits to see if it is tender, 50 to 70 minutes. Check the pie halfway through, and if the top crust is browning too quickly, cover it loosely with aluminum foil. When the pie is done, remove it from the oven and let rest for about 20 minutes, so the filling can firm up a bit.

Serve the pie warm, cut into slices.

Finding Pride in My Iraqi Heritage, and Breakfast

SHARED BY
Tami Shem-Tov

When I was a child, I always felt embarrassed. I was tiny and my hair was cut short, so I thought I looked like a little boy. I also couldn't read until I was in the third grade because I had a learning disability, but the worst was my father's name—the Arab name Sabich. Back then, in the 1970s, as Jewish Israeli kids, we were taught to distance ourselves from any connection to Arab culture.

One day, I asked my dad, "Why do you have an Arab name?" He told me: "My name is my identity. I'm an Arab, an Arab Jew." It's the same thing he told the immigration officers when he arrived in Israel from Iraq when he was eighteen and refused to change his name to the Hebrew Tzvi, like others with his name. Sabich comes from the word *sabah*, which means "morning." It can also mean dawn, the first light, the one you can see just before the sunrise, he told me. I became proud of him for refusing to deny his heritage for the sake of the Israeli melting pot.

But in my twenties, my embarrassment returned. *Sabich* had become the name of a very popular street food. Imagine if your dad were called

FAMILY JOURNEY

Baghdad → *Ramle, Israel* → *Kiryat Ono, Israel* → *Tel Aviv*

Tami and her father, Sabich, in Capetown, 1970

"Falafel" or "Pizza"? If you ask an Israeli what sabich is, they'll tell you it's hard-boiled eggs, slices of fried eggplant, fresh vegetables, and tahina stuffed into a pita. It's the basic ingredients of the Iraqi Shabbat breakfast, and they've been eating it for generations. We ate it every Shabbat at my parents' house, but we never, ever, called it sabich.

I found the man responsible for the sabich craze in Israel: a fellow Iraqi Jew named Sabich Tzvi Halabi, who used to sell snacks to bus drivers from a little kiosk in Ramat Gan. One Sunday, he brought leftovers from his Shabbat breakfast. In no time it became a hit, with people standing in line and shouting, "Sabich! Sabich!" because they all wanted this pita—and the name stuck.

Today no child in Israel is named Sabich anymore, but everyone knows the dish, which keeps an ancient tradition alive. I wrote a children's book called *Saba Sabich*, or *Grandpa Sabich*, about it, and I hope it helps kids feel more comfortable with who they are and where they come from. I dedicated the book to my father, who taught me how to be courageous.

Writer **TAMI SHEM-TOV** is a children's and young adult author who primarily writes historical stories and novels. She lives with her two daughters in Tel Aviv.

**TAMI SHEM-TOV'S
SHABBAT BREAKFAST**

Sabich
*Pickled Turnips, Eggplant,
Potatoes, Eggs, Tahini Sauce,
and Chopped Salad*
368

—*Serve with*—

pita, amba,
fresh parsley

Sabich

Pickled Turnips, Eggplant, Potatoes, Eggs, Tahini Sauce, and Chopped Salad

In Israel, sabich is the name of an iconic street food: pita stuffed with elements of the Iraqi Shabbat breakfast spread, like fried eggplant, overnight eggs, parsley, pickles, and amba, a tangy mango sauce. The origin of the dish's name, though, is actually up for debate. Some, like Tami, say it comes from Sabich Tzvi Halabi, a man who used to sell the sandwich in Ramat Gan, while others argue it comes from the Arabic word *sabah*, meaning "morning." In Iraqi Jewish homes like the one Tami grew up in, these elements are still served as part of a spread on Shabbat mornings.

While fried eggplant is traditional, roasted slices work well and make the meal easier to prepare.

Be sure to start the pickled turnips at least 4 days in advance so they will be ready. (You can make them up to 1 month ahead and store them in an airtight container in the refrigerator.) The chopped salad is best when the cucumbers are very crunchy, so dress and toss it just before serving.

If you like, serve this spread with Ron Arazi's pita (page 110). If you don't have time to bake it, look for fluffy pita at a bakery or grocery store.

MAKES 6 to 8 servings

FOR THE PICKLED TURNIPS

3 cups (720 ml) water

¼ cup (35 g) kosher salt

1 cup (240 ml) white vinegar

2 pounds (900 g) turnips (about 6 medium), peeled and cut into long rectangles ½ inch (1.25 cm) thick

1 small beet (about 4 ounces/115 g), peeled and cut into long rectangles ½ inch (1.25 cm) thick

1 garlic clove, roughly chopped

FOR THE EGGPLANT

2 medium eggplants, sliced into 1-inch (2.5 cm) rounds

2 teaspoons kosher salt

Extra-virgin olive oil for brushing

FOR THE POTATOES

¼ cup (40 g) kosher salt

6 Yukon Gold potatoes, scrubbed

FOR THE EGGS

8 large eggs

FOR THE TAHINI SAUCE

1 cup (250 g) raw tahini paste

⅔ cup (160 ml) ice water

Juice of ½ lemon

1½ teaspoons kosher salt

FOR THE CHOPPED SALAD

4 Persian cucumbers (about 1 pound/450 g)

4 medium firm but ripe tomatoes (about 1 pound/450 g)

½ medium red onion (about 4 ounces/115 g)

1 cup (30 g) chopped fresh flat-leaf parsley (optional)

2 tablespoons fresh lemon juice, or more to taste

ingredients and recipe continue

¼ cup (60 ml) extra-virgin olive oil,
or more to taste

2 teaspoons kosher salt

Freshly ground black pepper

FOR SERVING

6 to 8 pita, homemade (page 110) or
store-bought, or laffa

Flat-leaf parsley sprigs

Amba (mango sauce)

MAKE THE PICKLED TURNIPS: At least four days
in advance, prepare the turnips.

Put the water and salt in a medium saucepan,
heat over medium heat until very hot but not
boiling, and stir until the salt has completely
dissolved. Remove from the heat and let the salt
water cool completely, then stir in the vinegar.

Put the turnips, beet, and garlic into a large clean
glass jar or other nonreactive container with a
tight-fitting lid, pour in the brine, and seal the jar.

Let the pickles sit at room temperature for 4 to
6 days, then refrigerate.

MAKE THE EGGPLANT: Lay the eggplant
rounds in a single layer on a wire rack set over
a baking sheet. Sprinkle the exposed sides with
1 teaspoon of the salt, flip the rounds over, and
sprinkle the other sides with the remaining
1 teaspoon salt. Let stand for at least 20 minutes
and up to 1 hour.

Preheat the oven to 425°F (220°C).

Using paper towels, thoroughly wipe the salt and
moisture from the eggplant slices and pat them
dry. Generously brush both sides of the rounds
with olive oil and lay them on a baking sheet in an
even layer; use two baking sheets if necessary.

Roast the eggplant for 20 minutes, then flip
the slices and continue roasting until they are
golden brown and tender all the way through,
another 20 minutes or so. Remove from the oven
and set aside.

COOK THE POTATOES: Fill a large pot with cold
water. Add the salt and potatoes. Bring to a boil
over high heat, then reduce the heat to medium-
high and cook the potatoes at an active simmer
until they are fork-tender, about 20 minutes.
Drain the potatoes and set aside until cool
enough to handle.

Peel the potatoes using a knife and then slice
into ¼- to ½-inch (6 to 12 mm) pieces. Transfer to
a plate and set aside.

BOIL THE EGGS: Fill a large bowl with ice water
and set aside. Bring a medium saucepan of
water to a boil over medium-high heat. Gently
add the eggs to the boiling water, using a slotted
spoon. Boil the eggs for 7 minutes for soft-
boiled, jammy eggs, or for 12 minutes for hard-
boiled eggs. Immediately transfer the eggs to
the ice bath and let cool completely.

Peel the eggs and cut them into ¼-inch (6 mm)
slices. Set aside.

MAKE THE TAHINI SAUCE: Put the tahini paste in
a medium bowl and slowly add ⅓ cup (80 ml) of
the ice water, whisking until well blended. Whisk
in the remaining ⅓ cup (80 ml) ice water until the
mixture is blended and all the water is absorbed.
The tahini may stiffen at first, but eventually the
sauce will develop a creamy consistency. Add
the lemon juice and salt and whisk again to
combine.

MAKE THE CHOPPED SALAD: Finely chop the cucumbers and tomatoes into small cubes (about ¼ inch/6 mm). Chop the red onion into small dice (about ¼ inch/6 mm). Put the cucumbers, tomatoes, and onion in a large salad bowl and add the parsley, if using.

Just before serving, add the lemon juice and toss to distribute. Add the olive oil, salt, and pepper and toss again to mix well. Taste and adjust the seasoning if needed.

CREATE THE SABICH SPREAD: Arrange the pickled turnips, potatoes, eggs, and chopped salad in separate serving bowls and place the eggplant slices and pita on separate platters. Put the tahini sauce, parsley sprigs, and amba in bowls.

Invite diners to build their own sabich sandwiches, choosing their favorite ingredients.

A Moroccan Shabbat Feast by Way of Brazil

SHARED BY

Esther Serruya Weyl

I'm a professional chef, but before I left for a trip to Morocco with my mom in 2017, I hadn't thought much about the food we would eat there. We were focused on visiting Casablanca, my great-grandmother's hometown, and Tetouan, the city where my great-grandfather was born. I didn't realize eating in the country where our community came from generations ago would be such a powerful experience.

I come from a Moroccan community in Belem, a city in the north of Brazil. In the late 1890s, approximately three hundred Jewish families, including my own, immigrated there.

Cooks in the community found themselves faced with a completely different set of ingredients from the ones they'd used back home. They adapted everything they could to make their recipes survive. They replaced paprika with a seed called urucum, used preserved limes instead of lemons, and when they couldn't find semolina to make couscous, they substituted yuca flour. They also adopted local dishes like feijoada and made them kosher.

I grew up eating these recipes on Shabbat, when we always had two lunches. The first, called a seudah, was served at our synagogue. There was often dafina with brisket, potatoes and flour dumplings, or feijoada

---

FAMILY JOURNEY

Spain → *Morocco* → *Belem, Brazil*

Esther's grandma Esther at her wedding in Belem, 1953

with beef. After that, almost everyone in the community would go to their grandmother's or mother's house for another feast. We would spend the whole day together in this very special atmosphere until sunset.

When I returned from my trip to Morocco, I wanted to document our recipes. I started with my own family. My grandmother Esther Cohen had passed away, but a woman named Sandra who had cooked for her for twenty years spent two days teaching me her recipes. I started talking to other women in our community too. The Larrat sisters shared their recipes for an eggplant dip and for escabeche de peixe. My aunt Myriam and her mother, Doña Clara, taught me to make almoronía with layers of eggplant and chicken, and Helena Obadia Benzecry, one of the greatest cooks in our community, shared her meringue and citrus dessert.

When my mother and I were in Casablanca, a bookseller showed us a Moroccan cookbook with a dessert on the cover. For him, that sweet was Moroccan; for us, it was Jewish. It got me thinking: As Jews, we've had so many diasporas. We've made the food of the countries where we've lived our own and adjusted it to fit kosher laws and Jewish traditions. It's hard to define what Jewish food is, but when I look at the recipes I've collected, I know this is the taste of my community.

Raised in a small Jewish community in Brazil, **ESTHER SERRUYA WEYL** is determined to preserve her culture. A cook at the prestigious restaurant Blue Hill at Stone Barns in the Hudson Valley, she's working on a cookbook with recipes and stories from her community.

ESTHER SERRUYA WEYL'S SHABBAT

Fumaça
Roasted Eggplant Dip
376

Escabeche de Peixe
Marinated Fried Fish
376

Almoronía
*Baked Chicken with
Eggplant and Onions*
378

Dafina
Overnight Shabbat Stew
380

Meringue with
Orange Marmalade
382

—*Serve with*—

challah, tahini, peanuts,
limes, marinated olives

Fumaça
Roasted Eggplant Dip

Be sure to fully char the outside of the eggplant and cook the inside until completely tender, to give this dip an earthy-smoky flavor and a silky texture. If you're serving a spread of dips and salads, pair this with Jessica Solnicki's beet salad with cumin (page 75), which is similar to one Esther's family makes. Freshly baked challah (page 313) is perfect for scooping up the dip. *(Pictured on page 374)*

MAKES 6 to 8 servings

1 large eggplant (about 1¼ pounds/560 g)

1 large egg yolk

1 tablespoon white wine vinegar or white vinegar, or more to taste

1 teaspoon kosher salt

¼ teaspoon freshly ground black pepper

¾ cup (180 ml) mild extra-virgin olive oil or vegetable oil

4 cilantro sprigs for garnish

Extra-virgin olive oil for drizzling

Roast the eggplant using the method that works best for your kitchen: You can place the eggplant directly on a gas burner turned to medium-high heat and cook, flipping it frequently, until it is charred on all sides and tender inside, about 20 minutes. (Lay a few strips of foil around the burner for easy cleanup.) Or char the eggplant skin under a hot broiler, turning the eggplant frequently, and then finish roasting it until tender on a baking sheet in a 450°F (220°C) oven. Remove the eggplant from the heat and let it rest until cool enough to handle.

Halve the eggplant lengthwise and scoop the eggplant flesh into a blender. Discard the skin and stem.

Add the egg yolk to the blender and pulse until well combined. Add the vinegar, salt, and pepper and blend for another few seconds. With the motor running, slowly stream in the mild olive oil and blend until the mixture is thick and creamy. Taste and adjust the seasoning with more vinegar, salt, and pepper if needed.

Transfer the dip to a small serving bowl, garnish with the cilantro sprigs, and drizzle lightly with olive oil. Serve at room temperature.

Escabeche de Peixe
Marinated Fried Fish

You'll find escabeche, a dish of fried fish soused with a vinegar dressing, in many cultures. The idea of preserving and flavoring fish this way is centuries—possibly millennia—old. Sources differ on the origin of the dish, but the root of the name comes from the Persian word *sikbāj*, the name of a vinegary stew.

MAKES 6 to 8 servings

½ cup (65 g) all-purpose flour

½ cup (120 ml) extra-virgin olive oil, plus more for shallow-frying

1 pound (450 g) skinless red snapper fillets, sliced into 1-by-3-inch (2.5 by 7.5 cm) pieces

2 teaspoons kosher salt

⅛ teaspoon freshly ground black pepper

¾ cup (180 ml) white wine vinegar or white vinegar

½ medium onion, thinly sliced

½ cup (15 g) roughly chopped fresh cilantro

Put the flour in a small bowl and line a plate with paper towels. Arrange them both near your cooktop.

Heat about ½ inch (1.25 cm) of olive oil in a medium skillet or wide saucepan over medium-high heat.

Season the fish all over with the salt and pepper. Dredge a piece of fish through the flour and shake off any excess. Test the oil temperature by dipping a corner of the flour-coated fish into the oil—if it sizzles vigorously, the oil is ready; if not, heat the oil for a bit longer. Carefully place the piece of fish in the oil and repeat the flouring process with another 4 to 6 pieces of fish; don't crowd the pan. Fry the fish, turning once, until cooked through and golden brown, about 2 minutes on each side. Transfer the fish to the paper towel–lined plate to drain. Continue frying the rest of the fish in batches.

Put the vinegar, olive oil, onion, and chopped cilantro in a deep bowl or other container and stir to combine well. Add the pieces of fried fish to the bowl, making sure they are all submerged in the liquid. Cover the bowl with plastic wrap and set aside for 2 hours at room temperature to marinate, or transfer the fish to the refrigerator to marinate for up to 8 hours.

Serve the escabeche at room temperature.

Almoronía

Baked Chicken with Eggplant and Onions

"We can't talk about Sephardic cuisine, especially that from Morocco, without mentioning almoronía," explains Hélène Jawhara Piñer in her book *Jews, Food, and Spain: The Oldest Medieval Spanish Cookbook and the Sephardic Culinary Heritage*. The original recipe and name, she explains, come from the thirteenth-century cookbook *Kitāb al-ṭabīkh*, and Moroccan Jews still prepare it in the same way, with layers of fried eggplant, chicken, onions, and honey, which adds a surprising sweetness to the rich casserole. Serve it as the star of a meal with a salad or as part of a large Shabbat spread.

MAKES 6 to 8 servings

2 pounds (900 g) bone-in, skin-on chicken thighs

Kosher salt and freshly ground black pepper

2 large eggplants (about 2 pounds/900 g), not peeled, cut into ¼-inch (6 mm) rounds

Extra-virgin olive oil

4 medium yellow onions (about 1¼ pounds/ 560 g), thinly sliced

2 tablespoons honey

½ teaspoon ground cumin

½ teaspoon ground nutmeg

½ teaspoon ground cinnamon

Preheat the oven to 425°F (220°C).

Season each chicken thigh with about 1 teaspoon salt (make sure to sprinkle the salt on all sides of the chicken) and a pinch of pepper. Arrange the chicken on a baking sheet, skin side up, and roast until the chicken is golden brown and very tender when pierced with a knife (the internal temperature should be about 175°F/80°C), 45 to 60 minutes, depending on the size of the pieces. Remove the chicken from the oven and set aside to cool for about 25 minutes.

Reduce the oven temperature to 400°F (205°C).

While the chicken is cooking, fry the eggplant: Place the eggplant slices on a wire rack and sprinkle them on both sides with salt, about 2 tablespoons total. Set the eggplant aside for about 30 minutes to draw out the juices.

Pat the eggplant slices dry with a paper towel. Line a baking sheet with paper towels.

Heat ⅓ cup (80 ml) olive oil in a large skillet over medium-high heat. Once the oil is hot, carefully add 4 eggplant slices, or as many as will fit comfortably without crowding, to the pan. Fry, turning once, until deep golden brown on both sides, 5 to 8 minutes per side. Transfer the fried eggplant to the paper towel–lined baking sheet. Continue frying the rest of the eggplant in batches, adding more oil to the pan and adjusting the heat as needed. If the fried eggplant slices look oily, blot the top surface with paper towels. Set the eggplant aside.

Heat 2 tablespoons olive oil in a large skillet over medium-high heat. Add the onions and cook, stirring occasionally, until soft and golden brown, 20 to 25 minutes. Add 1½ teaspoons salt and the honey to the onions and stir to combine. Remove from the heat and set aside.

Once the chicken is cool enough to handle, pull the meat from the bones and shred it using two forks, aiming for bite-sized pieces. Cut or shred the skin as well (discard the bones). Put the shredded chicken and skin in a medium bowl. Add the cumin, nutmeg, and cinnamon and mix well to combine. Taste and add more salt and pepper as needed. Set aside.

ASSEMBLE THE ALMORONÍA: Arrange about half the eggplant in a 9-by-13-inch (23 by 33 cm) baking dish in an even layer, overlapping the slices as needed to fit. Spread half the shredded chicken over the eggplant in another even layer. Set aside about one-quarter of the caramelized onions and spread the rest over the chicken. Spread the remaining chicken into a layer on top of the onions, and top with the remaining eggplant pieces. Press gently to lightly compact the layers and make the almoronía easier to cut and serve, then distribute the reserved onions over the top.

Bake the almoronía, uncovered, until all the ingredients are hot, about 30 minutes. Remove from the oven.

To serve, scoop out portions, making sure to get a bit of each layer in each one, and arrange on plates.

Dafina

Overnight Shabbat Stew

One of the quintessential dishes of Sephardi cooking, dafina is a slow-cooked Shabbat stew that traces its history back to medieval Spain. It goes by many names, including hamin, dafina, and adafina, which means "buried" in Arabic, since the pots were either buried or cooked under a stone, depending on the source you consult. The dish is referenced in documents from the Inquisition, when preparing the stew on Fridays was given as proof that a Converso (someone who'd converted to Christianity) continued to practice Judaism in secret.

There are countless variations of the stew across the Sephardi Diaspora that vary by community and even household, but haminados, or eggs that are cooked in their shells until they turn brown, are a hallmark. In Moroccan communities like Esther's, chickpeas are commonly added. But sometime after moving to Brazil in the late nineteenth century, cooks in her community replaced them with flour dumplings called café de massa. This Portuguese term means "coffee dough," because "it was said that it was because the dough color [when cooked] looked like coffee," Esther explains.

Like cholent (page 358) and other Shabbat stews, this hearty dish cooks for a long time. Esther's recipe also requires marinating the meat for at least 8 hours, so plan accordingly. *(Pictured on pages 374–375)*

MAKES 6 to 8 servings

FOR THE BEEF BONE AND BRISKET MARINADE

2 or 3 beef marrow bones, about 3 inches (7.5 cm) long

2 pounds (900 g) brisket, chuck, or other beef stew meat, cut into 2-inch (5 cm) cubes

4 garlic cloves, finely chopped

2 tablespoons vegetable oil

1 tablespoon white vinegar

2 tablespoons kosher salt

FOR THE DUMPLINGS

1¾ cups (225 g) all-purpose flour, plus more as needed

1 large egg

½ cup (120 ml) water

½ teaspoon kosher salt

FOR THE DAFINA

2 tablespoons vegetable oil

2 large yellow onions (about 1 pound/ 450 g), thinly sliced

6 garlic cloves, thinly sliced

2 teaspoons ground cinnamon

2 teaspoons ground cumin

1 teaspoon ground nutmeg

½ teaspoon sugar

1 tablespoon kosher salt

¼ teaspoon freshly ground black pepper

2 large russet potatoes (about 14 ounces/ 400 g), peeled and cut into quarters

4 to 6 large eggs

About 5 cups (1.2 L) water

MARINATE THE BEEF BONES AND BRISKET:
Put the beef bones and cubed beef in a large bowl. Add the garlic, vegetable oil, vinegar, and salt and mix and turn the ingredients until all the meat and bones are coated with the marinade. Cover the bowl with plastic wrap and refrigerate for at least 8 hours and up to 24 hours.

Preheat the oven to 400°F (205°C). Line a baking sheet with parchment paper.

MAKE THE DUMPLINGS: In a large bowl, combine the flour, egg, water, and salt and stir until the ingredients come together into a dough.

Turn the dough out onto the work surface and knead until smooth, about 5 minutes. Divide the dough into 4 pieces. Lightly flour your work surface and roll each piece into a rope about ½ inch (1.25 cm) thick.

Cut one rope into ½-inch (1.25 cm) pieces. Roll each piece between your palms to form a spherical dumpling, and then poke a dimple into the center with your thumb. As you work, put the shaped dumplings on a plate or tray, keeping them separate so they don't stick together. Continue with the rest of the dough ropes until all the dumplings are formed. Sprinkle a generous few pinches of flour over the dumplings and toss until they're all lightly coated with flour, then spread the dumplings on the parchment-lined baking sheet.

Bake the dumplings until they are golden brown and crisp, 20 to 30 minutes. Remove from the oven and set aside. Reduce the oven temperature to 220°F (105°C).

COOK THE DAFINA: Remove the beef bones and brisket from the marinade (discard the marinade) and pat dry with paper towels.

Place a Dutch oven or other large heavy-bottomed pot (large enough to hold all the ingredients) over medium-high heat and add 2 tablespoons oil. Once the oil is hot, add the bones and beef to the pot. Sear the meat and bones until nicely browned on all sides, about 15 minutes total, taking care that the pan juices don't get too dark and burn. Transfer the meat and bones to a bowl.

Add about 2 tablespoons water to the pot, stirring and scraping the bottom of the pot to dissolve the pan juices, then simmer for a few seconds, until the liquid has evaporated. Add the onions and garlic and sauté until they are a deep golden brown, 15 to 20 minutes, adjusting the heat if the onions or garlic are getting too dark. Add the cinnamon, cumin, nutmeg, sugar, salt, and pepper and cook for another minute, stirring to distribute the spices.

Put the seared meat and bones back into the pot and add the potatoes and eggs. Add enough water to just barely cover the ingredients; it's fine if the bones are a bit above the water level. Gently stir the mixture to distribute the ingredients and bring the liquid to a boil.

Cover the pot with a lid and transfer to the oven. Cook the dafina for 1 hour.

Take the pot out of the oven, add the baked dumplings, along with any flour on the baking sheet, and gently stir the mixture. Cover the pot again and return it to the oven. Cook the stew for at least 8 hours longer or overnight. Remove from the oven.

Taste the cooking liquid and adjust the seasoning with more salt if needed. Remove the eggs, peel them, and return them to the dafina.

To serve, put some beef, potatoes, and dumplings into each serving bowl and then ladle over the cooking liquid. Distribute the eggs and marrow bones to a few lucky diners.

Meringue with Orange Marmalade

In Esther's community in Brazil, this meringue dessert is made with the Amazonian fruit cupuaçu, a relative of cacao that has bright acidity. But you can replace it with preserves—orange marmalade works beautifully, because the slight bitter notes from the orange peel are a nice contrast to the sweet meringue.

If you don't have a stand mixer, you can use a handheld electric one, but pouring the hot sugar syrup might be a bit tricky. You can steady the bowl by wrapping a damp kitchen towel around the base like a collar, which will free up both your hands. You'll want to make sure you have a candy thermometer for this recipe.

MAKES 6 to 8 servings

1½ cups (300 g) sugar

¾ cup (180 ml) water

6 large egg whites

6 tablespoons (90 g) orange marmalade

SPECIAL EQUIPMENT
Candy thermometer

Put the sugar and water in a small saucepan and bring to a boil over medium-high heat, stirring just until the sugar is dissolved; don't stir after that, or the sugar might crystallize. Cook the sugar syrup until it reads 240°F (115°C) on a candy thermometer (soft-ball stage); this will probably take 20 to 25 minutes.

Meanwhile, as the sugar gets closer to the soft-ball stage, in the bowl of a stand mixer fitted with the whisk attachment, whip the egg whites until they form soft peaks.

Remove the cooked sugar syrup from the heat and, with the mixer running on medium speed, very slowly drizzle the hot sugar mixture into the whipped egg whites. Continue mixing until the meringue forms stiff, glossy peaks.

Transfer the meringue to a large bowl, add 3 tablespoons of the marmalade, and fold the marmalade into the meringue with just a few strokes, to create orange streaks. Transfer the meringue to a large serving bowl and top with the remaining marmalade, swirling it into the meringue to make a pretty design.

Cover the meringue loosely with plastic wrap and refrigerate for 1 to 2 hours. Serve cold.

Bibliography

Brenner, Michael. *A Short History of the Jews.* Reprint ed. Princeton, NJ: Princeton University Press, 2012.

Butnick, Stephanie, Liel Leibovitz, and Mark Oppenheimer. *The Newish Jewish Encyclopedia: From Abraham to Zabar's and Everything in Between.* New York: Artisan, 2019.

Cohen, Stella. *Stella's Sephardic Table: Jewish Family Recipes from the Mediterranean Island of Rhodes.* Capetown: The Gerald & Marc Hoberman Collection, 2012.

Cooper, Jonathan. *Eat and Be Satisfied: A Social History of Jewish Food.* Northvale, NJ: Jason Aronson, 1993.

Dangoor, Linda. *Flavours of Babylon: A Family Cookbook.* London: Waterpoint Press, 2011.

Davidson, Alan. *The Oxford Companion to Food.* 3rd ed. Edited by Tom Jaine. Oxford, UK: Oxford University Press, 2014.

Davis, Mitchell. *The Mensch Chef: Or Why Delicious Jewish Food Isn't an Oxymoron.* New York: Clarkson Potter, 2002.

Gitlitz, David M., and Linda Kay Davidson. *A Drizzle of Honey: The Lives and Recipes of Spain's Secret Jews.* New York: St. Martin's Press, 1999.

Hassan, Hawa, with Julia Turshen. *In Bibi's Kitchen: The Recipes and Stories of Grandmothers from the Eight African Countries that Touch the Indian Ocean.* Emeryville, CA: Ten Speed Press, 2020.

Koenig, Leah. *The Jewish Cookbook.* New York: Phaidon Press, 2019.

Koerner, András. *Jewish Cuisine in Hungary: A Cultural History with 83 Authentic Recipes.* Budapest: Central European University Press, 2022.

Marks, Gil. *Encyclopedia of Jewish Food.* Hoboken, NJ: John Wiley & Sons, 2010.

Nathan, Joan. *Joan Nathan's Jewish Holiday Cookbook.* Rev. ed. New York: Schocken, 2004.

——— . *King Solomon's Table: A Culinary Exploration of Jewish Cooking from Around the World.* New York: Knopf, 2017.

——— . *Quiches, Kugels, and Couscous: My Search for Jewish Cooking in France.* New York: Knopf, 2010.

Newhouse, Alana. *The 100 Most Jewish Foods: A Highly Debatable List.* New York: Artisan, 2019.

Piñer, Hélène Jawhara. *Jews, Food, and Spain: The Oldest Medieval Spanish Cookbook and the Sephardic Culinary Heritage.* Brookline, MA: Academic Studies Press, 2022.

——— . *Sephardi: Cooking the History. Recipes of the Jews of Spain and the Diaspora, from the 13th Century to Today.* Brookline, MA: Cherry Orchard Books, 2021.

Rabinowics, Rachel Anne, ed. *Passover Haggadah: The Feast of Freedom.* 2nd ed. New York: The Rabbinical Assembly, 1982.

Roden, Claudia. *The Book of Jewish Food: An Odyssey from Samarkand to New York.* Later prt. ed. New York: Knopf, 1996.

Ross, Lesli Koppelman. *Celebrate!: The Complete Jewish Holidays Handbook.* Northvale, NJ: Jason Aronson, 1994.

Schauss, Hayyim. *The Jewish Festivals: A Guide to Their History and Observance.* New York: Schocken, 1996.

Schwartz, Oded. *In Search of Plenty: A History of Jewish Food with More Than 100 Classic Recipes.* Toronto: Culture Concepts, 1994.

Yoskowitz, Jeffrey, and Liz Alpern. *The Gefilte Manifesto: New Recipes for Old World Jewish Foods.* New York: Flatiron Books, 2016.

Other Resources

In addition to the books above, there are specific volumes cited throughout the text. We also found the websites of the United States Holocaust Memorial Museum, Yad Vashem, the Israel Museum, Centre Primo Levi, the Orthodox Union, and Chabad helpful resources, as were My Jewish Learning and the Jewish Virtual Library.

Acknowledgments

I WANT TO THANK the families who so generously shared their recipes and stories for this book and all of those who have shared theirs with the Jewish Food Society since its founding in 2017.

This book took a village to create and I want to thank my team at Jewish Food Society, past and present. Thanks for tolerating me, supporting me, teaching me, and drinking with me! This book is evidence of our shared passion for Jewish food and culture and our unique creative partnership. To the extended JFS community: Thanks for always showing up and especially to those of you who joined this book ride as recipe testers.

To Amanda Dell, for leading our photo shoots with so much grace and creativity, and for your overall partnership and friendship—JFS wouldn't be where it is without your magic. To Ellie Backer, for building JFS with me from scratch with tremendous talent and determination. To Yael Raviv, for your wisdom, calming energy, leadership, and endless dedication, working on this book and beyond. To Arielle Nir for raising our culinary bar and for bringing so much expertise and style to JFS and to this book. To Danielle Brodsky for working tirelessly and enthusiastically on getting the recipes just right. To Christina Whittaker, thanks for your kindness and dedication and for keeping us all on track! To Manami Takashina for all your

help. Chaya Rappoport for joining us at the finish line with your upbeat energy. Finally, to Devra Ferst, my co-author: choosing to work with you from day one of Jewish Food Society was one of the best decisions I've ever made. Thanks for your uncompromising and thoughtful approach to research and to writing, and for your tremendous part in shaping the Jewish Food Society's tone.

To the core book team: Penny De Los Santos—I'm so grateful we clicked at that Shabbat dinner in Red Hook in 2018. Your creativity and point of view are an integral part of JFS's visual identity, and I will cherish our partnership forever. Thanks to our recipe tester, Martha Holmberg, for applying your extensive experience to these precious family recipes. To Judy Haubert, the MacGyver of our set, thanks for your exquisite styling and for never giving up until it's perfect. To Vanessa Vazquez, your beautiful "grandma chic" props will make every savta proud! To our additional creative collaborators: Mariana Velásquez, thanks for bringing your killer sense of style and fashion to the Shabbat spreads in the Lower East Side and in Brooklyn. To Dan Perez and Nurit Kariv, collaborating with you on the Israel shoot was pure magic! Thanks Hamootal Radoshitzky for passionately orchestrating that shoot, too. To Armando Rafael, thanks for the gorgeous images in the book and many others in the JFS archive.

Thank you to my editor at Artisan, Lia Ronnen, for believing in this book and for guiding us with great sensibility, knowledge, and confidence. I learned so much from you! To Bella Lemos, thanks for your compassionate editing and meticulous care, and for Zooming with us around the clock. Thanks also to Jane Treuhaft and Suet Chong at Artisan for developing the visual identity of this book, and to Toni Tajima for the graphic design. To Emily Parkinson, your talent inspired me from the moment we met, and I'm delighted that your flower art brightens the pages of the book, and to Morey Talmor and Angus Plunkett for the perfect cover design. Your style shines bright.

Thank you Barbara Kirshenblatt-Gimblett, Ruby Namdar, Hedai Offaim, Avi Shilon, and Rabbi Jon Spira-Savett for generously reading sections of the manuscript and offering your expert advice. And to Muzna Bishara for your help with Arabic translation.

I also know that our work is made possible because we stand on the shoulders of those who lit the path forward, including cookbook authors Claudia Roden, Darra Goldstein, Gil Marks, Edda Servi Machlin, Joan Nathan, Gabriella Gershenson, Michael Twitty, Leah Koenig, Jeffrey Yoskowitz, Liz Alpern, András Koerner, Hélène Jawhara Piñer, Janna Gur, and others.

To Terry Kassel, for believing in me back in 2016 and giving me the opportunity to dream big and establish a home for Jewish food. It's an honor and a privilege to do this work, and I'm forever grateful.

To the entire Jewish Food Society board: Shari Aronson, Sara Bloom, Deborah Hochberg, Terry Kassel, Mark Reisbaum, Michael Solomonov, and Adeena Sussman. Thanks for your support and your belief in the power of food to effect real change.

Devra Ferst, my co-author, also wanted to add her thanks to her mother, Nancy, and her grandmother Marjorie, who are no longer here but inspired her every time she sat down to work on this manuscript.

To my support crew for life: Dafna Lustig, Yaara Keydar, Efrat Bigger, Yonatan Sagiv, Ido Mizrahy, Tamar Koren, and Noa Shadur. You are the most excellent people to eat, drink, cry, and laugh with—thank you!

Finally, to my love, Ilan Benatar, you are my greatest teacher (and critic!) and I love you for that, and much more. And to my sister, Halit Coussin, for being my best friend and my North Star. To my parents, thank you for raising me to believe in myself, and in the power of community.

Index

Add Your Family Recipe to the Jewish Food Society's Archive

Jewish family recipes tell the stories of who we are as individuals and as a people; how we live and love, celebrate and mourn. The **Jewish Food Society** works to preserve and revitalize these recipes and the stories behind them.

Do you have a special family recipe to add to our ever-growing digital archive? Visit **jewishfoodsociety.org**/**submit** to share it.

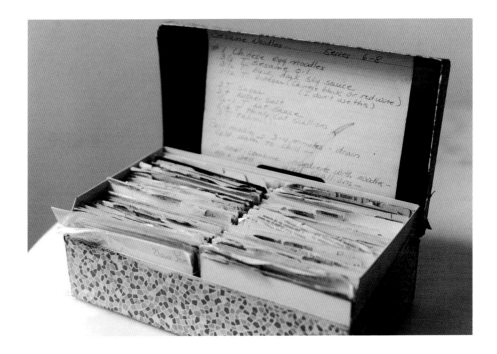

PHOTO BY TOMER APPELBAUM

Naama Shefi is a kibbutznik and New Yorker whose work sits at the intersection of food, culture, community building, and art. In 2017, she founded the Jewish Food Society, a nonprofit organization, which preserves and celebrates Jewish culinary heritage through a digital recipe archive and dynamic events. In the summer of 2021, she launched Asif: Culinary Institute of Israel, a center in Tel Aviv dedicated to exploring the diverse and creative food culture of Israel. She lives on the Lower East Side with her husband, Ilan, and their daughter, Ella.